Personal Being

Personal Being

A Theory for Individual Psychology

ROM HARRÉ

Harvard University Press
Cambridge, Massachusetts
1984

Library of Congress Cataloging in Publication Data
Harré, Romano.
  Personal being.

  (Ways of being).
  Continues: Social being.
  Includes bibliographical references and index.
  1. Identity (Psychology) 2. Individuality.
3. Self. I. Title. II. Series: Harré, Romano.
Ways of being.
BF697.H374 1983   155.2   83-12838
ISBN 0-674-66313-6

For Hettie

CONTENTS

PREFACE

In the past few years there has been an increasing tendency amongst theoretical psychologists to look towards social structures and processes for the ultimate explanations of psychological matters. The great bulk of this work has been European. At the same time, the demise of positivist conceptions of science has allowed a cognitivist revival based largely upon a conceptual scheme drawn from the technology of machine computation, the so-called 'artificial intelligence' field. The centre of cognitive psychology has been the United States. Like its sibling, the experimental movement in social psychology, it bears the marks of its origin in certain unexamined moral and political assumptions that are deeply embedded in the conceptual systems which have been built upon the basis of the machine analogy. In this context the assumption of individualism is involved, together with a pervasive predilection to substitute a causal – technical order for the moral orders within which human action is traditionally set. Ironically, neither cognitivism nor social constructivism manages to provide a way of understanding how it is that singular persons can emerge from socially created information-processing devices.

My aim in this sequel to *Social being* is to try to restore the consideration of moral orders to the techniques of psychological studies, and at the same time to address the problem of the emergence of personal being. In order to sharpen the focus of the theoretical arguments, I have added a research menu to each chapter, sketching some of the topics that could form the basis of work in a 'constructivistically' oriented psychology department. These proposals range from topics suitable for masters dissertations to projects requiring teamwork that could only be supported by substantial funding.

I have adopted a different method of reference citation from that usually found in contemporary psychological works. Reducing references within the text to a minimum has allowed me to append a short bibliographical essay to each chapter, offering a critical round-up of interesting reading. To my mind, excessive citation has become a vice in psychological writing and I would like to make a break with the all too easy insertion of the 'Budweiser and Schlitz, 1982' style of reference. Bibliographical essays are more trouble, but I think in the long run of more use.

I owe the original impetus to pursue the question of personal being to many conversations with J.-P. de Waele and with John Shotter. Each, in different ways, has made essential contributions to the field of personal psychology. I am also grateful to the State University of New York at Binghamton for the regular opportunity I have had to try out nascent ideas on many generations of students during my annual visits.

PART I

Social Foundations of Personal Psychology

CHAPTER 1

LOCATING PERSONAL PSYCHOLOGY

Theme: Neither the traditional experimental psychology nor the more recent cognitive approach is adequate for the study of personal psychology. The former systematically confuses causal with moral orders, while the latter has no way of representing the structural unities of belief and feeling that constitute individual minds.

Contents
1 Current state of theoretical psychology
       Causal mechanisms and moral orders
       Individualism and subjectivism in recent psychology
2 Cognitivism: the limits of subpersonal psychologies
       Late medieval psychology of action
       Psychodynamics
       Cognitive psychology
3 Social foundations of mind
       Social representations
       Origins of personal being
       Identity projects
4 Creation of personal being
       The semantics of theoretical concepts
       Person and self: preliminary distinctions
       The unities of personal being

The reorientation proposed here involves attributing the properties of mental—predicate ascriptions and avowals to the culture, not to minds.

                              (Coulter, *The social construction of mind*)

Popper was surely right to emphasize that bold conjectures contribute more to the progress of science than cautious inductions. This study is a linked sequence of bold conjectures, and is, of course, accompanied by the invitation — 'Go on, try to prove me wrong!'

1   CURRENT STATE OF THEORETICAL PSYCHOLOGY

Causal mechanisms and moral orders

Two images of human psychology compete for our attention. Academic psychologists, particularly those who work in the 'experimental' tradition, make the implicit assumption that men, women and children are high-grade automata, the patterns of whose behaviour are thought to obey something very like natural laws. Quite recently, thoughts and feelings have been reincorporated into the general ontology of psychology, but much of the subsequent work in cognitive psychology has preserved the automaton conception. It is assumed that there are programmes which control action and the task of psychology is to discover the 'mechanisms' by which they are implemented. Lay folk, clinical psychologists, lawyers, historians and all of those who have to deal in a practical way with human beings tend to think of people as agents struggling to maintain some sort of reasoned order in their lives against a background flux of emotions, inadequate information and the ever-present tides of social pressures.

I shall try to show that the great differences that mark off these ways of thinking about human psychology are not ultimately grounded in a reasoned weighing of the evidence available to any student of human affairs. They turn in the end on unexamined political and moral assumptions that show up in the choice of rhetoric, in morally and politically loaded ways of speaking and, more particularly, of writing. Although these profoundly different ways of interpreting and explaining human thought and action have their origin in preferred linguistic forms rather than any compelling facts of the matter, they do have profoundly different practical consequences. They carry with them very distinctive stances as to the moral, political and clinical problems with which modern people are beset.

To illustrate the role of hidden moral positions in psychology, I shall discuss a simple and fairly transparent case, where the conceptual confusion and methodological errors are near the surface. A study by Duval et al. called 'Self focus, felt responsibility and helping behaviour' was reported in the *Journal of Social and Personality Psychology*. The events, described by the authors as an 'experiment', went as follows: some young women, all psychology students, were first told a misleading tale about the episode they were to take part in. They were then left for a full minute to contemplate an image of themselves on a television monitor. Afterwards they heard a television programme, a lecture on venereal disease. Some of them heard the lecture immediately after they had been watching themselves, some four minutes later. They were then asked to fill in a questionnaire inviting them to comment on their willingness to contribute in various ways to remedial programmes for venereal disease. There is clearly something bizarre about all this — but exactly what?

The first clue can be found in the title of the article, 'Self focus, felt responsibility and helping behaviour'. Without as yet examining severally the viability of the three concepts here juxtaposed, it is clear that there is already a problematic conjunction between two conceptual systems with incompatible analytical models. The concepts of 'self-focus' and 'helping behaviour' are drawn from a system appropriate to describing human automatisms, while 'responsibility' — felt or otherwise — belongs to the representation of some moral order, the psychology of which would require judgement, decision, conscience and so on. It is clear that there is supposed to be a causal relation between 'self-focus' and the onset or degree of 'helping behaviour'. The effect of the insertion of 'responsibility' into this conceptual framework and the use of the phrase 'helping *behaviour*' is tacitly to propose that a form of conduct (*Handlung*) that is taken to be part of the moral order should be subject to a putative psychological law. The idea that the moral order is part of a technology (in this case a psychological one) is a highly culturally specific North American notion. The question of whether the North American mores which treats conduct as the behavioural output of trained automata is morally and politically acceptable, or generalizable to other cultures, is pre-empted by the way the 'experiment' is conceived. So we are presented with something as if it were empirical, which is heavily loaded with *unexamined* metaphysical and moral/political presuppositions. To look more closely at the conceptual apparatus, in terms of which the phenomena are created as 'facts', and reminding ourselves of Eddington's remark '. . . it is also a good rule not to put overmuch confidence in the observational results until they have been confirmed by theory', I turn to examine the specific concepts of this paper in more detail.

The key notions are 'self-focus' and 'helping behaviour'. The overarching theory which the experiment is supposed ultimately to test is Heider's well-known idea that people are more likely to become engaged in something with distinguishable moral qualities when they conceive themselves to be personally involved. However, there are several intermediate steps between that theory and the research programme of which the 'experiment' under discussion forms a part. The research programme began with some ideas of Duval and Wicklund in *A Theory of objective self-awareness*, which involved the forging of a dubious connection between Heider's general theory and the alleged state of consciousness called 'self-focus', by way of Mead's notion of the 'me'. To understand the problems in the design of the 'experiment', we must go back to examine the original confusions involved in the 'operationalization' of Mead's theory of the 'I' and the 'me', via the notion of 'objective self-awareness'. In Duval and Wicklund's earlier work there is not only a confusion between the assessment of actions within a moral order and the explanation of actions within a causal order, but also a failure to distinguish between an awareness of self and an awareness of aspects of self. On pages 1–9 of their first chapter, Duval and Wicklund claim to be defining a psychological condition corresponding in some way to Mead's 'me'. This they call 'objective self-awareness'. Its alleged importance lies in promoting self-evaluation; that is, it is supposed to introduce awareness of a proper subject of predication for concepts located in the moral order, such as 'responsibility'. Clearly, it can only be the self as moral agent that is the proper subject of moral evaluation, but the self in that sense is just the very thing that can never be an object of objective self-awareness. Our authors themselves acknowledge this on page 14 of the same chapter. Contradicting their original definition of self-awareness, they say that when someone focuses attention on him or herself the intentional objects are, for example, 'his consciousness, personal history or body'. But none of these entities can be the subject of those categories of moral evaluation that include 'responsibility'. The conceptual confusions of the 1979 paper are already laid down in the book of 1972. It is in this complex of confusions that automatization of the moral world of succour, aid and assistance begins. I shall now turn to examine the concepts at work in 'helping behaviour'.

Part of the source of our intuitions that there is something deeply wrong with the 'experiment' is that the scientistic terminology such as 'helping behaviour' is clearly equivocal in general and actually misapplied (outside any obvious equivocation) in this case. Taken literally, 'helping behaviour' might be thought to comprehend 'aid', 'succour', 'help', 'support' or 'assistance'. Now 'assistance', and in one of its senses 'help', is rendered to someone who is trying but not succeeding, who has some, but not all, of the requisites for a task. Here we have a determinable with a well-defined open class of determinates. But 'help' in the sense of 'succour' is an entirely distinct concept. Succour is rendered to someone already beyond trying, who is incapable of helping himself. The Samaritan gave both 'aid' (money) and 'succour' (medical attention) to the famous roadside victim. The moral order is involved in wholly distinct ways in assistance and succour. Scarcely anyone, of whatever political persuasion, would deny succour, but many on moral grounds ('It is good for you to struggle') or political principle ('It is a waste of national resources') would refuse assistance.

To one's astonishment, in this 'experiment', the 'helping behaviour' turns out to be none of these but something other — something one would be inclined precisely to exclude from helping behaviour. The young women involved (called oddly and significantly 'female subjects', a fairly clear indication of the assumed political stance of the experimenters) were not asked to render aid, succour, assistance or even help, but to fill in a questionnaire about prospective actions of various kinds not actually committing themselves, but recording whether they would, under certain circumstances, commit themselves. They were not asked whether they would give immediate help to someone, in either sense of 'help', but only whether they would act indirectly in a 'helping' programme.

So much for the 'effect' end of this study. What about the alleged cause? Again, we find equivocation rather than either the determinable–determinate or generic–specific relation. 'Self-focus' is alleged to be a specific state of consciousness, being induced by looking at oneself on the television monitor. But states of consciousness are, if anything is, intentional. How could 'self' be the intentional object of a state of consciousness of the self? Taken literally, the idea is a self-contradiction. Clearly, the concept must be being interpreted not as a focus on self, but a focus on some aspect of self as is clear from a consultation of the original text defining the research programme. There are large and diverse ranges of possibilities — general appearance, particular aspects of physical appearance, rings under eyes, skin cancer, expression, clothes and many more — even if we admit the constraints of the television monitor image as limiting the focus to what is being seen, a fairly static image of one's external appearance. None of these can be the proper subject of attributions of moral qualities such as 'responsibility'. Like 'helping behaviour', 'self-focus', taken now in the 'aspect of self' sense, is radically equivocal. In particular, there can be no certainty that 'self-focus', whatever it may mean, has induced a state of consciousness that in Miss A is psychologically commensurate with 'self-focus' as induced in Miss B, since the conditions of the 'experiment' were such as to remove all hints as to the meaning given to these strange events and in particular to looking at oneself on a television monitor, so that the myriad aspects of self one might pay attention to were undetermined. Was the appropriate psychological concomitant embarrassment, interest or self-consciousness? The young women involved were given no clue as to what it was proper for them to feel, since they were provided with no way of resolving the equivocation. The self as moral agent is, of course, the one thing that cannot be focused on via a television monitor image, since it cannot be an intentional object of awareness at all.

But, someone might retort, despite all the conceptual confusion evident in the way the events in question were written up for publication, did not *something* of significance happen? As Crowle has pointed out in his 'Deceptive speech in the laboratory', a very penetrating study of the equivocations in much 'experimental' social psychology, there are two dimensions to this. Perhaps something did happen that was essentially the *same* for each woman involved, but this, whatever it was, is capable of an indefinite number of competing explanations, each of which could be true of a particular but different woman. On the other hand, since the terms in which these events were described are essentially and deeply equivocal, the statistical results are equally compatible with the hypothesis that something essentially *different* happened to each person who took part, and only the vagueness of the conceptual apparatus is responsible for the apparent generality of the 'result'.

Individualism and subjectivism in recent psychology

Contemporary psychology is made up of two antithetical strands. First, there is the thoroughgoing individualism of the cognitivists who conceive of human action as the product of individual mental processes. Freud, Piaget and Dennett, each in their own way and each reflecting their own political and cultural assumptions, exemplify this strand. Secondly, there is the collectivism of the social constructivists, who conceive of human action as the joint intentional actions of minded creatures whose minds are structured and stocked from a social and interpersonal reality. Wittgenstein, Vygotsky and Mead exemplify the second strand, which has had little influence. For individualists, the deepest problem is how intersubjectivity is possible and their great philosophical problem that of our knowledge of other minds; for collectivists, the deepest problem is how individuality is created and sustained in so thoroughly social a world. For the former, individual being is given and social being constructed; while for the latter, collective being is given and personal being is an achievement.

The Cartesian distinction between subjective and objective experience involves a running together of two distinctions. To say an experience is subjective may mean that it is taken from a particular point of view (conceptual, moral or perceptual) that is currently 'occupied' by a person, but it may also mean 'within one consciousness'. That human beings cannot have each other's experiences (or, put picturesquely, enter into each other's consciousness) is a conceptual matter. However, points of view can be adopted, even if only with the practical aim of grasping how another person would feel or how the world would look from a particular angle, both literally and metaphorically. (J. Sabini and M. Silver in *Moralities of everyday life* give a detailed exposition of the multiplicity of meanings which the pair of terms 'subjective/objective' are capable of.) By eliding these distinctions, points of view become embedded within individual consciousnesses (or, as I will argue in a later chapter, persons become confused with selves), and so forever beyond the ken of another human being. Psychology becomes both speculative and individualistic. Before the introduction of information-processing models, the subjectivity of individual experience in this peculiar muddled joint sense led either to phenomenological meditation or to behaviourism, seeking the objective in a public physical space in which there were no points of view. But the information-processing models, formulated within the hypothetico-deductive conception of science, are still assumed to work within the subjective individualism of the traditional concept of mind. They are proposed as a way of getting round this subjectivism. It is presumed that they will enable us to grasp a 'hidden realm' of activity much as the atomic theory enabled chemists to grasp a hidden realm of exchanges which were the 'real' basis of chemical reactions (*see* M. Boden, *Artificial intelligence and natural man*).

In giving an account of any psychological phenomenon (and just what is to count as a psychological phenomenon is yet to be established), I will presume that reference to modes of reasoning and systems of belief is to be preferred to the invocation of automaton theories unless a special reason can be given in a particular case to justify the use of the latter approach. The complex of reasons for adopting this basic principle of method will emerge in the course of this work.

2   COGNITIVISM: THE LIMITS OF SUBPERSONAL PSYCHOLOGIES

You know how it is in the circus. The acrobat does something and the clown tries to imitate it, but the clown's not human, like the acrobat, he's just the creature with straw in his head. That's why clowns are at the same time funny and sad: they imitate exactly what human beings do, and if the *Nichomachean ethics* were right they really would become human. But no matter what they do, they remain just clowns.

(John Gardner, *Mickelsson's ghosts*)

For there to be a psychology in which we can recognize and represent personal being, personal powers and person-centred attributes must needs be preserved in the transition from culturally specific common understandings to a science of thought and feeling. Despite the advances in understanding achieved by recent cognitive psychology, it has failed to provide an account of the personal unities upon which human individuality depends.

A subpersonal psychology transfers the apparent psychological truths of commonsense psychologies into the scientific mode by the neat device of transforming personal functions into mental organs (or, in cybernetic terms, processing modules). Subpersonal psychology is nothing new. I shall illustrate the basic principle of the subpersonal approach and define its limitations by outlining three very diverse forms: medieval morality plays, contemporary cognitive psychology and Freudian psychodynamics. All three, according to the conventions of their times, turn functions and activities into things. None can represent what is essential to a person as a psychological unity.

It might be thought that the inter-relations of the processing modules could provide a structure sufficiently articulated to account for empirically observable cognitive organization. However, it will emerge in the course of the argument of this work that the most characteristic feature of the way modern people organize their experience involves them holding a quite specific theory about themselves. A theory, however powerful, cannot be a module or a structure of modules. It must be part of the contents of a cognitive system. It must be 'within' a module or structured on some ensemble of modules; it is part of the information processed.

Late medieval psychology of action

The morality play, as an extension of the sermon, was centrally concerned with the salvation of the soul. This interest defined the aspects of psychology dealt with in the play: the ways people 'fall into temptation and despair and how these could be overcome by repentance and by the operation of divine grace' (P. Happé, *Four morality plays*, p. 12). What were taken to be the relevant psychological facts were represented allegorically in a form of the same conceptual type as psychodynamics and cognitive psychology. A character trait, like humility, becomes a character. Humility, who helps the heroine Anima, the soul, against the machinations of Hypocrisy.

In these plays, the interaction between psychological and moral principles is overt, unlike psychodynamics and cognitive psychology, in both of which the moral element in the theory is hidden. Again, as Happé puts it, 'the hero is trapped into sin usually by the misguided exercise of free will which subjects him to the cunning of the vices who seek to destroy him' (*Four morality plays*, p. 16). The blending of psychological and moral issues appears again in the common theme of the hero entertaining a vice in ignorance. The psychology of reform and regeneration is based upon the principle that once a person begins to help himself, further support and assistance towards regeneration become available. The psychological effects of confession and penance are explored by the use of characters such as Hope.

In *Magnyfycence* by John Skelton (c. 1516) the psychology of will as wilfulness is explored. The hero, Magnyfycence, is led into trouble by being deceived by Fansy, who assists four vices, including Courtly Abusyn, to disguise themselves as virtues. So Counterfet Countenance appears as Good Demeynaunce. The effect of this is to let Lyberte escape from the oversight of Measure and Sad Cyrcumspecyon. Fansy can now be joined by Folly. From Happé (*Four morality plays*, p. 233) we see the psychological principles appearing in such dialogue as:

Fel . . .	Measure is worthy to have dominion
Liberty	Until that same I am right well agreed
	So that Liberty be not left behind.
Measure	Yea, Liberty with Measure need never dread
Liberty	What, Liberty to Measure then would be bound?
Measure	What else? For otherwise it were against kind
	If Liberty should leap and run where he list,
	It were no virtue, it were a thing unblest.

The psychological content in the play is expressed less in the action as in the discussion between the characters. It is in these exchanges that the relations between the subpersonal components are established.

In *The Castle of Perseverance* (c. 1415) it is mainly in the action that psychological theses are apparent and the model of thinking is expounded. The quotations in the following discussion are taken from *The Castle of Perseverance*, modernized by V. F. Hopper and G. B. Lahey in *Medieval mystery plays, morality plays and interludes*.

The seven deadly sins appear as characters, that is, as beings of the same kind as the hero, Mankind; temptation (the psychological play of impulse, motive etc.) is represented in conversational terms as one person tempting another. Sloth, for instance, advises Mankind:

> When the mass-bell sounds,
> Lie still man, and take no heed.

The psychological dynamics are based on the metaphor of 'advice'. Mankind accepts Envy as his Chief Counsel. This is a cognitive theory of the psychological phenomenon of the struggle against temptation (resistance to temptation has not been much studied recently though it has begun to reappear as a topic in studies of obesity, smoking and alcoholism). Treated this way thought appears as a kind of private dialogue, with the person, Mankind, adopting first one attitude and then another. For instance, Covetousness says:

> If thou be poor and needy and old,
> Thou shalt often evil find

offering a reason for accumulating wealth, just as Mankind could have offered himself.

We are presented with psychological functioning as dialogue. And this is the force of the convention by which the vices and virtues are presented dramatically. Similarly, Everyman is accompanied by Strength, Discretion, Knowledge and Beauty as companions, transformed from representations and attributes; as he nears death, Beauty and Strength literally depart. At this point a research project suggests itself: extract from both the content and the action of morality plays the main theses of late medieval cognitive psychology and compare the theories explicitly formulated by Aquinas etc. with modern attempts.

To an unknown extent subpersonal psychologies are dependent on the content of the allegories with which they express their psychological hypotheses. Dramatic allegory imposes on our understanding of psychological processes an 'internal conversation' or 'debate' framework by formalizing the psychology of temptation in terms of speaking characters. An important aspect of the psychology of temptation is the structure and conventions of personal (private) debate in which 'I' take one side and 'me' the other. Interestingly, late medieval psychologists saw that an account in terms of reasoning must be supplemented by a dimension representing the interplay of 'forces'. Debate between characters is succeeded by an outbreak of fighting in which superior force determines the outcome. Compare a modern account by Derek Wright in *The psychology of moral behaviour*.

In the exploitation of the allegories made possible by the dramatic way of representing psychological hypotheses an important feature of personal being is preserved, the unity of consciousness and agency of the hero. Despite the hiving off of some of his psychology to other characters (each itself a personal being), the hero is never divested of his psychological individuality. Even when Liberty and Measure have become disputing members of his entourage, Magnyfycence acts and suffers as a person. Though wholly failing to give an account of the personal unities, medieval psychology yet preserves them as given, playing a key role in the morally relevant psychological processes. In this respect, medieval subpersonal psychologies are very different from those of the twentieth century, where the allegories fail either to preserve or to give an account of the conditions of personal being.

Psychodynamics

In discussing psychodynamic psychology, as with medieval psychology and cognitive psychology, I am not proposing any kind of exhaustive critical treatment. I am not at all concerned with the insights these approaches have provided, but with the treatment of human individuality implicit in their structure as subpersonal psychologies. Whereas medieval moral psychology used a 'personal' allegory to give substance to psychological traits, motives and impulses, embodying them in dramatic modules (characters) represented as intentional beings, psychodynamics draws on an allegory that substantializes psychological processes as subpersonal modules as centres of force or activity. Id, Ego and Superego are not as fully personalized as Fancy and Measure are, but they strive and struggle with one another, taking over what commonsense psychology in the West treats as the activity of the person. In this sense, the classic Freudian theory is a subpersonal psychology.

The quasi-personalization of the subpersonal modules is very clear in the secondary psychodynamic literature. For instance, Blum in *Psychodynamics* talks of 'the task of the ego . . . the mediating between outer and inner forces. . .' (p. 33). 'The super ego can renounce its former alliance with the ego, in which case primitive urges from the id are more likely to gain expression' (p. 11). These quotations refer to what commonsense psychology regards as a discussion of various aspects of self-mastery or self-control. I now turn to Freud himself and his account of the famous threesome, Ego, Superego and Id.

The nature of subpersonal modules to which Freud transfers important personal functions is expressed in a distinctive allegory. In his *Outline of psychoanalysis* he writes, 'if the ego has successfully resisted a temptation to do something that would be objectionable to the super ego, it feels its self-respect raised and its pride increased . . .' (p. 122). Relative to this high degree of personalization both id and superego are automata, centres of psychic forces (reserves of psychic energy, libido etc.), illuminated by Freud in a series of non-personalist allegories. The quotations from Freud given in the following discussion are all taken from the *Outline of psychoanalysis*.

Freud calls the id a 'mental province or agency' which provides mental expression for instincts. The account of the ego is more specific in its elucidation of the psychodynamic allegory. The subpersonalizing step is made explicitly as 'the ego is in control of voluntary movement'. As voluntary movement is precisely the kind of action which the person controls, the introduction of a subpersonal module identified as performing that function eliminates the agency of the person.

Furthermore, the ego is a multi-function module since, according to Freud, it becomes 'aware of stimuli from without', and can 'gain control over the demands of the instincts'. The superego is also introduced as a 'special agency'. The interactions between and mutual influences among the three subperson modules are offered by Freud as the 'general pattern of psychical apparatus'. Mentation is the interplay of the three. For instance, Freud says: 'An action by an ego is as it should be if it satisfies simultaneously the demands of the id, of the super ego and of reality' (*Outline*, p. 16).

The personal unity of unities — of consciousness, agency and auto-biography, the understanding of which must be the core project of personal psychology — has been dissolved in the classic dynamic approach. (Interestingly, Freud gives a thoroughgoing realist account of his psychology of the unconscious, making his claim to founding a science just on the basis of a realist construction of physics and chemistry, *see Outline*, pp. 105 – 6.) Freud's description of his theory draws on a qualitative rather than a relational theory of consciousness. He speaks of 'these qualities of mental processes: they are either conscious, pre-conscious or unconscious'. By choosing this descriptive convention, rather than speaking of a person standing in three different 'awareness' relations to a mental content, Freud quietly eliminates another central unity, the one (person) to many (contents) organization of a personal field of knowledge.

In treating psychodynamics as a subpersonal psychology, I have interpreted the three organizing centres, id, ego and superego, as functionally defined modules. Such a treatment presumes that there are such distinctive functions. Equally one might take them to be names for clusters of beliefs, interpreted feelings, conventionally sanctioned structures of cognition and so on. Looked at this way, psychodynamics shifts from a putative analysis of mental formations engendered by some sort of process — say, learning to cope with the interplay between social relations within a family and biological maturation — to a competitor to other socially founded theories upon which to build one's mind. Instead of the duality of indexical 'I' and referential 'I', and the socially grounded separation of 'I' and 'me', the mind of a person growing up within a society which has institutionalized the psychodynamic point of view will take on the tripartite form the theory represents, struggling against the insidious pressures of the traditional grammatical models. Further pursuit of this idea would take us into the study of social representations, where an important beginning has been made by the French school of social psychologists (*see*, for example, Moscovici, *La psychoanalyse*).

Cognitive psychology

In psychology we can see a tacit change of the philosophical foundations of academic psychology, from positivism to realism, closely matching Freud's position. It appears not only as the attempt to bring back the study of thought to psychology, but as proposing a powerful theory of thinking based on the use of the realist apparatus of theory construction. Through the 'artificial intelligence' link, a powerful source model for controlling theory construction is deployed, namely machine computation. Why then seek to pass beyond it, since unlike radical behaviourism as a successor to classical behaviourism, it meets all the most stringent demands required of a study to be reckoned to be scientific.

The limitations of cognitive psychology arise from disparities between its source model, the general computation machine treated system-theoretically, and the client, a human being. The honest efforts of Dennett to develop the foundations of cognitive psychology have revealed the limits to this approach as well as signalled its successes. There seems to be no way that the necessary unities of human psychological functioning, the foundations of personal being, can be expressed in the concepts available within this framework. In particular, there is no place in this representation for the sense of personal identity through which one conceives of oneself as having an autobiography, nor the necessary unity of each person's consciousness, nor the asymmetrical structure of each person's experience of his or her powers of action. To be true to its subject matter, cognitive psychology must be transcended in just these respects. This issue has a very close parallel in the problem Hume bequeathed to Kant. If 'the self' is not an empirical concept, how is the experienced unity of personal being to be accounted for? Kant's philosophical innovations can be looked on as contributions to a general psychology in which the unities of experience are accounted for through applications of the doctrine of synthesis. In the Kantian view, the experienced unities of personal being are actively created out of an undifferentiated continuum of experience. I believe Kant's solution to be essentially right. Thanks to an excellent exposition of the nature and assumptions of cognitive psychology by Colby in 'Modelling a paranoid mind', the strength and limits of cognitive psychology can be defined quite precisely in two steps: the subpersonalizing step and the AI step.

The subpersonalizing step

A personal activity, such as deciding, is described as an entity, a decision module, which merely belongs to a person. A person's decisions are made by a subpersonal component or system of components. Initially these subpersonal components or modules are the reified analogues of personal capacities and activities, that is, mental functions, that are identified and individuated by folk psychology. This step has the effect of setting up cognitive psychology as a realist scientific project, since information processing by subpersonal components constitutes a generating 'mechanism' for explaining noticeable patterns of talk and meaningful actions. The ontological status of subpersonal modules will be considered below.

The AI step

To create a generating 'mechanism' out of the subpersonal components of mind, a source model is introduced, machine computation (called by Colby 'an algorithmic model') whose explanatory force is 'related more to its generative power than its predictive power'. This imposes certain structural features on the system of modules, and sharpens the way they can be conceived to function. Each human individual is conceived as an AI-like system.

Two features of this scheme stand out: (a) the person as psychological agent and actor is systematically eliminated in favour of the person as owner (but not manager) of a bunch of 'machines' and, (b) the subpersonal components are parts of an individual. These two features are enough to specify the limits of cognitive psychology quite precisely.

Limit one: psychological unities are necessary but cannot be
represented.

Limit two: sociopsychological dualities are necessary but cannot be
represented.

I borrow a 'layout' (from an unpublished paper by Justin Leiber) to illustrate the nature of the argument to these limits. The following schema represents possible subjects of mental predications:

				Psychic	
Species Societies Families		PERSONS	Organisms Brains	modules (mental organs)	Cells
Suprapersonal structures			Subpersonal components		

The centre point at persons provides a model for all mentalistic predications, but the subjects of thinking, knowing, believing, acting feeling predicates are always 'persons' and persons 'have' unity. Precise answers to the question of the limits of cognitive psychology as subpersonal psychology will depend which of the mentalistic predicates in ordinary language involve unity concepts *of necessity*, and which involve collective concepts *of necessity*: the former I call the 'unities' and the latter the 'dualities'.

The conceptual clusters around personal identity, consciousness and agency necessarily involve 'unity' and so cannot be analogically re-applied to either the domain of subpersonal modules or suprapersonal structures. But many conceptual clusters, it seems, can be reapplied to subpersonal modules without conceptual incoherence, that is, without violating any necessary conditions for their intelligibility, for instance 'remembering'; others can be reapplied to suprapersonal structures, for example, 'reasoning'. However, there will be some which can be applied suprapersonally, but not subpersonally.

The 'dualities' appear as defining a limit because, while they cannot be reapplied to suprapersonal entities without some change in meaning (as, for instance, in speaking of a nation as intending or of a crowd as angry), they do involve among the necessary conditions for their application, certain properties of collectives of which their ostensible bearers are a proper part.

These restrictions on cognitive psychology can be expressed in another way. Again, to quote from 'Modelling a paranoid mind' by Colby: 'As a type of theoretical psychology, AI takes as its entities of enquiry, representations of mental processes. Its vocabulary is a mixture of terms from folk-psychology . . ., scientific psychology . . ., linguistics. . ., and computer science.'

There are two ways in which the vocabulary of folk-psychology could engender a fragment of the terminology of cognitive psychology, depending on the analogy relations between the referents of the terms in question.

(1) Person attributes $\rightleftharpoons$ 'unconscious' processes and
analogous to cognitions,

exemplified in familiar psychodynamic relations such as that between 'conscious wish' and 'unconscious wish'. Some have argued that the analogy relation is used to create a terminology for a top-down taxonomy for physiological states and processes. This, it is clear, is *not* how cognitive psychology is created.

(2) Personal attributes $\longrightarrow$ thinking modules.
subpersonalized

This is not an analogy relation but exemplifies the process socio-linguists call 'relexicalization', that is, using a term with a set of onto-logical presumptions radically different from its 'transparent' use. So to speak of 'my memory' instead of 'I remember' (to take an example of Colby's is to shift remembrance from its 'transparent' place as a personal achievement to a point in a network of conceptual relations that ramify from its having a thing-like status.

Personal attributes which involve essential reference to unified selves cannot be relexicalized in this fashion. The change of ontological commitment of the concepts in cases which are permitted is not a fallacy since the new entities are hypothetical beings, thought modules whose workings are supposed to explain the pattern of personal attributes, identified relative to the pre-relexicalized use of the descriptive term. In short, the workings of the memory module are supposed to explain remembering. All other terms but memory in that phrase, i.e. 'working' and 'module', are derived from the AI source model. Whether this has been a useful development can be empirically tested by running the module as a simulator. In so far as its behaviour is analogous to 'someone remembering' then so far is it proved plausible in the familiar manner of the natural sciences.

I began with the suggestion that the relation between cognitive psychology and computer science could be exhaustively understood by assuming that the latter provided a source of models for the mechanisms responsible for functions and processes identified by the commonsense psychological distinctions built into the former. The creation of 'modules' or 'mental organs' by relexicalizing personal action, process and achievement concepts suggests that the role of AI is not just to be a source of models but is also a descriptive rhetoric. But a rhetoric for a description of what?

There seem to be only two possibilities. First, it is a rhetoric for redescribing commonsense psychology; for instance 'pattern recognition' in AI is what is called 'noticing' in commonsense psychology. Or secondly, it is, as Freud took his psychology to be, a mentalistic rhetoric for describing physiological processes; or both. The former runs into the difficulty we have spotted with much laboratory psychology of slipping by virtue of rhetoric alone, without substantial argument, from moral to causal orders, from thinking to information processing. The latter imposes a cognitive module as mental organ structure on the physiological description of brain activity. While it is patently clear that stomachs digest and hearts pump, as opposed to whole bodies, families etc., it is not at all clear that contemporary brain physiology will admit of a memory organ remembering or a language organ speaking. So far as I can understand him in *Brainstorms*, Dennett does not require direct physiological reference for the terms of his AI rhetoric.

I have discussed the cybernetic theory in rather simplistic fashion concentrating on the subpersonal modular structure; but, to be taken seriously, the analogy between machine computation and thinking needs more careful examination, particularly the reading given to the distinction between programming languages and machine languages. Looked at closely, the idea that machine computation could be the analogue of thought is easily disposed of. Computers do not compute in the programming language chosen, but in a 'machine language', an electronic code. The question upon which the viability of the machine computation as an analogue for thought depends is whether, in a relevant sense, machine language is a language. The relevant sense has to do with its cognitive attributes, if any. I think it is clear that the 'machine language' neither has nor could have any cognitive attributes, hence it is not a language in the relevant sense and so could not be an analogue for thought.

The proof is simple. When a computer is programmed, an essential step in the process is the transformation of strings of programme language units, which do have meaning and whose syntactical constraints are significant, into sequences of electromagnetic pulses whose sequential manipulation is a product of the physical structure of the machine. The point is banal, but of enormous philosophical significance. In this respect computers are no more sophisticated than egg sorters. The instruction 'Sort eggs into large, standard and small' is realized in flexible plates with different-sized holes in them. But the relation between the holes is physical; it is the machine language version of the semantic distinction between 'large', 'standard' and 'small' of the programming language.

In a simple case like this the structure of the physical relations of the relevant components of the machine maps neatly on to the semantic structure of the concepts in the natural language. If this kind of mapping is the justification for supposing that there is a computational 'language' the argument is very weak. The machine 'language' of the brain, the basis of the structured patterns of electrical impulses and chemical diffusions that go on when we think, is not a language in any reasonable sense. Fodor supposes that it is just obvious that 'the organic events which we accept as implicated in the etiology of behavior will turn out to have two theoretically relevant descriptions *if things turn out right*: a physical description by virtue of which they fall under causal laws and a psychological description by virtue of which they constitute steps in the *computation* from the stimulus to the response' (my italics). But by what right is it claimed that there is a 'psychological' description in terms of which thinking appears as 'computation'? Fodor simply begs all the important questions by asserting on p. 99 that 'the available models of cognitive processes characterize them as fundamentally computational' and uses this claim to *exclude* English, Russian etc. as languages of cognition. We have one very good model of cognitive processes, namely ordinary language, which characterizes such processes precisely as non-computational. Until it has been *shown* that for an English native speaker the medium of cognitive processes cannot be English, the introduction of a 'computational engine' is gratuitous. (See further Fodor, *The language of thought*.)

Fodor simply takes for granted the logicism (that is the principle that the representation of cognitive processes should be in terms of formulae of formal logic) that should have been the matter at issue.

3   SOCIAL FOUNDATIONS OF MIND

The fundamental human reality is a conversation, effectively without beginning or end, to which, from time to time, individuals may make contributions. All that is personal in our mental and emotional lives is individually appropriated from the conversation going on around us and perhaps idiosyncratically transformed. The structure of our thinking and feeling will reflect, in various ways, the form and content of that conversation. The main thesis of this work is that mind is no sort of entity, but a system of beliefs structured by a cluster of grammatical models. The science of psychology must be reshaped accordingly.

Social representations

I hope to show that not only are the acts we as individuals perform and the interpretations we create of the social and physical world prefigured in collective actions and social representations, but also that the very structure of our minds (and perhaps the fact that we have minds at all) is drawn from those social representations. At the centre of the argument will be a treatment of the three central aspects of human psychology, consciousness, agency and identity, and above all their reflexive forms, self-consciousness, self-mastery and autobiography, tying all this together in one, very general, empirical hypothesis. For me, a person is not a natural object, but a cultural artefact. A person is a being who has learned a theory, in terms of which his or her experience is ordered. I believe that persons are characterized neither by their having a characteristic kind of experience nor by some specific genetic endowment. They can be identified neither phenomenologically nor biologically, but only by the character of their beliefs.

There are two primary realities in human life: the array of persons and the network of their symbiotic interactions, the most important of which is talk. I begin with the presumption that privatization and personalization of part of that network is thought. These realities are irreducible to one another, but each is a necessary condition for the possibility of the other. The network of symbiotic interactions appears to people in the form of two secondary realities; these are the social systems of material production and of the creation and maintenance of honour and value, both of which are mediated by meanings and stabilized by ritual.

Given these primary realities, where are cognitive processes aboriginally located? Are they in the public – collective/social realm of talk or do they belong in the private – individual/personal realms of individual experience? The basic premise of personal psychology is that cognitive activities are primarily public and collective, located in talk. They become personal activities of individual people by developmental processes of the kind Vygotsky in *Thought and language* called 'appropriation', for example, the process by which we come to learn to talk to ourselves. Personal appropriations occur, I shall try to show, only in the course of the redistribution of demands upon individuals to make contributions to the public performances of thought and feeling put on them by psychologically symbiotic arrays, that is, socially structured groups of people. A simple competence – performance distinction is too unstructured to help us understand this. Not only are many of the items of the stocks of knowledge that should be included in competence not individually represented, they may be socially created in the course of collective action, as may be the very beings themselves. Personal beings, as I shall try to establish, must be thought of as social productions if we are fully to understand their nature. Personal beings appear in our psychology in much the same way that gravitational fields appear in physics. The ambiguity of this remark is deliberate. They appear both in our mental life *and* in our science of mental life in much the same way. Our mental life, I shall argue, is the result of the acquisition of a theory. Though personal beings are real, they are the product of theoretical activity. They are not, for instance, the result of biological maturation.

This duality comes about because much that we take to be metaphysically ultimate in psychology are referents of theoretical concepts. The case I shall concentrate on is the 'self'. By believing the theories in which concepts like the self have a place, we so structure our experience as to create them: different theories, different mental organization. Everything that appears to each of us as the intimate structure of our personal being, I believe to have its source in a socially sustained and collectively imposed cluster of theories. What then remains as native psychological endowment? I think this question is much more difficult than most discussions of the nature/nurture controversy would have it. (*See* Moscovici, *Society against nature*.)

It has been shown that from their earliest moments infants make demands upon their mothers and other caretakers that provoke the very talk and action from the mother that promotes the kind of development towards personal being implicit in the viewpoint here expounded. If my general thesis is right, each level of sophistication of public — collective activity in which a developing person joins is prepared for, not by a maturing natural endowment, but by the previous level of that inter-personal, public and collective activity. The infant's apparently native contributions are already emerging from the personalization of the social structure within which it is being established. The outcome of contemporary studies of how development proceeds is a highly socialized theory of maturation, but in my view it is not yet socialized enough.

The arguments of this work, designed to show the plausibility of the view that to think, to perceive, to be rational and to experience emotions are cultural endowments not native achievements, fit neatly and tightly into recent advances in developmental psychology. In addition, as I shall propose from time to time, they shadow forth a sheaf of research menus, for much yet remains to be done to prove that a conceptual system as radical as the one proposed is indeed instantiated in mankind. An irony will be that ethnocentric theories like those of Piaget and Kohlberg will be able to be shown to be instantiations themselves of the theory of personal being. The conclusion of the argument is the idea that a person is a being who orders his or her activities according to a theory of his or her own nature. To realize that one is a person is to learn a way of thinking about and managing oneself. It is not to be prompted to make some kind of empirical discovery.

Both cognitive psychology and psychodynamics fail to give an account of the unities which constitute persons as individuals, and which make possible their personal being. The proof that these unities are artefacts is the centrepiece of my study. I propose to show that the unities of consciousness and of agency which constitute a sense of personal identity are acquired as the result of learning theories of personhood in which various notions of 'the self' figure as theoretical concepts. My project is Kantian in that I do not believe that the unities that are the basis of selfhood are given in experience. However, unlike Kant, I believe that it is possible to give an account of their origin in empirical terms, but the terms are social. Contrary to Kant, who held that transcendental objects had only transcendental properties, I hold that at least some important transcendental objects have social properties.

The detailed arguments which follow are each an application of a general theory of the semantics of theoretical concepts, a theory which shows how it is possible for concepts which refer to entities beyond any experience to have empirical content.

Origins of personal being

To be psychologically an individual is to be self-conscious and self-activating and controlling. The former includes a knowledge of one's history as well as one's current unique location in the array of persons. The latter includes one's capacities to initiate action upon things and persons other than oneself, as well as to undertake reflexive intervention in oneself, and so requires the mastery of the concept pair 'myself'/'not myself'.

Neither self-consciousness nor self-activation and intervention is sufficient to establish personal being, since the structures of mind upon which they depend and the forms they take are derived from the social structures and linguistic practices of the communities within which people, to become people, must live. Personal being arises only by a transformation of the social inheritance of individuals. It is essentially a semantic transformation and arises through the use of cognitive processes typified by metaphor to transform the social inheritance. This capacity is itself a social inheritance and there may be societies whose members never can achieve personal being because the practice of individual transformation of social resources does not exist.

All this has profound consequences for the psychology of moral orders and for our views as to the apprenticeship of moral agents. I propose an alternative view of the transformation of social puppets into moral agents to that of Piaget and Kohlberg — the analogue in the moral order to the psychological transformation of social into personal beings.

Identity projects

The central role of the social environment in the formation of persons, an environment which takes particular form in languages and other semiotic systems, poses the complementary human predicament to that with which I was concerned in *Social being*. In that work I aimed to show how it was possible for individual thinkers to come together to form collectives and to engage in structured, coordinated action. I was concerned, too, with how social identities are created and how people come to feel themselves to belong to human categories of various kinds. In this work I am concerned with the problem of uniqueness, of how it is that creatures whose very minds are the product of social processes can nevertheless so distinguish themselves from their social equals that they can stand out truly as individuals. For marginal men and women, the achievement of social identity, of blending into a background, of acquiring camouflage, is a primary task. It has been the main research interest of those psychologists who are themselves in one way or another marginal people. In this work I am concerned with the predicament of those who have too much social identity, who have been born into families, classes or nations which provide them with a very detailed mode of social being. Their problem is to stand out from the crowd. So while it is true that people strive to show themselves to be what the best authorities tell them they are, it is also true that many among them make strenuous efforts to be at least in some respects different from those they find around them and in terms of which their category of being is defined.

4   CREATION OF PERSONAL BEING

If to be a person is to have a grasp of a theory, an important part of personal psychology will overlap with the philosophy of science. The study of how theoretical concepts come to have meaning will be a matter of common interest.

The semantics of theoretical concepts

In the natural sciences theories exist to explain patterns of phenomena. But patterns of phenomena are not given, they are abstracted from a very complex matrix of experience. It seems that some sort of analytical 'tool' is in use to make the abstraction systematically. In many cases I believe it can be shown that the analytical tool is an analogy. For example, by exploring the analogy between springs and gases, Boyle devised his original apparatus, in which the effect of compressing air could be accurately measured. His law describes a pattern of phenomena revealed only on the condition that air is treated as if it were a spring.

This can be transferred to the social sciences with a crucial modification. Whenever we presuppose that the analytical analogue helps to reveal natural patterns, we must first suppose that, in the human case, the analogue helps to create them. I hold that people create themselves and their patterns of interaction by virtue of the psychological and social theories to which they subscribe. To follow this thought through, we must explicate the relation between explanation and analysis, since the prime role of theory is in explanation. There is an explanatory task coordinate with the analytical task. It is to answer the question 'By what means are the revealed patterns engendered?' In general, these means are not available to observation, at least when the question is first posed. How are we to find the means to describe something which cannot be experienced? And how are we to ensure that the description is not of some mere fancy?

First, let us think of the content of a theoretical discourse, and then of the semantics of its descriptive vocabulary. Whatever one imagines as the productive process of a known pattern of observation must satisfy two criteria:

(1) Its imagined manifest behaviour must be treated like the real manifest behaviour of the real productive process, behaviour which is revealed in the patterns of phenomena, abstracted by the use of the analytical analogue. So the gross behaviour of the imagined constituents of gases, molecules, must be similar to the behaviour patterns of real gases as revealed by Boyle's use of the analogue of the spring. This is the criterion of the behavioural analogy.

(2) Its imagined nature or defining characteristics must be like that of some real thing or process of which we already have some empirical knowledge. The effect of this material analogy is to ensure the plausibility of our imagined productive process as something that could be real, as a possible object of observation. In philosophical terms this constraint determines the rules of natural kind to which the components of our imagined productive process must comply. This is the criterion of the source analogy.

It is not suggested that there should be a material identity between the source analogue and the explanatory process we have imagined. This would be altogether too conservative. There seem to be many controversies within the sciences which could be interpreted as disputes about the limits to which a material analogy can be drawn without the imagined process losing its plausibility as a possible existent. In the physical sciences radically new natural kinds are introduced as explanatory agents by cognitive processes different from those described here. This methodology is appropriate to problems of explanation where the explanatory agents are for some reason assumed to be of a familiar kind, though instances may be unobservable as such.

The central pivot of my argument is this: the semantics of the conceptual cluster around the general notion of the 'self' is to be understood as if the 'self' were a theoretical concept like those of the natural sciences, judged by its behavioural and material analogies and its degree of coordination with the analytical analogue that is in use in abstracting experiential patterns, which are to be explained by invoking it. Unlike the natural sciences, in the human sciences the productive process, and in particular the beings involved in it, are themselves products of 'educational' processes in which these very theoretical concepts play an indispensable part. These beings are what they are partly by virtue of holding this or that theory. It is my belief that empirical research built around these ideas will show that that 'partly' is actually 'mostly'.

The flow of the following argument is determined by my belief that the central constructing concept of individual human psychology is a concept of 'self', but that it is a theoretical concept whose source analogue is the socially defined and sustained concept of 'person' that is favoured in the society under study and is embodied in the grammatical forms of public speech appropriate to talk about persons. Our personal being is created by our coming to believe a theory of self based on our society's working conception of a person. I can change my personal being only if I can come to believe a theory of self derived from the concept of a person current in another and different society. It is the societal element in this process which makes it virtually impossible for people to acquire the genuinely Oriental selves they need to be adepts of Eastern religions while they live in a practical order dependent on an incompatible concept of person.

Person and self: preliminary distinctions

For the purposes of exposition I propose to rework the twin concepts of 'person' and 'self' to differentiate them a little more sharply than is customary in ordinary language or in philosophy. However, I believe that in doing so I am highlighting a working distinction in the concepts appropriate to a discourse about human individuals. By 'person' I intend the socially defined, publicly visible embodied being, endowed with all kinds of powers and capacities for public, meaningful action, very much the concept as elucidated by P. F. Strawson in his *Individuals*. By 'self' I mean the personal unity I take myself to be, my singular inner being, so to speak. The self, in this sense, is that for which Hume searched but which he could not find. I believe that it is a concept quite essential to the elucidation of our personal being, but that its status has not been fully or correctly explicated even by Kant. It has been neglected by psychological science in which the 'self-concept' refers to something quite different, namely a system of beliefs that one has about oneself. The conditions predisposing to such self-ascription are central to my enquiry. The principal endeavour of this work is the elucidation of the nature and origin of this traditional 'self' through a study of the acquisition of the concept of personal unity.

While 'person' is an empirical concept which distinguishes beings in a public – collective realm, 'self' (in the sense I am using it in this work) is a theoretical concept acquired in the course of social interactions. This is not the self-concept of the psychologists, but a more primitive notion presupposed by it. Psychology, both lay and professional, takes for granted that human experience is organized as 'person-centred modules'. I would like to find out how this organization comes about. To undertake such a project a conceptual structure must first be built.

First, I shall show how selves are constructed and discuss some of the consequences of that demonstration. In the course of the argument, the important idea of psychological symbiosis is introduced. Next, I shall demonstrate in detail how the self, as a theoretical concept, functions in creating the unities of personal identity, consciousness and agency. Finally, I shall reveal in detail, with various illustrative examples, the essentially social nature of a range of typical personal psychological states and attributes, in particular intentions and emotions. The bases of personal being will appear in the form of a sense of identity, a capacity for self-consciousness and in reflexive powers to act, agency directed to oneself.

The unities of personal being

Sense of personal identity
I distinguish the socially defined fact of personal identity, in which the particularity of personal embodiment plays a central part, from the personal sense of identity through which a person conceives of him or herself as a singular being with a continuous and unique history. The latter is a necessary condition for the acquisition of a theory of the self, which is experienced as the sense of identity.

Self-consciousness
In studying the second pillar of personal being, 'self-consciousness', my first step is to argue for the cultural diversity of the structures or forms of consciousness that is taken as known experience. As a form of knowledge, consciousness must take on the structure of the grammatical forms in which personal knowledge is expressed in psycholinguistically distinct cultures. I argue for a distinction between consciousness as the experiencing of something and consciousness as knowing that one is experiencing something. Certainly the latter is propositional and, as I shall argue, is structured in accordance with grammatical forms. I shall show that the experiential aspect of consciousness can be expressed by the use of the concepts of 'awareness' and 'attention'. The further study of the phenomenon of consciousness as experience is of biological and physiological interest (*see* J. M. Davidson and R. J. Davidson, *The psychobiology of consciousness*).

A theoretician's interest will be caught by such problems as whether 'aware of' and 'attend to' can be properly predicated of creatures who do not (or perhaps better seem not to) make use of concepts. Where do we draw the line in the organic world between those creatures whose awareness is intensional as well as intentional, that is, depends on concepts and is directed to objects and those with simpler preconceptual cognitive systems?

Consciousness as knowing involves both knowing what one is experiencing and that one is experiencing it; in short, in consciousness experience is rendered both propositional and self-attributable. Grammatically speaking, this must involve the capacity to make some form of self-reference. I shall try to show that in its most general form this requirement is met by the capacity to use indexical expressions, typically pronouns and equivalent forms, which do not involve any metaphysical assumptions about 'inner' organization of thought and require only a public – collective concept of 'person'.

In English first person pronouns (and second and third person too) have a dual function. They serve to index a speech as the utterance of a particular person, that is, to locate the utterance and all its moral consequences, such as commitment etc., in an array of persons — the sociopsychological 'space'. They are also taken, in our culture, to refer to an inexperienced theoretical entity — the self — which is the centre of the field of conscious experience, both perceptual and meditative, and the subject of psychological attributions, as, for example, feelings, emotions, decisions, thoughts and perceptions. To be able to make the second kind of self-reference it is necessary, I believe and undertake to show, to be in possession of a theory. In any particular culture it will be just the very theory that others use to make psychological attributions to a person, many of which will belong in a moral order as, for instance, exhortations, complaints, condemnations, congratulations and so on.

The distinctions I am making are not, I hope, unfamiliar. That between consciousness and knowledge is very close to Dennett's distinction in *Content and consciousness* between awareness of cues to action and awareness of what might be said, though I am not happy with his treatment of these in detail. The distinction between the socially defined person of person predications and the theoretically defined 'self' of self-predications is close to Mead's distinction between the 'I' and the 'me' in *Mind, self and society*; it is not that between Kant's empirical and transcendental selves. While the latter is the self of my account, the Kantian empirical self seems to be close to the 'self-concept' of the psychologists, the object of a bundle of beliefs without a well-defined subject, slipping about between the concept of a socially defined person and a theoretically defined self.

Between the simply experiential and the plainly propositional lies the philosophically tantalizing territory of prepropositional knowing. One knows what one is experiencing without at that moment being ready to declare it. To identify something, to know what it is, rather than merely to react to it as a stimulus, requires the use of a system of categories and types, amongst some of which it belongs and others it does not. It seems to me quite proper to say of an animal that it knows what it is watching, hunting, perhaps even expecting, though quite improper to say that it knows that it is watching a bird, hunting a mouse or expecting its dinner (*see* R. Harré and V. Reynolds, *The meaning of primate signals*). This implies that while animal psychology may need categories and concepts (that is, involves intensions) it does not need propositions.

Agency
The third component of personal being is agency. To be an agent is to be something more than a creature with a subpersonal psychology formed of active components like drives, motivations, intentions and desires. To be an agent is to conceive of oneself as (hold a theory that one is) a being in possession of an ultimate power of decision and action. A pure agent is capable of deciding between alternatives, even if they are equally attractive or forceful. A pure agent is capable of overcoming temptations and distractions to realize its plans. It can adopt new principles and it can curb its own desires.

The argument for an ultimate source of agency *above*, as it were, subpersonal powerful particulars, such as desires and intentions, depends on treating *akrasia* ('weakness of will') and bloody-mindedness as socially defined proofs of autonomy, inexplicable by reference to structures of subpersonal mental components. Both sorts of failing are instances of public acts of personal defiance of the imperatives to action usually represented in the means—end pairs like intention—rule sets that are taken as mandatory forms of cognition, at least in contemporary Western societies.

The theoretical entity (at least in our cultures) at the heart of our theories of self-awareness and of agency is the very same entity 'oneself', belief in which our sense of personal identity depends upon. There is no necessity in this unity of unities since one could imagine cultures in which a pair of distinct entities did the job, one to each role. I believe that what is transcendental to experience is none other than the social conditions under which persons are created from mere organic beings by their acquiring a theory appropriate to their society. To be self-conscious and to act freely are not, I believe, mysterious capacities, but particular ways of thinking about what one is experiencing, planning, executing and so on. It follows that there ought to be hints, in anthropological reports, of cultures with different theories of the self, and perhaps even cases in which, unlike the Kantian West, one theory is used to organize awareness of one's states and activities and another to control action. Julian Jaynes, in his *Origins of con-*

sciousness, has suggested as much in his distinction between cultures where one instructs oneself to act and cultures where instructions are thought to emanate from elsewhere, for instance from the gods.

The conceptual edifice created in this study rests, inevitably, on unexamined foundations. The most important of these is the notion of belief. A proper investigation of this concept would be a massive undertaking beyond the scope of this work. I must rely throughout, therefore, on the indulgence of an intuitive understanding of the notion.

RESEARCH MENU 1

Much work remains to be done in bringing out the subtle ways that cultural presumptions, both moral and political, are at work in psychological theory and method. The most fruitful field at present is social psychology, where there continues to be a tradition of experiment of a rather naïve sort. This field shares with moral development psychology a widespread use of the documentary method, that is experimental subjects work with documents — descriptions of people and events and questionnaires to fill in and scales to mark up. The idea of personal interaction through documents is a very modern innovation and its moral, political and psychological groundwork needs careful examination.

Three areas stand out:

(1) Attribution theory, where the situational effects on the asymmetries of explanation of action (or inaction) seem to cry out for evaluation relative to local moral orders.

(2) The organization of attitude research around the idea of attitude change is an obvious candidate for a historical study of the social and political attitudes of those who first set about such a study.

(3) Perhaps the most interesting study would be to look into the assumptions that lie behind the premise that intergroup processes are founded in social comparisons and occur in taxonomic or unstructured groups. A comparison between Sabini and Silver's theory of the holocaust in *Moralities of everyday life* with that implicit in the work of the late Henri Tajfel would be most instructive, (see his generalization of 'in-group'/'out-group' theory in *Differentiation between social groups*).

A fascinating study in subpersonal psychology, based upon Medieval plays suggests itself: Extract from both the content and the action of morality plays the main theses of implicit late medieval cognitive psychology; compare them with the theories explicitly formulated by Aquinas, and with modern attempts to define the principles of human reasoning, say the 'balance' theories inspired by F. Heider.

BIBLIOGRAPHICAL NOTES 1

Since de Schamm's remarkable study of the politics of agoraphobia, the idea of a change in psychology with a change in social conditions can hardly be denied by the most naïve universalist. Agoraphobia appeared amongst women just to the degree that the streets became safe for them to venture abroad. Much that we take to be psychological ways of acting, such as self-control, see N. ELIAS, *The civilizing process*, vol. 1 (Oxford: Basil Blackwell, 1978), or psychologically distinctive categories of beings such as children, see P. ARIES, *Centuries of childhood* (trans. R. Baldick, London: Cape, 1962) and C. JENKS, *The sociology of childhood* (London: Batsford, 1982), is of recent origin but is now very well established.

In this work I cannot pretend to have proved the reality of psychological relativity. Rather I have tried to cast doubt on naïve theses of psychological universality and to develop a conceptual scheme within which the question of psychological relativity can be raised empirically. 'Experimental' psychologists have paid no attention that I can discern to the mass of material assembled between the publication of Z. BARBU, *Problems of historical psychology* (London: Routledge and Kegan Paul, 1960) and P. HEELAS and A. LOCK, *Indigenous psychologies* (London: Academic Press, 1981). See also B. LLOYD and J. GAY, *Universals of human thought* (Cambridge: Cambridge University Press, 1982). This omission is partly the outcome of ignorance, but partly the result of the inability of the automaton conceptual scheme to accommodate the idea of human action as the product of belief systems, whether the automaton is Skinnerian, Freudian or cognitive. Further citations of empirical studies relevant to the issue will be found in the bibliographical notes to chapters 2 and 5. For an important discussion of the ambiguity of 'experiments', see A. J. CROWLE, 'Deceptive speech in the laboratory' (in *Life sentences*, ed. R. Harré, London: Wiley, 1976).

G. H. MEAD's great work, *Mind, self and society* (Chicago: Chicago University Press, 1933) had very little influence on the direction of psychology, despite the clarity of its proposals (*see* p. 150). Two further conceptual innovations were required to put its ideas to work in empirical research. L. VYGOTSKY's idea of the way speech develops 'from the social to the individual' in *Thought and language* (Cambridge, Mass.: MIT Press, 1962, p. 20) is neatly summarized by A. R. LURIA, *Language and cognition* (Washington: V. H. Winston, 1981): '. . .what the child at first does with help, and on the instructions of the adult, he later begins to do by himself, supporting himself with his own speech; that speech as a form of communication with adults later becomes a means of organizing the child's own behaviour, and that function which was previously divided between two people later becomes an internal function of human behaviour'. Also important are Wittgenstein's investigations of grammatical models at the heart of language games of thinking, deciding, expressing feelings, acting and so on. For the general theory of 'grammars' see J. CANFIELD, *Wittgenstein, language and world* (Amherst: University of Massachusetts Press, 1982). See L. WITTGENSTEIN, *Remarks on the philosophy of psychology* (vol. 1, eds G. E. M. Anscombe and G. H. von Wright, trans. G. E. M. Anscombe; vol. 2, eds G. H. von Wright and H. Nyman, trans. C. G. Luckhardt and M. A. E. Aue, Oxford: Basil Blackwell, 1980) and, of course, L. WITTGENSTEIN, *Philosophical investigations* (Oxford: Basil Blackwell,

1953). Wittgenstein's contribution to psychology is admirably summed up by G. P. BAKER and P. M. S. HACKER, 'The grammar of psychology: Wittgenstein's *Bemerkungen über die Philosophie der Psychologie'* (*Language and Communication*, 2, 1982, 227−44).

A perfect example of universalist−positivist distortions in the theory of socialization is R. R. SEARS, E. E. MACCOBY and H. LEVIN, *Patterns of child rearing* (Evanston, Ill.: Row Peterson, 1957). For the contribution of the infant to the conditions of its own cognitive supplementation see C. TREVARTHEN, 'Communication and cooperation in early infancy: a description of primary intersubjectivity' (in *Before speech: the beginning of interpersonal communication*, ed. M. Bullows, Cambridge: Cambridge University Press, 1979).

The work that parallels most closely the study I have undertaken in these pages is the excellent and unjustly neglected J. COULTER, *The social construction of mind* (London: Macmillan, 1979). Coulter uses both ethnomethodology and linguistic analysis as his foundational methods and arrives at treatments of 'self', 'consciousness' and 'emotions' that are encouragingly similar. There are also similarities in spirit, though not in style, with Lacan's general psychology. See J. LACAN, *Écrits: a selection* (London: Tavistock, 1977, § 3 and 5.

Two works in theoretical cognitive psychology are of great importance: D. C. DENNETT, *Brainstorms* (Hassocks: Harvester Press, 1978) and J. A. FODOR, *The language of thought* (Hassocks: Harvester Press, 1976). For a comprehensive review of the 'state of the art' see D. A. NORMAN, *Perspectives on cognitive science* (London: Academic Press, 1981) and M. A. BODEN, *Minds and mechanisms: philosophical psychology and computational models* (Hassocks: Harvester Press, 1983). Despite the wonderful title, there is no real attempt to deal with the personal psychological unities in D. R. HOFSTADTER and D. C. DENNETT, *The mind's eye* (Hassocks: Harvester Press, 1981).

Additional works cited in the text are G. S. BLUM, *Psychodynamics: the science of unconscious mental forces* (Belmont: Brooks-Cole, 1975); M. BODEN, *Artificial intelligence and natural man* (Hassocks: Harvester Press, 1977); R. M. COLBY, 'Modelling a paranoid mind' *(The Behavioural and Brain Sciences*, 4, 1981, 515−18); J. M. DAVIDSON and R. J. DAVIDSON, *The psychology of consciousness* (New York; Plenum Press, 1980); S. DUVAL, V. H. DUVAL and R. KNEALEY, 'Self focus, felt responsibility and helping behaviour' (*Journal of Social and Personality Psychology*, 1979, 1769−78); S. DUVAL and R. A. WICKLUND, *A theory of objective self-awareness* (New York: Academic Press, 1972); S. FREUD, *Outline of psychoanalysis* (trans. J. Strachey, New York: Norton, 1949); J. GARDNER, *Mickelsson's ghosts* (New York: Knopf, 1982); P. HAPPÉ, *Four morality plays* (Harmondsworth: Penguin, 1979); R. HARRÉ, *Social being* (Oxford: Basil Blackwell, 1979); R. HARRÉ and V. REYNOLDS, *The meaning of primate signals* (Cambridge: Cambridge University Press, 1983); D. R. HOFSTADTER and D. C. DENNETT (eds), *The mind's eye* (Hassocks: Harvester Press, 1981); V. F. HOPPER and G. B. LAHEY, *Medieval mystery plays, morality plays and interludes* (New York: Barron, 1962); J. JAYNES, *The origins of consciousness in the breakdown of the bicameral mind* (London: Allen Lane, 1976); S. MOSCOVICI, *La psychoanalyse: son image et son publique* (Paris: Presses Universitaires de France, 1961); S. MOSCOVICI, *Society against nature* (Brighton: Harvester Press, 1976); J. SABINI and M. SILVER, *Moralities of everyday life* (Oxford: Oxford University Press, 1982); P. F. STRAWSON, *Individuals* (London: Methuen, 1959); H. TAJFEL, *Differences between social groups* (London: Academic Press, 1978); L. VYGOTSKY, *Thought and language* (Cambridge: Mass: MIT Press, 1962); D. WRIGHT, *The psychology of moral behaviour* (Harmondsworth: Penguin, 1971).

CHAPTER 2

PSYCHOLOGICAL DIMENSIONS

Theme: The Cartesian distinction between an inner – subjective and an outer – objective realm has proved a poor theoretical basis for psychology. I propose and illustrate a more complex conceptual space based on the dimensions public – private, individual – collective and active – passive.

Contents

If we believe that the structure of ordinary language reflects and in part creates the psychology of the people who use that language, through the embedding of implicit theories in terms of which experience is organized, then we need an analytical scheme for understanding ordinary psychological concepts. On this view the analysis of these concepts must be the starting point for any technical or scientific psychology. The foundation of my argument is the assumption that it is in terms of commonsense psychologies that everyday folk construct themselves as persons and criticize the psychological activities, the reasoning, emotional displays etc. of others. Whether the process of construction of minds on the basis of theories introduces an ultimate universal foundation for all peoples in a 'Ur-psychology' (cf. G. Kelley's man-as-'scientist') is a matter, I believe, for empirical research. But I shall discuss the possibility of an argument to reveal the transcendental conditions for cognitive self-construction of a cognitively active being.

1   DIMENSIONAL AND COMPONENTIAL ANALYSIS OF CONCEPTS

A distinction presupposed, but not explicitly stated, in much analytical philosophy, is that between the legitimate field of application of a concept and the root ideas and implications which are its meaning; positivistic theories of meaning would be unable to make this distinction. A field of applications can be presented as a space. Taking the metaphor a step further, I shall call the critical study of fields of application 'dimensional analysis' and the teasing out of root ideas in complex psychological concepts 'componential analysis'. In this chapter I shall undertake a dimensional analysis of certain mentalistic concepts whose componential analysis I shall merely sketch without detailed argument.

The distinction can be illustrated with concepts from other systems, for instance, the concept of 'disease' in medicine. Consider a one-dimensional space representing a spectrum, from physical to mental disorders. Traditionally, diseases were confined to the general category of physical disorders, and the concept of disease was not used for war wounds or accidental injuries. Recently, 'disease' has been used for mental disorders, taking into this application its original system of root ideas and implications, such as the distinction between symptom and cause. From the traditional corelativity of cure to disease, the idea of treatment has been imported into the sphere of mental disorder, and this has various moral implications. The middle ground of the one-dimensional space of disorders includes psychosomatic complaints and remains interestingly clouded; even the medical profession does not speak of psychosomatic diseases, rather of conditions or complaints. A detailed analysis and discussion of the various matters outlined here would be a formidable undertaking. Such a project would produce a full-scale dimensional analysis of the concept of 'disease', presupposing a componential analysis. The componential structure of the concept would need to be kept under constant review since it would be liable to be influenced by changes in the range of application, revealed by dimensional analysis.

One might object that talk of dimensional and componential analysis of a concept or concept-cluster is just a pretentious way of reintroducing the traditional distinction between the extension and intension of a term. The similarity is evident. I have two reasons for taking an oblique approach via my neologisms.

(1) The extension of a term is rarely explicitly considered, nor is its structure analysed in any detail. It is usually treated as given ('the

members of such-and-such a set') and more importantly as unstructured. Philosophers should perhaps have drawn a moral from one aspect of the problems that arise with attempts to understand mentalistic concepts. Though we may have a clearer account of the intension of a term (the root ideas it comprises), the range of application of the term may be problematic. This point is evident in much of the discussion of mental concepts that has followed Ryle's treatment of mental attributes as dispositions in his book *The concept of mind*. If 'intelligence' is not a state or condition but a summary expression of adverbial qualifications of the verb 'to solve', ought we to include physical manipulations such as football within its range, with or without accompanying cognitive implications? In this chapter I want to emphasize the way fields of application of a concept are structured, and to illustrate the importance of giving an account of that structure in elucidating the workings of a concept or concept-cluster. Philosophers have tended to follow the way of thinking of taxonomists, for whom the extension of, say, the concept *Lepus caniculus* is just the undifferentiated population of rabbits.

(2) To some extent positivistic theories of meaning are still with us, theories in which meaning is elucidated through that to which a term refers. Sortal terms tend to be explicated extensionally. The extension of a term can hardly be thought to be problematic unless one already has some idea of the meaning of that term (of the root ideas in the concept), the field of application of which one is trying to discuss. To carry out componential analysis independently of dimensional analysis implies that the elucidation of the intension of a term can be undertaken independently of the study of the structure of its field of application.

2 FOLK PSYCHOLOGY AND SCIENTIFIC PSYCHOLOGY

There are many ways in which folk psychology is incomplete and there are many psychological processes for which folk concepts provide an inadequate analytical scheme. As the empirical investigation of human life proceeds, new terms will be needed to enable us to express novel hypotheses and new distinctions. Although the folk do construct themselves in accordance with their theories of how people are supposed to be, they do not have explicit knowledge of a wide variety of psychological processes, those we could call automatic or habitual. Such processes involve causal chains, some of which are physiologically based and some perhaps more perceptively analysed as the product of habits. The latter will have been acquired by processes, only some of which are conscious and many of which are social. An adult, accustomed to act in accordance with unconsidered social habit, may

not have an adequate conceptual system for describing, let alone understanding, the sources of some of the general features of his or her
activity. It is clear, then, that new terms will be required as patterns of
social action and habits of thought and feeling that are usually taken for
granted come to the attention of detached observers. I can illustrate the
point with Goffman's concept of the tie-sign in *Relations in public*. A
tie-sign is something we display to indicate to others that we are with
someone, even when we are alone awaiting their return. Introducing
the concept enables us to pick out solitary people from those who, while
temporarily alone, are, in Goffman's phrase, 'half-withs'. But tie-signs
are sociopsychological phenomena of which no one has been aware
except, perhaps, actors preparing to simulate a slice of life on the stage.
To be acceptable as a part of a conceptual system for analysing and
understanding social life, the 'tie-sign' will have to be coordinated with
adjacent concepts of the commonsense system, such as 'marks of
affection', 'stand-offishness' etc.

I propose to adopt the principle that psychological conceptual
systems, which have been developed to deal with the psychological
activities occurring in ordinary life, ought to be generalized to control
the introduction of technical terms for novel hypotheses and new distinctions. In the course of this discussion I shall be arguing for a set of
dimensions that come from reflection on commonsense psychological
concepts. These dimensions are intended both to facilitate the analysis
of ordinary language and its associated folk psychology and to control
the introduction of neologisms.

The growth of explicit knowledge of existing phenomena is not the
only kind of change that needs to be dealt with. Social and
psychological practices change, and some of these changes are wrought
in the field of application of psychological concepts. As Wittgenstein
pointed out, no conceptual system is prepared in advance for all possible applications, so that moments of decision as to which of various
ways to treat a phenomenon are likely to occur. They seem to arise in
two ways. New phenomena appear within an existing field of application that call in question the internal structure of a concept. For
instance, the concept of disease with its traditional root ideas and implications is unprepared for the discovery of physical malfunctions that
derive from a genetic defect. In calling sickle cell anaemia a disease,
we have effectively chosen amongst several possible terms. By making
the decision one way rather than another, the structure of the concept
of disease is changed. It may also be that some change occurs (perhaps
a technical innovation) that suggests the application of the existing concept, with its existing structure of root ideas and implications, to a new
field of phenomena. For instance, the appearance of organized, inter-

nationally linked, terrorist gangs tempts one to apply the concept of war to conflict between these gangs and state security forces. But this application reflects back upon the internal structure of the concept which, let us suppose, once included the root idea of national conflict.

In the following discussion I offer tentative dimensional analyses of some commonplace psychological concepts. These will involve both the above cases. First, I shall develop a three-space of dimensions appropriate for locating psychological concepts. This will lead to the examination of the constraints the scheme imposes on the introduction of neologisms, constraints which would explain how the range of a concept is coordinate with existing uses. Then I will set out two contrasting cases of the use of commonsense notions. In one case new applications have taken root without serious confusion. In another, despite technical innovations which might have led to conceptual change, the concept has remained undisturbed.

3   REJECTION OF CARTESIAN DIMENSIONS

Despite much criticism of the Cartesian way of understanding psychological concepts through the polarization of the mental and the material/behavioural on a single dimension, discussions are still carried on in terms of the traditional pair of dimensions, subjective−objective and inner−outer. In most discussions these dimensions are mapped on to each other, so that the subjective and the inner are treated as coextensive, while the outer coincides with the objective.

It is necessary to go over some familiar ground to re-emphasize the need to abandon these dimensions for graphing psychological concepts. Though they are plotted on to each other, the distinctions embodied in the traditional dimensions depend upon radically different ways of dividing psychological reality. But the matter is not so simple. The subjective−objective distinction is, I think, a complex of dimensions, the product of two further distinctions as I suggested briefly in Chapter 1. This inner complexity leads to a characteristic equivocation in the way the distinction is used. Sometimes it seems to be used to emphasize the difference between attributes which are person-dependent, such as thoughts and feelings, and those which are person-independent, such as physical properties. This distinction, I suspect, reflects the conceptual truth that for an entity to have a subjective attribute, for example to be able to entertain thoughts, it must necessarily be a person. However, anything corporeal can have physical attributes, such as mass. This is not sufficient to account for the way the subjective−objective distinction has been taken. It also appears to depend in part on the difference between inter- and intrasubjectivity. If this is correct, the distinction is related to the way in which some items can be present to only one consciousness, such as sensations or memories, whereas others, such as material things and their physical properties, can be present to many consciousnesses at once; or at least it is so arguable. To maintain the distinction in this form one would have to resist a traditional philosophical argument against the propriety of accepting any intersubjective objects of experience. There are arguments for sense-datum theory, which would have the effect of legitimating only the intrasubjective pole. For my purposes it is immaterial whether one accepts such an argument. Even to frame it one must admit, at least in thought, the conceptual distinction between inter- and intrasubjectivity. The distinction is required even if one of the poles represents an empty category. Sabini and Silver, in Chapter 10 of *Moralities of everyday life*, discern a yet wider range of senses in the use of the subjective−objective distinction, amongst which are those I have emphasized in this argument.

The inner−outer distinction is usually treated as coextensive with some version of the subjective−objective distinction. Sabini and Silver demonstrate that the problems of the subjective−objective distinction are worse than a mere equivocation, so the argument against the distinction could be strengthened still further. The distinction between inner and outer states is clearly related to the body. Without further argument it seems to dissolve into a rather feeble metaphor by which the surface appearances of the body are treated as non-mental, while the mentalistic attributes are supposed, somehow or other, to be inside the skin, behind these appearances. We speak of concealing our thoughts by the control of facial expressions, that is, of the outer surface of the body which is visible to other people, by not making a grimace of disapproval or drooping in disappointment. If the disapproval which is not being expressed is the 'inner' to which a grimace is the 'outer', the implication is that the *real* disapproval is within the body.

Among the many ways that the subjective−objective distinction can be taken, two have had important consequences for the method of psychology. In some contexts 'subjective' refers to the taking of a personal point of view. Each person sees, interprets and socially responds to the world subjectively, that is, from a point of view. It is possible for other people to occupy that point of view, though perhaps never with a perfect reproduction of the original perspective. The simplest case is space−time location, easily taken up by another. The systems of belief which constitute the personal points of view in the usual metaphorical sense can also be adopted, even if only hypothetically, and perhaps never with their original charge of passion. In this sense of 'subjective' there is no in-principle exclusion of other people. What is subjective in this sense can be interpersonally explored, even if imperfectly. Objectivity, by contrast, would be achieved by taking other points of view into account; for instance treating geometrical projections of physical shapes as 'views'. Even colour blindness can be treated as objective in this sense. Another person can grasp that the colour-blind person does not see a certain figure in the presented array of coloured dots.

However, 'subjective' can also be used for that which is among the contents of my consciousness. It is logically impossible for you to have my subjective experiences in this sense. To say you can have experiences like mine is to invoke subjectivity in the other sense. In which sense are my thoughts and feelings subjective? In both — in so far as they are subjective in the second sense, they can form no part of the subject matter of psychology. For instance, the phenomenal quality of experiential fields, such as hue, fall under that prohibition. But in so far as the subjectivity of thoughts and feelings is just that they are imbued with a personal point of view, they can be part of the content of psychology.

To talk of the hidden thought, by contrast, as 'inner' is to slip into thinking that what is concealed is hidden within the body. Without investigating the muddles involved in this view in any detail, it is clear that the inner — outer distinction is a vivid but dangerous metaphor.

Neither 'subjective — objective' nor 'inner — outer' is a useful distinction for categorizing psychological properties and to treat them as co-extensive is to confuse the issue still further.

Arguments which collapse the conjoint distinction by denying one of the poles are exemplified in a good deal of traditional philosophy. I have in mind, for example, the paradoxes of interactionism. If the extensional identity of inner with subjective experience and of outer with objective attributes is maintained, and the former are attributed to mental substance and the latter to corporeal substance, we have a classic Cartesian distinction. I note in passing the two extreme forms of solution to the problems engendered by that form of the distinctions. There is the proposition that interaction is ultimately an illusion (materialism) and there is the proposition that it is miraculous (Leibniz's pre-established harmony). Neither seems to me to have much appeal if one can find reasons for rejecting the distinction from which the problems of interaction arise.

More recently the argument has turned on a slightly different issue which has surfaced in the debate between Husserl and Schutz. By indulging in a phenomenological reduction and experiencing (achieving) the first and second 'epochés', Husserl found himself firmly ensconced within his own subjectivity. In *Cartesian meditations*, no. V, he began to brood on the problem of how one could return from the verge of solipsism to the intersubjectivity upon which the human relations characteristic of ordinary life would depend. As he put it, 'How could intersubjectivity be transcendentally constituted; how could it be shown to be a necessary condition for the possibility of experience?'. As an argument it turned out to be very weak, though perhaps Husserl never intended it as a transcendental argument — only a study of the phenomenal markings of intersubjectivity. He seems to have thought that only by assuming that the bodily appearances of other people are animated can we return from a phenomenological reduction to inhabit an intersubjective world. In such a world we can presume that others see us as we see them, that is, as animated bodily appearances. Only with the joint domain of persons can there be agreed experiences of unitary material things. In his commentary on this problem, Schutz in *Collected papers*, reverses the trend of the argument. He proposes that we should take intersubjectivity as given. We should then ask how subjective activity, that is, personal experience which is ours and ours alone, is constituted from the given intersubjectivity. Put this way, the problem no longer seems to be philosophical. It could be treated, as indeed I think Merleau-Ponty treats it, as an issue in developmental psychology. Students of human development should be able to find out how as a matter of fact we learn to refrain from public display of our thoughts and to conceal them, as we say, from each other. How do we come to grasp that the point of view from which we understand a public thing creates for us, as individuals, distinctive appearances from those experienced by people differently placed? Developmental psychologists have tried to build up an account of how individuals come to have the idea of experiences being theirs and theirs alone. Newson, Shotter and others have proposed the idea of psychological symbiosis (see their 'How babies communicate'). Mothers who continuously complement the psychological and social deficits of infants by talking to and of their child as if it had the full complement of psychological capacities, in particular as if it were a fully competent self, seeing and acting upon the world from its own standpoint, eventually create adult human beings. This story hints at other ways of mapping mental concepts than the Cartesian.

4 CONCEPTUAL SPACE FOR PERSONAL PSYCHOLOGY

The dimensions I propose to develop depend on a foundation of basic considerations for which I shall not provide detailed arguments. I hope they will be recommended by their utility.

Consideration A: Human life is lived as one amongst many. Even when momentarily solitary and acting for him or herself alone, an individual's linguistic capacities and knowledge of conventions ensures the presence of the many through the persistence of collective conventions and interpretations of what can be thought and planned. Nevertheless, a human individual has some idiosyncratic attributes, for example, a unique biography, and often conceives and acts upon personal projects.

Consideration B: Consider a list of attributes traditionally taken as characteristically the province of psychology — feelings and emotions, knowledge, intelligence, consciousness etc. In different cultures, and indeed different moments in one's own life, these attributes may differ greatly in the degree to which they are displayed to others or kept to oneself. Schoolboy culture generally requires knowledge to be kept to oneself and publicly displayed only to teachers. Even consciousness need not be displayed — in an emergency one may pretend to be asleep.

Whatever may be the origin of the human tendency to form groups, be it a genetically transmitted physiological structure or a culturally maintained adaptive device invented by human ingenuity, it is characteristic of human beings to form collectives of all sorts for a variety of purposes, both expressive and practical. Some human attributes have both an individual and a collective realization. For instance, agency can be realized both in individual and collective exercises of power. By taking these basic considerations together, we get the following dimensions.

(1) If we consider the possibilities for the display of one's psychological attributes, it is clear that these can be undertaken with oneself as the only audience, e.g. mulling over one's plans to oneself, or one may go so far as to reveal a project publicly for the attention of anyone who cares to take notice. I shall call the poles of the dimension of display 'private display' and 'public display'. Since displays range from revelations and productions for quite specific personal and private purposes to general and open performances, the pole of display private—public encompasses a dimension which we could imagine to be continuous.

(2) Certainly, some apparently psychological attributes can be realized as a property of one or of many, and in differing degrees, provided the 'many' are not a mere rabble (an aggregate) but a collective. For instance, one human being can impose his will upon a multitude of others. Groups of people as collectives, for instance institutions, can be agents of a sort and can exercise power. A group may impose its will upon an individual. There is some middle ground since an individual

can act through collectives and vice versa, and that in differing degrees. I propose a second continuous dimension, the poles of which I shall label 'individual realization' and 'collective realization', against which a variety of psychological attributes can be considered. A second way of interpreting the individual – collective axis is based on the grounding of psychological attributes — what is their source and where could we look for their maintenance and validation? For example, the 'rules' of grammar and the semantic structures of language are collectively, not individually maintained, but they may be individually realized, for example, someone might be the authority on proper usage.

(3) Further dimensions could be created as they are required. Another useful dimension will mark the degree to which, in possessing a psychological attribute or using a skill, a person is active or passive, is an agent or patient, is exercising power or suffering liability. We can reasonably treat this dimension as orthogonal to the other two since both individuals and collectives can be active or passive, and activity or passivity may be privately or publicly displayed.

To illustrate the application of this three-dimensional system, let me offer as a preliminary example a brief dimensional analysis of the commonsense concept of intelligence, say as expressed in terms like 'clever' or 'smart'. We can ask whether intelligence is a private attribute or whether it can be publicly displayed? I would be inclined to say that, although the notion does have private applications, its essentially comparative nature suggests that it is fundamentally an attribute of public performances. Is it the exercise of a power that is individually located or is intelligence a feature of actions or projects that stem from the activities of a group? I think the answer is clear. As it is ordinarily understood, intelligence is an attribute exemplified in individual exercises of competence or skill. Is it exemplified in the creation of order among the personal aspects of life or is it merely a passive, automatic response? I would be inclined to say that we regard the exercise of intelligence and the active creation of cognitive order to be almost synonymous. It is a power to create a certain kind of order in any kind of intentional object, personal or social, e.g. personal belief system or social institution, and that fundamentally its display is public. Its dimensional analysis can be represented in figure 2.1 as a plane.

The axes of the three-space are represented as orthogonal in figure 2.1, that is, as independent of one another, so that display, realization and agency are features of human life which can vary independently relative to the 'one : many' distinction. This is clearly true of the relation of the private – public axis to each of the others. The axes of realization (or grounding) and of agency are also orthogonal. Consider the exercise of power or agency. Order, for example, may be imposed upon a group of people by the exercise of power by a single individual who achieves his plans for the structuring of the activities of a group, e.g. the authoritarian scout master who sees to it that all the pup tents are neatly in line and that all lights go out together.

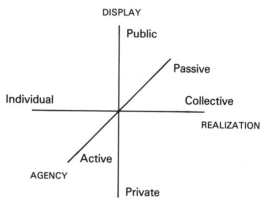

FIGURE 2.1

Each of eight cells offers possibilities for the use of psychological concepts. The location 'private – collective – active' allows for the attribution of quasi-psychological concepts to such pseudo-entities as firms. For instance, the concept of 'information' could be applied to this location in the three-space. We might speak of concealing information from other firms.

A psychological attribute need not be forever fixed in a particular application. The development of a human being would typically involve a time-dependent displacement of attributes through the three-space. For instance, small children have not learned to keep their intentions to themselves. The concept of 'intention' for a two-year-old would be located in the region public – individual – active. A year and a half earlier, at the stage of psychological symbiosis, when his mother is formulating his intentions for him, the concept would be located in the region public – collective – passive, the social region.

However, the long history of the Cartesian distinctions must reflect some important aspects of the psychological functioning of human beings. It can hardly have convinced so many if it were wholly without some empirical foundation. In what follows I shall consider only the basic two-space of display and realization or grounding (figure 2.2). The nearest application to that distinction in the two-space would be a major conjoint axis running through the space from the cells private – individual or personal to the public – collective or social. If I may remind the reader of the argument of the first section, I particularly want to deny that attributes located at the private−individual pole of the conjoint axis are to be identified with inner states and processes, while those at the public−collective pole are thought of as the outer or visible events or conditions. This association would collapse the new dimensions back into the Cartesian distinctions. Though the major conjoint axis represents an important distinction, the use of the two-space as a form of representation allows us to consider whether other cells in the space are also empirically realized. For example, important cells are the public−individual and the private−collective. I shall try to show that certain important psychological attributes ought properly to be located in one or other of these spaces.

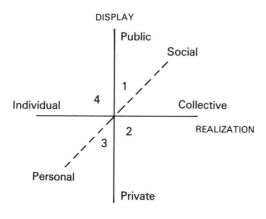

FIGURE 2.2

It is worth emphasizing that I do not want the poles of my dimensions to be taken as distinctions, dichotomizing the conceptual structure of folk psychology and by the covert role of commonsense concepts in professional psychology determining the conceptual structure of that field as well. I am proposing that the dimensions are continua. A psychological concept can be considered as more or less privately displayed. The continuity of the dimensions is mediated by language and other symbolic systems which span the space between the poles. I offer the following formulae by way of explication. In the private−public dimension: language is understood as a common *instrument of representation*. In the individual−collective dimension: language is understood as a common *instrument of action*, e.g. 'I order . . .' compared with 'It is required that . . .'. I have introduced these dimensions schematically and with the minimum of argument. In order to secure a measure of conviction I will try to show how they would be employed in dealing with some particular cases.

If the four quadrants, identified by the Cartesian product of the display dimension, public to private, and the location dimension, collective to individual, define a cycle, quadrants 1, 2, 3, 4, or appropriation and testing of knowledge, could it be merely arbitrary or contingent that the cycle is described as starting in quadrant 1, the public – collective quadrant? If it were arbitrary, then we could admit the categorical scheme without it having any particular implications for developmental psychology, since it would admit of 'repunctuation', starting a developmental cycle as easily at quadrant 3 as in quadrant 1. So we need a further argument to establish that the zero point is in quadrant 1. Indeed, there seem to be two arguments: temporal – factual and logical – conceptual.

(1) Vygotsky in *Thought and language* shows that grammar is acquired through first joining in the public – collective conversation, talking 'out loud' so to speak. So my intentions appear first as avowals, as speech acts. Only later do children make these avowals 'in thought', as speech acts in a private conversation, whose grammar is at first the same as that of the public conversation. By about eleven years of age, individual sentential thought as private conversation begins to develop idiosyncratic features, for instance of grammar. So there are good empirical reasons for putting 't_0' in quadrant 1, that is, sentential thinking starts as public talking.

(2) If emotions are individual feelings and feeling displays coupled with collective interpretations in specific social structures (cf. Sabini and Silver, *Moralities of everyday life*), then personal emotions (as contrasted with personal feelings) must be logically – conceptually dependent on public – collective practices of labelling feelings and feeling displays in socially defined situations. So there are good reasons for putting 't_0', at least for some psychological states in quadrant 1. (I hope I have proved the case for consciousness in a later section.) Hence the punctuation of the cycle as beginning at quadrant 1 is non-arbitrary.

5   ILLUSTRATIONS OF THE USE OF THIS SPACE

Knowledge

Implicit in the discussion is a distinction between the problem of determining location(s) of the application of a psychological concept and the problem of discovering the internal structure and implications of that concept. The possibilities of application are partly determined by the semantic components of a concept which are themselves adjusted to presuppositions about the range of entities, properties and processes to be covered in its extension. Thus if 'knowledge' is construed as 'justified true belief', one is committed to a field of application carved out of whatever is the field of application of 'belief'. Arguably the concept of 'belief' covers a range of attributes, dispositions or states which are individual. When we talk of 'shared beliefs', I think we mean 'similar individual beliefs', rather than some quality of a collective. Construing 'knowledge' as 'justified true belief' would tend to confine the field of application of that concept to the person cells of the space.

The conceptual structure of psycholinguistics recommends itself as a non-behaviourist format for any branch of psychology by virtue of the distinction between theories of competence and theories of performance, that is, between theories concerning the cognitive resources required for competent action and theories concerning the productive processes by which those resources are employed by particular actors to create coordinated action sequences. To avoid too close an identification with psycholinguistics, I shall refer to competence theories in general as 'resource theories' and performance theories in general as 'action theories'. Referring these theory types to my analytical space, it is immediately evident that action theories are necessarily social. Acts as intentions must be matched by interactors' interpretations for an action of a specific sort to have occurred. Resource theories, it might be thought, ought to be person-centred and individual, since an actor uses his knowledge to form his intentions and an interactor uses his to interpret what the actor is doing. Knowledge, understood as resources for action, would seem, although socially deployed, to be individually realized, though it may be collectively stored (*see* Schutz and Luckman, *The structures of the life world*).

However, this would be too simple. In many cooperative enterprises actors have to be prompted, controlled or corrected by reference to a knowledge resource other than their own individual representations of locally correct means – ends principles. Cases can be found in the practical order of apprentices working under a master craftsman, and in the expressive order of participants in a ceremony who have to be taken through their contributions step by step by the officiating chief of protocol. Resource theory must, therefore, allow forms of knowledge which are collectively located and socially ordered.

These considerations suggest that in examining the extension of the concept of knowledge with respect to the above three-dimensional system in which the individual – collective dimension is interpreted as 'realization', we may find ourselves required to accept a generic account of knowledge, wider than but including that which emerges when knowledge is studied only relative to Cartesian limits. In particular, aspects of the use of the concept for some specific forms of knowledge which have dropped from sight through the use of the Cartesian dimensions may become visible. Let us consider the location of knowledge as a psychological attribute on the three dimensions which I have proposed above.

(1) *Private—public*: While it can hardly be denied that there is private knowledge, it seems clear that some items of information are permanently and impersonally displayed. For example, wall maps of the layout of an underground railway could be said to represent knowledge which is neither private nor personal. Anyone who has the necessary skills to interpret these diagrams has access to that knowledge: it is, you might say, public knowledge. As Popper has pointed out in his book *Objective knowledge*, the invention of ways of recording discoveries makes it reasonable to speak of 'objective knowledge', information which has become detached from any particular knower. Ziman has made a somewhat similar point in his work *Public knowledge* by arguing that a concept of 'public knowledge' is needed to understand the epistemology of institutionalized science.

(2) *Individual—collective*: Sociologists' complaints about philosophers' ways of treating knowledge have hinged on the way in which the cognitive resources deployed in the successful performance of social practices are distributed throughout a collective. In such cases no one individual knows everything that is required in order to perform the practice successfully. A performer may have to be prompted by others, and sometimes everyone involved may have to consult a manual or script. This feature of a knowledge system that is distributed through a collective can be found in all kinds of social activities. For example, the knowledge needed by the workers in constructing a building may be distributed through a collective so that a team is required to complete the activity successfully. In the expressive order it seems that very complicated informal rituals, such as football 'aggro', draw on a knowledge system distributed through the collective of fans. The criterion for completeness of the corpus or system must be derived from the social demands on the completeness of the action. Particular individuals are known to have fragments of the knowledge.

The introduction of the idea of a social order relative to social knowledge leads to a hitherto relatively neglected (except by Schutz and Luckman, *The structures of the life world*) feature of knowledge becoming 'viable'. The human collective through which a body of knowledge is distributed might be a structured society, the persons making it up being ordered in some way. We would expect, then, if a corpus of knowledge were distributed through the collective and the collective were structured, that the corpus of knowledge should be treated as having a structure dependent on that order. If knowledge is socially organized, then the possibility of differential access to knowledge has to be considered. Persons in different role positions might have very different degrees of access to the body of knowledge. Perhaps by the very fact of belonging to the same social class as those who are the personal repositories of important fragments of the corpus of knowledge, some people have access to knowledge that others cannot attain. Sociological studies show that this is true of many forms of professional knowledge, the most notorious being medicine.

(3) *Active—passive*: Is knowledge 'active' or 'passive', or is the knower neither one nor the other? If we think of knowledge as certified or authoritatively promulgated fact, typically expressed in that which follows justified assertions of 'I know that . . . ' and similar expressions, then an act of commitment goes along with a claim to knowledge. To claim to know something is actively to engage one's moral standing in the matter. To have made such a claim and to be forced to withdraw it is a serious matter, perhaps leading to a loss of face in the associated expressive order. If the psychology of knowledge concerns the use of the verb 'to know', then clearly knowledge ought to be located among those 'attributes' in the displaying of which a person is active. In short, claims to knowledge do not just happen to a person.

Looked at from another angle, that of the acquisition of that of which we may speak authoritatively, the psychology of perception, particularly as revised by Gibson in *The senses considered as perceptual systems*, calls for active exploration of the very possibility of acquiring reliable information with one's sensory equipment. Philosophical analysis, for instance by Campbell in 'Evolutionary epistemology', points in the same direction. Knowledge is the product of active trial and the management of error, not the result of passively receiving sensory stimuli.

However, the relocation of the concept of knowledge in the analytical three-space represents a historical process. Nothing could have pre-empted the way the concept developed. The decision to call the information stored in libraries or in computer memories 'knowledge', even if qualified as public or impersonal, is strictly arbitrary. In proposing the category 'objective knowledge', Popper is not just making a philosophical point, but reporting a fact of historical linguistics.

To relocate 'knowledge' in psychological 'space', I shall begin by raising a doubt about the propriety of the traditional philosophical account that knowledge is 'true belief'. Though it would probably be possible to defend a notion of collective belief, philosophers who treat the concept of knowledge as representing a special form of belief clearly have an individual rather than a collectively located concept in mind. Ambiguity infects this notion because convincing reasons can be given both for treating beliefs as mental states and for treating them as behavioural dispositions. Couple this with the qualification of the philosophical conundrum 'true', and we have a psychologically unusable concept.

However, if we reflect on the role knowledge plays in a social order we can move some way towards a better notion. Again, two concepts seem to be coupled in the social concept of knowledge. First, knowledge is a kind of reflective source in both know-how (practical) and know-that (contemplative) aspects. It can be regarded as something that a member can draw upon to use for carrying out some project; there is also a knowledge used for identifying projects. Since any social order within which a resource exists will be differentiated, rights to display and rights to draw upon a resource will also be differentiated. In this respect knowledge is no different from any other resource. 'Knowledge' is a competence concept. Studies of knowledge as a socially differentiated resource can be found in Schutz and Luckman's *The structures of the life world*; note, for instance, their distinction between men's knowledge and women's knowledge.

The second element in the concept of knowledge is represented by the performative operator 'I know that . . .'. Familiar arguments show that the prefixing of the operator 'I believe that . . .' creates an intentional context, that is, the truth of the overall statement 'I believe that p' does not depend on the truth of p, the embedded statement. However, 'I know that p' is different. If p turns out to be false, I did *not* know that p; if p is true, nothing follows about whether 'I know that p' is true. I might not know that particular truth. How can this difference be explained? If we read 'I know that . . . ' not as an avowal of some personal mental contents but as a performance of a social act, the disparity is resolved. Reflection on how the phrase is used suggests that it is a performative of trust; roughly, 'I assure you that p can be relied on (as a resource) for your actions'. Thus, if what I said to you authoritatively turns out to be unreliable, you have cause for moral complaint. Trust has been violated. And anyone else within earshot has more or less the same right to complain if I should turn out to be unreliable. Clearly, I have been describing certain complex social relations in explicating the workings of 'I know that . . .'. At least some of what we mean by knowledge is located in the public–collective quadrant, and its psychology is part of the psychology of social relations.

We can refine this distinction a little further. If knowledge is a trusted resource for various kinds of practices, both cognitive and material and has no particular individual location, it may be that no individual has that resource as a personal property at all. It may be that no one ever learns the layout of the underground railway in London but has always to consult a printed, that is a public, representation of the layout in order to find his way about.

We can now undertake an analysis of 'I know that *p*' in the categories of Austin's speech act theory, from *How to do things with words*.

(a) Locutionary force: 'My belief in *p* is well grounded.'
(b) Illocutionary force: 'Trust me, *p* can be relied on.'
(c) Perlocutionary force: the confidence you have in *p*.

The basis of the illocutionary reading by you of my utterance comes from our social relations, in particular that I am an authoritative speaker and have access to locally defined practices for thinking my belief to be well grounded. This could be anything from a library ticket to a skill in performing analyses by chromatography.

Memory

Philosophical controversy about memory has turned on whether memory should be thought of as a certain continuous state representative of the matter remembered or as a disposition to recall that matter. The argument for the latter position is based upon a construction of the act of remembering as an achievement ('I've got it!') rather than as a task ('I'm looking for it'). An argument for the former position might concede all the points about dispositions and achievements, but insists that dispositions must be grounded in some continuous state of the being to whom they are attributed. To be in the state grounding the disposition to recall is the nub of what it is to have a memory. Despite the essentially personal location of the memory-grounding state, there are problems about the authoritativeness of memory which prompt one to consider whether perhaps memory might not have a public aspect too. To claim to have remembered is prima-facie evidence that the recollection is true or appears to be true. However, evidence from documents or from the recollections of the events by others may cast doubt upon the claim. So, upon the question of whether a recollection is a genuine memory, a person, however certain he or she may be, is not necessarily authoritative.

In the Cartesian one-dimensional space, remembering is a mental process so memories as mental phenomena must be inner events or states. Neither the process nor the phenomena occur publicly on the outer surface of the body. The association of the subjective – objective cluster of distinctions with the inner – outer dichotomy is part, I think, of what has made memory puzzling. There is evidently no secure subjective criterion for definitively assigning an inner state to the favoured epistemic category of memory, i.e. correct recollection of things past. So something seems wrong with making memory inner−subjective; yet the category inner−objective is ill formed within the Cartesian scheme. Let us try mapping memory onto the three-space of dimensional analysis instead.

Relative to the individual−collective dimension, it is clear that, as currently employed, items from the conceptual cluster around the notion of memory are applied to matters located at the individual pole. This reflects the conceptual truth that an act of remembering, when genuine and performed by me, is my memory and not someone else's, but once we introduce considerations of authority, social structure appears. For instance, a mother's recollections are more authoritative as to the genuineness of the infant recollections of her offspring than the feelings of conviction that accompany that offspring's own recollections of their childhood. On these grounds we should say while remembering is individual, memories are located in a social order since their validation is not a personal matter. Though the signs of having remembered are often publicly displayed (the self-congratulatory tap on the forehead with the heel of the hand), the memorial experience seems essentially private. Since notoriously memories return most readily when not actively sought — though one can pursue a train of recollection — memory is found along the whole of the active−passive axis. Relative to the three-space, memory seems to be located in the plane parallel to the active−passive axis, passing through a line in the sector private−individual.

In the first section of this chapter I remarked that technical innovations and changing social practices sometimes bring pressure on to a conceptual system well adjusted to traditional concerns and ways. This can lead to moments of decision. The current rules for using a concept or concept-cluster can run out, not being prepared for a novelty yet to be described. A community can institute new uses of existing concepts or introduce new concepts to deal with such moments. There is presently a certain amount of pressure on the memory-cluster in both the individual−collective and the private−public dimension.

Diaries, engagement books, chronicles and so on have long been part of the equipment of civilized men and women. They are clearly devices for the extension of individual memory, but they have not influenced the concept. Most are actually, and all are potentially, public. Perhaps for that reason they have been conceptually set off as *aides-mémoires*, as mnemonic devices and so on. Even the conceptual system for dealing with electromagnetic recording has followed the same trend since tapes and discs are treated as the memory of the gadget, not as the memory of the person (or corporation) whose equipment it is. Tendencies to personify such gadgets have perhaps helped to direct the conceptual innovations to cope with such developments in the direction they have actually gone, but I can see no a priori reason why they should have gone that way.

On the other hand, record keeping, and particularly secret record keeping by institutions, such as government departments, firms and banks has led to the use of terms in the memory-cluster to talk about those records. Remarks like 'Some institutions have long memories' have begun to appear. Philosophical treatment of this kind of development must turn on whether 'memory' is here used metaphorically, preserving its original sense, or whether the new domain of application reflects the appearance of a new specific term corresponding with traditional usage, requiring us to recognize the coordinate formation of new generic concepts to cover both old and new specific usages. The implications and potential misunderstandings deriving from the innovation will be very different in each case.

It seems that our present conceptual system preserves the range of application of the traditional concept-cluster with which we deal with the ordinary human faculty of memory. But if all our psychologies are to be organized around the joint search for resource theories (competence) and action theories (performance) and, thanks to technical innovation, some of the resources we call upon for recollecting and correcting recollections are to be located in the public – collective cell, the psychology of memory is thereby transformed, since the resource theories component is transformed. It seems to me that if I routinely use a computer to assist my recollection of past events, the faculty that is ordinarily called 'memory' is not the same for me as for some country cousin not so equipped. In principle, memory banks of a computer are public, limited only by the contingent rules governing access.

To sum up these considerations, it is quite clear that the conceptual system in which memory is embedded is not prepared for advances in modern technology. The tendency in our culture has been to confine memory to personal recollections without public helps, the latter being treated as mnemonics, records etc. In order to give some motivation for extending the psychology of remembering, under the pressure of contemporary innovations, to include our relations with gadgets, I owe notice of an intermediate case to a personal communication from L. Heit. He pointed out that even in the old conceptual system we admit the notion of a shared memory. This concept applies in the sort of case where two or more people contribute to a conversational reconstruction of events in which they too took part. Each contributes to and amplifies the recollections of each other. A psychological study of shared memory would require an investigation of the conditions under which a contribution from one served as a reminder for the other. Under what conditions did one allow his recollection of an experience to be corrected by the other, and so on?

These considerations could be extended to included a number of other important classes of psychological concepts, such as intentions and emotions. I have argued elsewhere that intentions are complex in just the way that we have seen knowledge to be complex. We need to use the whole three-space for the representation of the location of the concept. Similarly, Sabini and Silver, *Moralities of everyday life*, have given a convincing argument for the use of a similar analytical scheme for understanding some of our emotional concepts such as 'envy'. It seems clear that traditional psychological theory as embedded in everyday English benefits in clarity of exposition from the use of the more elaborated scheme I have proposed as an alternative to simple Cartesianism. If the underlying metaphysical issue is resolved in such a way that we can take it that it is a necessary property of psychological concepts that they be considered as possibly able to be located somewhere in the three-space, then we have an a priori structure for controlling the introduction of new concepts. So, for example, the use of a concept like 'attribution' to pick out the psychological phenomenon of giving praise and blame to others by the ascription of dispositions would have to be considered against its mapping onto the three-space. To what extent are attributions public rather than private? How far are they able to be composed by individuals or determined by the acceptance of the community? And in what way do they structure human interactions to give them social form?

It follows from the argument so far set out that knowledge is partly socially located and distributed. A general psychology of social action requires knowledge as a necessary component of competence, that is, of the cognitive resources of someone able to act adequately as occasion demands. If these are genuine features of the use of the concept, as it is located in ordinary explanations and accounts of ordinary life, then the theory of action which is coordinate with ordinary understandings cannot be a wholly individual psychology. The resources on which an actor draws in forming the intentions to act, which he may realize if the conditions are right, may be knowledge which is not his own personal possession. So, although action must be individual and the performance theory aspect of an action psychology must deal with individual processes, the competence theory may not be individual at all.

It seems clear that knowledge is not necessarily a personal property either philosophically or functionally. I have argued that, though in its ordinary usage the concept of memory seems to be closely tied to the personal and private capacity for recollection, technical innovation could lead us to modify the field of study of the psychology of memory in such a way that we should include a person depending on public and collective ways of storing and recollecting events in his own past. In this case the individual—private or personal component of memory would be reduced to two capacities: knowing where to look to find the external storage of representations of one's past and the capacity to understand the deliverances of machines, that is, knowing how to interpret the recording conventions.

RESEARCH MENU 2

(1) The social construction of memory has been expressed by Coulter in *The social construction of mind* (pp. 59−61) in the following observations:

(a) To remember is to be correct about some past event, not to have any particular kind of experience.

(b) Utterances declaring memories are constructed by reference to the interests and presumed state of knowledge of the recipient.

(c) There are social norms concerning what one is permitted to remember and to forget.

These principles suggest two interlocking research projects: how far are there institutions of remembering and do they differ from family to family, culture to culture; and are memorial utterances concerning the same topic actually adjusted to the presumed knowledge and interests of the hearer? For the first topic, one would need to find out whether there was a social structure to the verification of memories, for instance that one person (or one type of role-holder) had a pre-emptive right to declare a recollection a memory or to rule it out. The second topic might not be too distorted by performing a series of experiments, though ideally it should be studied naturalistically.

(2) A great many projects could be set up to explore the social structuring of bodies of knowledge. An important condition would be to keep rights of display and competence clearly separated. Gender distributions of technical knowledge have been studied, but there is little on child—adult distributions (the dimension of rights of display being almost wholly ignored) and there is little on the social organization of bodies of knowledge other than the medical, as for example the legal. A reworking of the row over the publication of information on how to commit suicide (the EXIT affair) would be illuminating in revealing presumptive rights concerning knowledge of how to kill.

The three-space I have proposed is only one among many possibilities for expanding the basic two-space of the dimensions of display and realization. Another dimension could be future-directed v. past-directed. It would be interesting to examine emotions in the light of a three-space of concepts so constituted, for instance 'hope' and 'regret'. Can one presently 'regret' what one 'will have done'? A time axis could also be introduced with the contrast time-independent v. time-dependent. On that axis 'hope' and 'regret' would be contrasted with 'anger' and 'pity'.

The three-space proposed in this chapter could be used for defining the research arena for many other 'psychological' matters. One could use it to sort out 'negative' intelligence concepts, which cry out for systematic study. There is at least 'folly', 'stupidity', 'unreasonableness', 'dullness', 'being "thick"' and many others. Far too much attention has been paid to the solving of problems, and not nearly enough to the helplessness and confused frustration of those occasions when problems are not solved.

As in most topics raised in this study there is a cross cultural dimension. The discovery by DeVos, reported in his *Socialization for achievement* that in that other hotbed of the 'protestant' work ethic, Japan, achievement motivation is defined relative to groups, has some interesting consequences. It suggests that the locations which are found for local psychological matters, such as the realization of a motive for achievement in individuals, may not be generalizable to other cultures, even when the psychological matter in question seems to be much the same in form and content.

Finally the work of Pearce and Cronen in *Communication, action and meaning* has shown how a conversation can have cognitive and other properties which are not intended by the conversationalists and yet are severally accepted by them as the marks of a 'good' interaction. The techniques they have developed could be put to use in a wide variety of contexts to find out the range of cognitive attributes that a collective discourse might have.

BIBLIOGRAPHICAL NOTES 2

In defending his view of objective knowledge, K. R. POPPER, *Objective knowledge* (Oxford: Clarendon Press, 1972) has added a 'third world' whose ontological status is puzzling. Impersonal knowledge is discussed less dramatically by J. ZIMAN, in *Public knowledge* (Cambridge: Cambridge University Press, 1968) and is more or less what I have in mind in speaking of knowledge in my public—collective quadrant.

Though not admired quite unreservedly — see criticisms by R. L. GREGORY in *Mind in science* (London: Weidenfeld and Nicolson, 1981) — J. J. GIBSON, *The senses considered as perceptual systems* (London: Allen and Unwin, 1966) makes a convincing case for active knowledge gathering as the basis of perception. D. CAMPBELL argues for a similar but more general idea in 'Evolutionary epistemology' (in *The philosophy of Karl Popper*, ed. P. A. Schillp, (La Salle, Ill.: Open Court, 1974), part II, ch. 12, 1974).

The debate about dispositionalism in mental science can be exemplified by the contrast between the use of dispositional concepts by G. RYLE, *The concept of mind* (London: Hutchinson, 1947) and the necessity that D. ARMSTRONG, *A materialist theory of mind* (London: Routledge and Kegan Paul, 1968) sees to ground dispositions in continuous states of the entity which 'has' them.

Functionalist theories of mind have been vigorously defended by many, but I very much like the economical manner in which the case is presented by D. BROADBENT, 'Non-corporeal explanations in psychology' (in *Scientific explanation*, ed. A. F. Heath, Oxford: Oxford University Press, 1981). See also H. PUTNAM, *Philosophical papers*, vol. 2 (Cambridge: Cambridge University Press, 1975) and D. C. DENNETT, *Brainstorms* (Hassocks: Harvester Press, 1978).

Additional works cited in text are J. L. AUSTIN, *How to do things with words* (ed. J. O. Urmson, New York: Oxford University Press, 1965); J. COULTER, *The social construction of mind* (London: Macmillan, 1979); G. A. DE VOS, *Socialization for achievement* (Berkeley: University of California Press, 1973); E. GOFFMAN, *Relations in public* (Harmondsworth: Penguin, 1972); E. HUSSERL, *Cartesian meditations* (The Hague: Martinus Nijhoff, 1973); M. MERLEAU-PONTY, *Consciousness and the acquisition of language* (Evanston: North Western University Press, 1973); J. NEWSON and J. SHOTTER 'How babies communicate' (*New Society*, 29, 1974, 345−7); W. B. PEARCE and V. CRONEN, *Communication, action and meaning* (New York: Praeger, 1980); J. SABINI and M. SILVER, *Moralities of everyday life* (New York: Oxford University Press, 1982); A. SCHUTZ, *Collected papers I* ed. M. Natanson, The Hague: Martinus Nijhoff, 1973), part II; A. SCHUTZ and T. LUCKMAN, *The structures of the life world* (London: Heinemann, 1974), 3 A §3, 4 A §2.

CHAPTER 3

THE PRIMARY STRUCTURE: PERSONS IN CONVERSATION

Theme: The primary human reality is persons in conversation. In this context people are simple beings, the locations of speech acts. The fact that they are naturally embodied in a spatiotemporal manifold is important, but there are other modes of embodiment possible, particularly for modern people as collections of documents or files.

Contents
1 Referential grids
2 People as places
3 Time structures
4 The conversation
5 Rights of occupation
6 Persons and selves
7 Natural embodiment and the autonomy of psychology
8 Other modes of embodiment: consequences in the moral order
    File-selves and real-selves
    File-speak

1 REFERENTIAL GRIDS

The psychology of human beings is currently embedded in the same metaphysical substructure as that in use for the sciences of the physical world. That world is conceived as a causally interacting group of things, located in and individuated by physical space and evolving in physical time. The metaphysics subscribed to tacitly by most psychologists is Newtonian and Euclidean. Causes are deterministic and space and time are independent and flat. On a cosmological scale, the independence of physical space from time vanishes, and the essential locating roles of these grids are taken over by space−time but the scale of psychological processes makes this development irrelevant to the metaphysics of domestic space and time.

As conceived within this metaphysics, people are a specialized class of causally interacting things, of some internal complexity, located within the referential grids of space and time. I shall try to show that for most of the purposes of psychology this metaphysical foundation is quite seriously inadequate. An indication that this might be so can be found in studies of human perception and use of space and time. Social significance imposes a texture on the spatial and temporal manifolds of ordinary life, so that in much research space and time appear as systems of belief about access, danger and so on quite as much as they serve as locating guides. A more fruitful alternative can be found. I call it the 'primary structure'.

The primary structure will bear some analogy to the grids of space and time. It is the system by which psychological items, whatever they be, can be distinctively located. By means of their distinct locations, qualitatively identical items can be numerically distinguished. The primary structure will emerge from a comparative analysis of the conditions of speaking in the physical world and of speaking in the socio-psychological world, though I have yet to show that these worlds are distinct. By examining the logical grammar of indexical expressions we can make out the primary structure of the physical world. Speech acts are bound to a particular place and time (indexed for location) by expressions such as 'here', 'now', 'this', 'there', 'then', 'that' etc., all of which work by virtue of relations to the current acts of speaking in which they occur. 'Do it now!' indexes the order for execution at the time of utterance. 'Put it here!' does the same for place. And so on. The locating grids are space and time.

The names of space and time locations make up a comprehensive set of referring expressions defined in a pair of abstract grids, one for space and one for time. They are anchored to the real world by the use of the indexical expressions 'here', 'now' and their equivalents. 'At the third stroke it will be three fifty-nine and forty seconds, beep beep beep!' I do not believe a referential model is adequate to explicate the logical grammar of indexical expressions, but that is a technical issue in logic which it would not be apposite to pursue here. I shall simply take the indexical expressions of a form of talk to be a system distinct from the proper names of places and times, those we find expressed by latitude and longitude in space and by calendars and clocks in the temporal referential system. By marking the place and time of their utterance, indexical expressions anchor the abstract system of referents to the real world of things and events. Once that grid is anchored, we can use the grid itself as our referential net. So, to tensed questions like

'Where and when was the Crucifixion?' we can answer with replies like 'It took place on Golgotha at 3 p.m. on 25 March 32 AD'. This reply can make sense only for those enquirers who know where they stand themselves on the maps of space and time. On town plans displayed for tourists helpful municipal authorities glue on little arrows with the legend 'You are here'.

In founding a science of psychology a suitable referential grid must be created for the location and tracking of thoughts, feelings, intentions, commitments and so on. The history of physics teaches us that however beguiling and deeply embedded in our practices is the grid of the commonplace world of domestic objects and events, it may be misleading as the referential grid for a science. To my knowledge this issue has never been systematically addressed in psychology. (The remarkable intuitions of Lewin in *Une théorie du champ dans les sciences de l'homme* have been very largely ignored.)

In the case of the physical system the choice of grid was determined by the conditions for and criteria of numerical identity of the material things which were traditionally taken as fundamental beings. The metaphysics of the appropriate indexicals is thereby determined and with it their logical grammar. They should label a sentence with its place, 'here', and a moment of utterance, 'now'. By studying the logical grammar of the physical indexicals labelling utterances with locations, we could have discovered the role of the space and time grids as the basic locational system for the physical world, and perhaps worked out a good many of its properties. Can we develop a parallel system for a psychoreferential grid? Perhaps the study of the logical grammar of 'I', 'we' and so on can reveal the referential grid for psychological and social reality.

The corresponding device by which speech acts are indexed for location in the psychosocial world are the first person pronouns. 'I' and 'we' are used indexically in ways parallel to the uses of 'here' and 'now' for speakers of English, French and languages with similar grammars. It is not at all clear that the 'natural metaphysics' of languages in which indexical reference is secured by other grammatical devices is the same as that of the major Western European languages. This is an issue of great importance for the foundations of personal psychology and I shall return to it in some detail. We can pick out the primary structure of the psychosocial world, at least for the speakers of Indo-European languages, by identifying what it is that these indexicals use to label speech acts. It is persons, not places and times. And what they label with its speaker is a conversational moment. Tense indexes speech acts by reference to the moment of utterance, not to the calendrical instant.

Through their fundamental connection with conversational acts, and in many cases being realized only in those acts, thoughts, feelings, intended actions and so on are indexically located at persons, at the time of their utterance, just as things are located at places at times. The set of places is space and the array of persons provides a basic referential grid with similar powers for social and psychological entities, properties and processes. Things can be at some places and not at others, and they can move from place to place. In parallel ways, thoughts can be entertained by some persons and not by others, and they can be communicated from person to person. Remarks like these pre-empt how we are to understand the criteria for 'sameness of thought', 'one and the same thought' and so on. By choosing amongst the more obvious alternatives here, a metaphysical foundation for the appropriate indexicals could be determined. I believe the personal pronouns by which persons identify themselves as 'speakers of the moment' are a lexical system parallel to the 'here' and 'now', 'this' and 'that' of physical space and time. The study of the logical grammar of 'I' and 'we' should therefore reveal the referential grid for psychological and social reality. It is the array of persons since it is to persons that utterances are anchored by the pronominal indexicals by using 'speaker' as the utterance label. In the primary structure persons are not like things, they are like places.

The spatial manifold of places is dense and continuous. Things cannot exist unplaced, but there are more locations than there are things. In the physical world there are both actual and possible places, though it is not clear whether we should admit times without events. Thoughts, feelings, declarations of love cannot exist except as located at people, but there can be people who lack any or perhaps in some extreme cases, all of such psychological objects — truly empty places. In this metaphysics psychological phenomena are not attributes of people, but entities (having their own attributes) located at people.

2 PEOPLE AS PLACES

All spatiotemporal locations are, were and will be, in principle, available for occupation by things and events, restricted only by the physical existents already there. Are these principles, distinctions and restrictions also to be found in the workings of the psychological locating grid? Various comparisons are instructive.

(1) To empty places there should correspond silent people, that location in the array of persons not occupied by a speech act or other intentional performance. More light can be thrown on the psychological

world by considering why someone is silent. It may be because they have nothing to say, but in many cases a person or category of persons is silent because they have no right to speak (the stenographer at the company meeting, the public in the courtroom, those children who are seen but not heard). As a 'space', a set of possible and actual locations, the array of persons is non-Euclidean. It is structured by moral and political considerations, rules and conventions. It is not anisotropic. It is Einsteinian since it has structure.

(2) There are also some important dissimilarities between the array of persons and the grids of space and time. In particular, there are the important psychosocial locations to be found at former persons and possible persons, but there cannot be former places and possible places in this sense of 'possible'. Possible locations are actual places in physical space, and so too for instants of time.

Former persons are important locations for psychosocial items such as speech acts, for instance the making of wills. (I shall be using the term 'speech act' to cover both vocal and written performances of illocutionary acts.) This raises the issue of the temporal persistence of speech acts, an issue to which I shall return. The sociolegal devices by which wills are witnessed and 'proved' turn metaphysically on the positioning of certain acts at the location in the array of persons proper for the making of a will. (Again the structuring of the location system by rights and by duties is important.) The curious Mormon custom of retrospective baptism of the dead, turns on the metaphysical propriety of including former persons within the array of persons as psychosocial locations for acts of baptism. Equally the arguments of the anti-abortion lobby turn on finding a place in the locutionary grid for possible persons, on whose behalf the campaigners claim to speak.

What of libraries, magnetic tapes and the like? Does the existence of these entities force us to admit the insertion into psychological reality of categories of conversational objects not locatable in the grid of the primary structure, the array of persons? I propose to treat written and printed sentences as possible speech acts, their actuality being achieved by their being put to use, for instance by being read or cited at some location in the array of persons, that is, by someone. (To read, for instance, is to perform a speech act occasionally for others, but more often for oneself.) But that person must have the right so to use the sentence. The printed Riot Act is only psychosocially realized in so far as a magistrate reads it out.

How far should the array of persons be extended? Does the use of indexicals by machines require us to include them as members of the array? In so far as the states and processes of machines are taken as intentional, that is, as thoughts (and here the huge question of the way to deal with the distinction between simulation and reproduction of mentation is begged), those machines are to be recruited to the array of persons as places where cognitive objects can exist. The 'space' and 'time' of psychology is thereby extended to comprehend new locations. We might want to extend the array of persons to include signing chimpanzees were we to have good reason to think that their signings too were intentional.

3 TIME STRUCTURES

If the array of persons is a referential grid like space, how is time to be incorporated into the metaphysics of psychology? A thoroughgoing parallel would require the order of psychological events to define the time element in the pseudo-space and time of the array of persons, as it does for the array of places. But there is a complication. There are psychological events (soliloquy, for example) which have been taken out of the public realm and made private. In trying to communicate with other people it soon becomes apparent that our 'thought rates', in the sense of the rate of flow of our *sotto voce* conversations do not always match. When I have reached the third thought in some fairly standard sequence you may have already reached the fifth, using the flow of public conversational elements as a common time-frame.

The problem of creating a kind of unified time system from the infinite number of possible inertial frames, each with its own rigidly mounted clock, is solved for physical time by devising a set of rules for communicating between any two frames each of which has its own clocks providing a local reference system, and none of which has any claim to be absolute and universal. However, those rules must be such that the form of the laws of nature are always the same, in whatever frame they are studied. These rules are the Lorentz transformation. An analogous set of rules is needed for the time of person – space. We might require the conservation of the rules of grammar and polite discourse.

The flow of conversational contributions creates a discrete event manifold, relations of coincidence and succession of which define a 'time' for each distinct episode. For modern people there is no absolute conversation the succession of the speech acts of which defines an absolute time within which the speech acts of subordinate conversations are to be embedded, and so absolutely ordered. The problem of the coordination of 'times' in distinct conversational episodes is exacerbated by the fact that the social and psychological past is not fixed. Emotions can be reinterpreted, insults can be nullified by apologies and transformed by explanations, claims to knowledge can be weakened and so on. The distinction between past, present and future, on which the numerical identity of the events that are located in the simple ordering of physical time depends, does not go over into psychological time. Amongst the many analogues of the Lorentz transformation by which physical times are related to one another, there are social conventions such as the rules of evidence, depositions before notaries, signed statements and so on, by means of which the conversational episodes relevant to the conduct of a trial are welded into a coordinated flow. Furthermore, by means of these devices, speech acts are stabilized, made resistant to reworking, taking on many of the attributes of past events in physical time. These matters deserve a great deal more attention than they have received (*see* research menu 3).

The importance of vagueness in human communication has been noticed, for instance by Brenner in 'Actors' Powers'. Given the usual malleability of the informal social and psychological past, through the deployment of further speech acts of redefinition, reinterpretation, apology, qualification and the like, and the importance of these acts in their influence on the consequential changes in the social and psychological present and future, it is important that our actions should have a certain vagueness as acts. We are thus prepared for renegotiation of their meanings should the need arise. Psychotherapists may have to work to make vague what was precisely defined for the client.

As I have remarked, contemporary society (at least where electronic surveillance is rare) is characterized by the absence of an absolute conversation to which all episodic conversations can be referred and matched up in time. This was not always so. In more pious times God's conversational presence as ubiquitous listener and occasional speaker provided a universal conversational framework for the psychosocial world. In prayer the human conversation was extended to include God. Further research into the effects of the existence of this absolute reference frame would be of great interest (*see* research menu 3).

4 THE CONVERSATION

So far I hope to have shown that an array of persons has certain important properties that are brought out by comparing that array with the grid of locations that are physical space and time. Just as ordinary things and events have locations in the grids of Newtonian space and time, so commitments, avowals, rememberings and feelings have locations at persons in the psychosocial array. I take the array of persons as a primary human reality. I take the conversations in which those persons are engaged as completing the primary structure, bringing into being social and psychological reality. Conversation is to be thought of as creating a social world just as causality generates a physical one.

Relative to this scheme there are secondary structures. I take the secondary *social* realities to be the practical order of work, more or less as it was understood by Marx, and the expressive order, generating honour, respect, contempt etc., more or less as it was understood by Veblen. These orders come into being, as I argued in *Social being*, as relational networks through the interactions of persons interpreted and mediated in conversation. By 'conversation' I mean not only speech exchanges of all kinds, but any flow of interactions brought about through the use of a public semiotic system, such as that involved in the meaningful flying of flags, the wearing of uniforms, ballroom dancing, gestures and grimaces, a *concours d'élégance* and so on. I am not suggesting that persons and their talk exist prior to social reality and engender it as an effect. People and their modes of talk are made by and for social orders, and social orders are people in conversation. I shall be arguing for a thoroughgoing reciprocity between the social and the personal.

The secondary *psychological* realities are human minds. Each person, a mere location in the primary structure, is formed as a secondary structure, essentially as a semi-systematic cluster of sets of beliefs. The psychological secondary structure is a reflection of the primary structure, the array of persons and their conversation which is the primary reality of the society which brings them into being. It follows that not only human individuals, but collectives too can have 'psychological' attributes and be the locations of psychological processes.

5 RIGHTS OF OCCUPATION

The discrete person-manifold happens to be located in the continuous space and time of physical reality. For most practical purposes that space and time can be treated as Newtonian/Euclidean. Though this is a contingency of our world it is an important one. Persons are embodied beings located not only in the array of persons but in physical space and time. The relation between the consequences of our joint location in both manifolds is mediated by the local moral order, particularly the unequal distribution of rights upon which I have already remarked. For example, one may be physically present with others in the same space and time of a meeting, but, in the position of secretary, may not have the right to contribute to the cognitive processes proceeding in the flow of the conversation.

So persons, as the elements of the array by which indexicals can be used to label psychological items and as embodied beings located in the referential grids of physical space and time, can be thought of as having careers extending in a plane. One axis of the plane represents the rights one has as a member of the moral order of society and the other the physical world space. The locations in space and time that one can (legitimately) occupy are an *umwelt*, a product of one's rights and one's world-line in physical space and time. Not all the points of view and of action theoretically open to one in the course of life can properly be occupied. Part of what is involved in having a point of action, relative to any project one has proposed, is to be so located in a moral order that one has or has not the right to act in the required ways and to be in the required locations in the space and time of the physical world. There may even be rights involved in perceiving the social world from some particular point in the array of physical locations. Only some persons can rightly squint through key holes or tap phones, and only some can legitimately demand an individual's personal recollections.

6   PERSONS AND SELVES

The distinctions between the primary and secondary realities will emerge in various ways as the theory of personal being unfolds. One of the most pervasive will be built around the way human individuality is manifested in each structure. Pronouns, or their grammatical equivalents in languages which do not use such devices for personal reference, are used in our Western societies not only to locate speech acts in the array of persons ('I admit I took the money'), but also to refer to a theoretical entity 'the self' in the deployment of the concept of which the psychological unity of persons as secondary structures is brought about. It is partly through coming to see both how central is the separation of indexical and theoretical aspects of self-reference for our mental economy as persons, and how culturally distinctive and local a feature it is, that we shall be brought to realize the relativity of psychological theories and discoveries to the cultures in which they have been made. It is on the varying extent of the diversity between the concept of the public—collective person and the concept of the private—individual self that my theory of personal being is to be built.

Perhaps some of my readers may remember the good old days of radio, when the adventures of the Lone Ranger entertained us. A remarkable feature of the dialogue between the hero and Tonto, his faithful Indian, was the distribution of ways of self-reference. While the Lone Ranger was permitted the doubly functional 'I', displaying him as one who was both a public person and a private self, the Indian was restricted to the use of his own name, Tonto, for the same job. But Tonto was the name of a public person. There was a pretty clear implication that while the Lone Ranger had a rich and diversified personal psychic life, the simple Indian had no need for the niceties of reference to personal psychic unities. His public or social being would do. (The script would repay further study. 'Tonto' is Spanish for 'blockhead', and very young children typically use their proper names for self-reference.)

7 NATURAL EMBODIMENT AND THE AUTONOMY OF PSYCHOLOGY

If I am justified in adopting a generally anti-Cartesian line, on the grounds that the Cartesian way of talking about thought and action is not warranted, then how is the commonplace distinction between the brain as a thinking, feeling machine and its thoughts and feelings to be expressed? Having disposed of Cartesianism in the wake of Wittgenstein, the commonplace distinction no longer constitutes a problem, that is, an intellectual predicament calling for a solution. But it does require a discussion of good and bad ways of describing it.

I would like to recommend that we should treat the distinction (or rather cluster of distinctions) on the same lines as that between colour as hue and colour as the disposition to reflect light of this or that specific wavelength, or between warmth and molecular motion. I do not believe that there can be a theoretical account to explain why molecular motion is experienced as warmth. To have the possibility of such an account would require that the experience of molecular motion and the experience of warmth should be distinct beings, their relationship mediated by some third being (perhaps a causal influence). But if, as seems to be the case, warmth is how people having a certain kind of neurological apparatus experience molecular motion, there are not two beings whose relationship could be the locus of a problem. Since people experience grosser motions as motions, the traditional distinction between primary and secondary qualities seems apt to describe the way thoughts and feelings and neural states, processes and structures, can all be experienced by people under appropriate circumstances. The way I experience the condition of my nervous system when my body is flooded with adrenalin is as excitement, fear etc. One is reminded that in Bhuddist psychology 'mind' is treated as a *sense*, along with sight, touch etc.

Whereas there is a constancy in the way a kind of physical state of bodies other than my own (and most parts of my body) appears to me, in that molecular motion is usually experienced as warmth by our kind of sentient being, there seems to be reason to believe that though there are commonalities of thought and feeling mediated by shared semiotic systems, including language, similar thoughts and feelings are, or may be, experiences of different physiological states in different people. This is the relation called 'token identity', and the essentials of the argument for it have been presented most recently by Broadbent in 'Non-corporeal explanations in psychology', who argues for the abandonment of the naïve assumption that the same software structure and content must always have the same realization in hardware. (The Strawsonian concept of person depends on the natural way persons are embodied in the corporeal *frame* of *Homo sapiens* — see Strawson's *Individuals*.) I shall keep to this way of talking, not because I think there is a problem for which the distinction between primary and secondary qualities provides the form of a solution, but because I think there is no problem, only some facts to be described. Why bother, then, with an antique distinction? Why not simply let the facts speak for themselves?

At this point it is necessary to defend the autonomy of psychology. The most obvious defence follows directly from Broadbent's argument (a somewhat similar line of thought has been proposed by Putnam in *Philosophical papers* and Dennett in *Brainstorms*). If it is only in psychological terms, and particularly those most linked to the traditional psychological vocabularies of daily life, religion, the law etc. that the commonalities between persons can be identified and described, then if psychologists claim to be saying anything about people in general, they can avoid begging the question of token-type identity only by treating psychology as autonomous.

There is a second, more powerful argument. Even if at some degree of fineness of analysis there were physiological commonalities between people, relevant to psychological matters of interest, such as the physiology of the emotions, memory, manual and intellectual skills, how would they be identified? It must be by exploiting psychological distinctions to partition and classify physiological states, conditions and processes via some intermediate system of theoretical representation. Only if we have the prior distinction between anger and fear can we begin to look for a physiological distinction between those who are angry and those who are afraid. There are probably an indefinite number of ways that people differ from one another physiologically at any time. Which of these ways is relevant to locating the physical basis of a psychological process cannot be determined by examining them ever so closely in physiological ways alone. Could not one look for behavioural differences that would be within the physical world and so make the requisite distinctions that way? But distinctions in movements, say, do not always mark the same or even any distinction in psychological kind as, for example, one may express an intention to leave a room in an indefinite number of ways, exploiting situational disambiguations of a wide variety of movements.

A powerful argument against physiological reduction of personal being to the identity of a body would be to show that there are other modes of embodiment, where personal identity is constituted *not* by the physical identity of the body but by a conceptual cluster defining this *as* an embodiment of the person in question. The person is prior to embodiment.

8 OTHER MODES OF EMBODIMENT: CONSEQUENCES IN THE MORAL ORDER

File-selves and real-selves

An unvoiced assumption in all that has gone before is that the people being 'made' by the people-makers of a moral order are embodied in the common flesh and blood of the human frame. We are so accustomed to think when philosophizing of persons as embodied in human beings, and perhaps in certain primates and some complex machines, that we overlook the possibility of other modes of embodiment which may have important consequences for growth and life in a moral order. Contemporary bureaucratic civilization routinely deals with persons embodied in another way. In many important events, persons appear as documents and, in particular, as files. I distinguish between a 'real-self' and a 'file-self' or 'selves'. Each is capable of multiple self-presentations, depending on episode, that is, on interactors in the one case and on readers in the other.

In discussing the occasions of interaction as file, I shall take the nature of a file to be a collection of documents unified by their common referent, the person *A*. On many occasions important to his or her career, *A* appears not as a real-self but as a file-self. For instance, in the early rounds of processing by an appointments committee, job applicants are presented to the committee only as files. It is not until the short-list is settled and interviews begin that real-selves begin to take part in the interaction. Currently, credit appraisals, parole decisions etc. are made of file-selves, rarely of real-selves. Frequently, one's first consultation with a specialist in the medical profession is in the form of a referral letter from the general practitioner to the consultant. The intensity of such interaction depends on the care with which the file is read. As a file-self, a person has only limited ways of drawing attention to him or herself, perhaps by making sure that his or her file is 'interesting'. Most file-selves figure in brief encounters during a mere skimming of the file. The bulk of a file can be deceptive. In typical file encounters readers look for the salient documents. A person's fate hinges on a very small selection from the available file material. Since most file encounters involve some sort of assessment of a person relative to a moral order, the fate of one's file can play an enormously important part in one's life.

A person as real-self is, amongst other things, a store of information, some of it reflexive. As a file-self, a person is almost wholly reduced to such a store. There is a further difference. A real-self is a hotch-potch of contingently acquired bits and pieces, but a file-self is usually an assembly controlled by a principle of selection or central relevance. The decision as to what is relevant to the aspect of the person that is embodied in the file is made by the file-master, not by the person. Though a person has only one real-self, he or she will be accompanied through life by a flock of file-selves of unknown extent, each member of the flock representing an aspect of a person as defined by the appropriate file-master. To go more deeply into the fatefulness of files, we need to look closely at their metaphysics.

Unlike his or her real-self, a person in the form of file-selves can be present at many different places and so take part in many different episodes at once. A person may be playing tennis as real-self, while at the same time involved in a job application and a credit check, a police investigation and a medical consultation, all at the same time. When consulted, the file-self replies: the person as file-self is not mute. Any part of the file can be read, but in file-self a person cannot produce a tactical lie, extemporize or elaborate, nor can a file-self correct mistakes in the corpus of information. As a social actor, the file-self is passive and obedient. A person as file-self cannot initiate a conversation, nor can he or she unilaterally close it. As file-self a person cannot be an agent. The psychology of personal being as file-self is reduced to biography and, to a limited extent, to autobiography.

Much of the corpus of knowledge and belief recorded in the real-self is available to a person and indeed as a self-conscious being the process of self-scrutiny is also knowable. Many file-self embodiments may be outside an individual's 'sphere of consciousness'. In the form of an isolated file-self, a person is neither conscious nor self-conscious. Unlike the contents of the real-self memory, the file-self memory, though a set of biographies, cannot be accessed at will, except under exceptional circumstances. But unlike real-self memory, notoriously unreliable, file-self memory is normally incorrigible. By that I do not mean that it contains truths, but that it is normally impervious to self-reconstruction.

In defining the central characteristics of persons as we construct them for most human societies, self-consciousness, reflexive agency and autobiography stand out as being as near essential to persons as anything could be. This discussion shows that that conclusion is relevant to a person's embodiment in the normal human frame; strict characteristics of a person depend upon his neurological mechanisms. Of the three central characteristics, file-selves have neither consciousness nor agency and, lacking their reflexive developments, are not immediately available for consultation by the person in a real-self embodiment mode.

A new dimension of developmental psychology opens up, the principles and dynamics of the construction and growth of files. From the point of view of the relation between personal development and the moral order, the relationship whose complexity will be revealed in the discussion of psychological symbiosis, the state of one's file is a crucial matter. It is yet another feature of the psychology of personal life, that is irreducibly social. The efforts by various movements to gain a right of access to files can be seen as an attempt to regain personal control over all that is personal. It corresponds to the use of Freudian psychotherapy to gain control of those repressed memories which are subtly influencing one's decisions and emotions; that is also an attempt to gain personal control over aspects of the self that are plainly personal. But unlike file-selves, which exist in the public−collective domain, repressed memories are part of the third quadrant of psychological space, the private−individual domain.

Both self-knowledge and self-mastery are limited by the existence of personal files to which one has no access. The fact that the issue of access to the file is treated as a moral problem and discussed in terms of the balance of rights over the pragmatic advantages of confidentiality, as in job references, suggests we are close to the moral core of personal being.

File-speak

There are special features of the vocabulary of files, and these have consequences for the nature of vicarious personhood. The psychological study of the content and structure of files is still a fairly undeveloped field. In this section I report an empirical study of the vocabulary of psychiatric files to illustrate the kind of work that might be undertaken in the pursuit of file psychology. In this empirical study one feature stands out: the degree to which the vocabulary of files reflects a simplification of the material features of the real-self it represents. The vocabulary that is actually in use contradicts the theory of file-construction, tacitly adhered to by those who create files.

Moreover, it is clear that the medical prescription, as it were, for the creation of a file by the taking of a history, is not fulfilled. The descriptive vocabulary is very much related to situation. However, in the vocabulary of psychiatric files there is a preponderance of terms which refer to moods, feelings and current cognitive states and processes. It was wholly unexpected to find that there are very few terms which could be reckoned as identifying long-term traits which might be relevant to personality. Here is a preliminary classification of the lexicon:

(1) *Feelings*: felt shivery, felt disgust, feeling in throat, heavy feelings during the night.

(2) *Moods*: nervy, gets very dark moods, gets low, not nervous, suicidal, unhappy, no interest in doing things, mood-swings, very dejected, not too bad now.

(3) *Cognitive states and processes*: confused, perplexed, repeats thoughts and over, knows the answer but just can't get it out, knew he would get caught, feels she partly blames him.

(4) *Current behaviour terms*: sits and stares into space, just sits doing nothing all day, sleeps badly.

(5) *Self-intervention*: shakes himself out by doing things, builds up a complex fantasy world.

This is a fairly complex vocabulary, covering a wide range of attribution, though from the nature of the case, the sort of moods and states that are reported to a psychiatrist are likely to reflect the darker side of human experience.

A small number of trait-terms appear rather rarely in psychiatric files. These fall into two fairly sharply distinguished categories, social traits and psychic traits. Typical of the former are: children get on well with him, gets bullied, has to be less active than she should be, always wins arguments; typical of the latter are: lacking in confidence, felt shy as a child, wants to be a woman, has no further urges, preoccupied with such and such. Within these roughly classified psychic traits, some complexities appear; in particular, features of the interview during which the file is constructed obtrude. For example, the remark 'doesn't think about the future' is in ethnomethodological terms accountable. The appearance of the qualification or account that it is too painful following that confession warrants the admission of a psychic trait which is generally not expected amongst human beings who, if anything, are expected to be concerned about the future.

There is virtually no reference in the many files which formed the empirical basis of this study to the history of the condition that the person is complaining of or to their past lives. The file-self springs into being at the moment at which the complaint starts and disappears from the scene when the complaining stops.

The distillation of the file into the medical letter, and its history, show an interesting asymmetry. In the letter from the general practitioner to the psychiatrist, a good deal of simplifying psychology appears. For example, 'repressed emotions' are referred to as 'unexpressed affect', and the predicament of someone who no longer has confidence in his capacity to manage his life is expressed in the vague term 'loss of self-esteem'. A rhetorical transformation has taken place as the file content is distilled into the general practitioner's letter. To my surprise, letters from psychiatrists to general practitioners revert to commonsense vocabulary for everyday complaints and represent a retranslation of the initial translation from everyday vocabulary into psychiatric terminology. The subtle distinctions embodied in the ordinary vocabulary are eliminated by the general practitioner's choice of very technical terms, which then are rendered back into ordinary language by the specialist. It is not surprising to find, from time to time, that the psychiatrist's reinterpretation of the general practitioner's translation of the original commonsense term does not correspond to the sense of the original complaint. It is possible, then, to examine the process of file-construction, the nature of the representation of a person as a file-self.* I believe that there would be considerable interest in pursuing this research much further (*see* research menu 3).

RESEARCH MENU 3

(1) Most psychologists take for granted that everything that happens (and particularly everything that happens in their empirical studies) is determinate. But every event is capable of many different interpretations and there are social processes by which conversational moves and other interpersonal happenings are stabilized and fixed to take on the character of a concrete 'pastness'. The psychological ramifications (for instance, its effect on memory) would be worth exploring, both as to intentional strategies and to the effects of interpersonal fixing on intrapersonal belief structures.

(2) Historical research into the consequences of belief in a transcendental divine order in which actions were fixed would contrast interestingly with a study of the techniques by which publicly and privately we 'get away with it', reworking our pasts.

(3) The study of file-embodiment and its fatefulness needs to be vigorously pursued. School files, credit ratings and so on need to be included with a careful categorization of vocabularies, and the effect these have on the avail-

*I am most grateful for permission from the Oxford 'Ethics of Research' Committee to consult the psychiatric files upon which this study is based.

ability of assessments of the file-self so embodied. The brief study reported in the text shows that the way files are actually compiled is different from the theory of their compilation subscribed to by the person who makes up the file, even when file keeping has been part of their formal training.

BIBLIOGRAPHICAL NOTES 3

K. LEWIN was responsible for the original idea of socially structured space and time, *Une théorie du champ dans les sciences de l'homme* (Paris: Librairie Philosophique J. Vrin, 1968), dating from the 1930s. More recent is E. GOFFMAN, *Relations in public* (Harmondsworth: Penguin, 1972).

For the theory of indexicals see bibliographical notes 4 and Y. BAR-HILLEL, 'Indexical expressions' (*Mind*, 63, 1954, 359−79). A discussion of the relation of 'now' to tensed statements can be found by R. M.GALE, J. J. C. SMART and I. THALBERG in the *Philosophical Quarterly*, 12, 1962 and 13, 1963. See the tidy summary by B. RUNDLE, *Grammar in philosophy* (Oxford: Clarendon Press, 1979, ch. 2 and 6) and also H. PHILIPSE, 'The problem of occasional expressions in Edmund Husserl's *Logical investigations*' (*Journal of the British Society for Phenomenology*, 13, 1982, 168−85).

For a defence of intentional notions in primate psychology see R. HARRÉ and V. REYNOLDS (eds), *The meaning of primate signals* (Cambridge: Cambridge University Press, 1983). M. BRENNER's tragic death in 1982 prevented the publication of his more recent critique of the over-determinate analyses promoted by the 'rule-following' picture of human action. His only published discussion of this issue is 'Actors' powers' in M. VON CRANACH and R. HARRÉ (eds), *The analysis of action* (Cambridge: Cambridge University Press, 1982, 213−30).

The cyclical interaction between social orders and personal belief systems has been discussed by many authors. The clearest and sharpest account is R. BHASKAR, *The possibility of naturalism* (Hassocks: Harvester Press, 1979, ch. 2, s. 3). There is a close parallel with the idea of 'structuration' in A. GIDDENS, *Central problems in social theory* (London: Macmillan, 1972, ch. 2). The metaphysical implications of the thing-like way we are ordinarily embodied has been developed by P. F. STRAWSON, in his now classic *Individuals* (London: Methuen, 1959).

Additional works cited in text are M. BRENNER, 'Actors' powers' (in *The analysis of action*, ed. M. von Cranach and R. Harré, Cambridge: Cambridge University Press, 1982, 213−30); D. BROADBENT, 'Non-corporeal explanation in psychology' (in *Scientific explanation*, ed. A. F. Heath, Oxford: Clarendon Press, 1981); D. C. DENNETT, *Brainstorms* (Hassocks: Harvester Press, 1978); R. HARRÉ, *Social Being* (Oxford: Blackwell, 1979); H. PUTNAM, *Philosophical papers* (Cambridge: Cambridge University Press, 1975, vol. 2).

CHAPTER 4

DUALITY ONE: PERSONS AND SELVES

Theme: People need be taken as no more than social atoms for an analysis of public conversation, but they do have a secondary structure, namely their mental organization as individuals. I argue that the structure of mind as the thoughts, feelings and actions of a self derives from belief in a theory.

Contents

1 PRIMARY AND SECONDARY STRUCTURE

In chapter 3 I proposed a conceptual system for investigating the individualizing of speakers in the human conversation as persons. This represents, in a general way, the structure of the distribution of psychological attributes, processes, states and so on that are found in quadrant 1, the public – collective realm of my proposed psychological dimensions. I have called this the primary structure.

In the primary structure people appear as locations for speech acts. As such they are metaphysically simple without internal structure, just as the point locations of physical space are. Real human beings, however, are not mere locations: they are 'internally' complex. This internal complexity I call the secondary structure. The multi-dimensional space of psychological dimensions developed in chapter 2 can be used to represent the relations between primary and secondary structure, by adding a dynamic order to the quadrants. This will be taken up in chapter 5.

By virtue of individually located secondary structures, the speech acts of the human conversation can be grounded in mental activity and treated as the product of expressions of personal intention interpreted by other members of a collective by virtue of their secondary structures. The social constructivist thesis, that each secondary structure is a variously imperfect reflection of the primary structure, will turn out to be true, I hope to show, only in a limited way. The properties of the primary structure of a social world once appropriated by an individual as a secondary structure are then modified to a greater or lesser degree by intrinsic personal processes. This is represented in the psychological dimensions scheme by the transition from quadrant 2 to quadrant 3. Detailed consideration of the formal properties of secondary structures, including the organization of experience, thought and action as mine, requires, I hope to show, a second centring of the psychological, the concept which I shall call a 'self'.

I propose to amplify a tendency noticeable in recent philosophical writing to work towards a distinction between the individuality of a human being as it is publicly identified and collectively defined and the individuality of the unitary subject of experience. Recent arguments about the basis of personal identity have turned on the relative weight to be given to public bodily continuity and maintenance of behavioural style over against some felt unity of experience.

In this chapter I hope to justify the introduction of a new duality into the metaphysics of psychology, a duality between person and self. Persons as social individuals are locations in the primary structure, and so are identifiable by public criteria. The intentionality of their actions and speeches is interpreted within a social framework of interpersonal commitments rather than as the outward expression of some inner state. Selves are psychological individuals, manifested in the unified organization of perceptions, feelings and beliefs of each human being who is organized in that fashion in their own regard. There may be human beings whose belief systems, imaginary anticipations and so on are organized in some non-unitary way. Necessarily all human beings who are members of moral orders are persons, social individuals, but the degree of their psychological individuality, their personal being, I take to be contingent. The distinctions to be drawn out in this work as founding hypotheses for personal psychology are but the empirical counterparts of the oppositions displayed in Strawson's stern warning 'The concept of pure individual consciousness — the pure ego — . . . cannot exist as a primary concept in terms of which the concept of a person can be explained or analysed. It can exist, if at all, as a secondary non-primitive concept, which itself is to be explained, analysed in terms of the concept of a person' (Strawson, *Individuals*, p. 102). Why should this distinction be introduced to play so fundamental a role? I shall support it by demonstrating its power to resolve certain persisting philosophical issues, and by its utility in making intelligible a dimension of intercultural differences brought out by comparative anthropology. The duality of person and self is thus fitted to be the conceptual foundation of a programme of psychological research.

At this point it will be well to distinguish social constructivist theories of self from the social learning theories of such as Bandura, in *Social learning theory*. Social learning theorists claim (no doubt correctly) that certain traits, dispositions and the like are the result, not of native development, but of the acquisition in social contexts of beliefs and habits. The social constructivist, however, goes much further, asking whether the self-'centred' structure of our system of beliefs, or any other structure personal systems of belief may be found to have, such as the triple agency structure proposed by Freud, is itself a belief. For those who answer this question in the affirmative, not only the content but the form of mind is socially acquired.

Finally, I want to emphasize that my concern is not with the 'self-concept' as it is currently understood in psychology. As Rogers introduced the term in 'A theory of therapy', it is clearly to be taken to refer to a belief system: 'The organized, consistent gestalt composed of the characteristics of the ''I'' or ''me'' and the perceptions of the relationships of the ''I'' or ''me'' to others and to various aspects of life, together with the values attached to these perceptions' is the self-concept. It is also usually taken to include what a person thinks they would like to be. However, self-concept is often carelessly spoken of as 'self'. For instance, in *Personality* Liebert and Spiegler remark 'The person defends himself from . . . impending danger by a process of defence which maintains the self (sic) as it exists at that time'. Sometimes there is a correlated concept of 'identity' which treats the belief systems of each as their identity. This is a qualitative concept presuming the grasp by each of his or her own numerical identity. In a word, identity crises are not crises of identity. To be troubled as to who I am requires that I know that I am.

My concern is with the origin and nature of the structure of that belief system and the relation of that structure to the generally 'centred' structure of experience I shall refer to throughout this work as the 'sense of self'. It is that which, as Doris Lessing has put it, is 'kept burning' behind our many roles.

2   PHILOSOPHICAL ISSUES CONCERNING PERSONS AS SELVES

The quest for the true bases of the person, the sense of individuality and continuous self-identity of human beings, is a persistent theme in philosophy. I shall somewhat artificially separate my treatment into grammatical and metaphysical investigations.

Grammatical investigations

The philosophical grammar of proper names and personal pronouns should throw some light on the nature of the beings to which they are used to refer. For my purposes in this chapter I need consider only the first person pronoun 'I', whose modes of use one might think are closely related to conceptions of personhood and self. Some philosophers have argued that 'I' is non-referential, that is, it is not used to ascribe properties to the individual substance or entity to which it is tied. Others have thought that it was referential, though there have been great differences in their views as to the nature of that referent, roughly whether it is body or mind (soul).

Referentialists differ further as to whether the referent is a collection or bundle of properties, states etc. or an entity. Hume's 'bundle of perceptions' view of personal psychological unity, in *A treatise of human nature*, stands in the strongest possible contrast to McTaggart's claim that 'I' is a logically proper name, that is, a name used referentially for speaking of a being of which one has immediate acquaintance (*The nature of existence*). In McTaggart's view, recently endorsed by Madell, in *The identity of self*, to be aware of the referent of 'I' is not to know that some particular cluster of properties has been realized. McTaggart's argument turns on the alleged point that I could not know that some description applied to me unless I knew not only the property ascribed but the 'myself' to which it is ascribed. This proposal will be seen to dissolve, as an argument, as we proceed.

There are various ways to make the step to the non-referential theory, but the basic thought is simple. After all the properties, physical, mental, dispositional and so on have been enumerated, the claim that *I* am that person expresses an additional piece of information, not included among either the corporeal or mental attributes of the person in question. A person could, for example, imagine him or herself to be of a different nation, culture, sex or time, and yet think that *he* or *she* was that person, without contradicting any current facts true of that person. But what is the force of the extra element in first person statements? First person assertions such as 'I am here' and 'It's me' are non-empirical in the sense that there are no conditions under which their utterance would be false. According to non-referentialists like Vesey (*Personal identity*), Anscombe ('The first person') or Coval (*Scepticism and the first person*), the irreducible extra element such statements introduce into the discourse is the display or indication of uniqueness, the feature I have called 'location in the primary structure'. Anscombe's conclusion that 'there is no subject to which "I" refers, there are just "I"-thoughts' is adequate only for the primary structure in which 'I' functions as a person label. Her argument (and indeed I think the arguments of all non-referentialists) supports only the view that there is no *given empirical* subject to which 'I' refers in the declaration and ordering of thought. There are indeed only 'I'-thoughts, unified into clusters in the public world by indexing to simple locations in the array of persons. But we know full well that they are also unified in personal experience, and that unification is not empirical. Contrary to McTaggart's claim in *The nature of existence*, I do not believe that we have experience of our psychological 'centres', but it does not follow that because there is no empirically given unifying *entity* that there is no unifying *concept*.

I must certainly have the concept of myself as a subject of experience to be able to order my beliefs, memories and plans the way I do, but awareness is not the only way a concept can be acquired. So 'awareness of myself' is not necessary for me to have the concept of myself. As in the physical sciences, so in this case, a concept can be acquired by a semantic displacement. 'I' as self is a concept acquired by semantic displacement of the concept of 'I' as a person.

I believe that no resolution of the antithesis between referential and non-referential uses of 'I' that has emerged is possible through generalizing one of the alternatives in an attempt to provide a unified account by subsuming the other. The reasons for identifying each of these uses of 'I' in current English, each with its appropriate metaphysical theory, seem to be sound. In each case the making of counter-arguments can be treated merely as demonstrations of the need to admit the viability of the other concept in our socio- and psycho-linguistic practices.

A passage from Madell's *The identity of self* (p. 29) cries out for a dualist resolution. In commenting on the view that 'I' is used indexically to indicate or display the speaker as the person committed to an utterance he says:

> . . . even if the arguments that 'I'm here' or 'It's me' is some sort of truth valueless indication were successful, the suggestion that we could then go on to generalize this and claim that, even in assertions like 'I am increasingly aware of the difficulty of this topic', 'I' is being used as some sort of indicator, without awareness of a subject, looks thoroughly implausible.

Indeed it does. An awareness of one of my own states as mine is certainly presupposed in that remark, and so is the knowledge that it is mine and with it is presupposed the concept of myself. There is the difficulty that is being experienced, and the location of that difficulty within an ordered framework of experience that is mine. The most elegant resolution of the irreducibility of this kind of sentence to an indexical (non-referential) form is to see that no more than the self as a theoretical concept is being invoked. In this sort of context 'I' refers to an entity without empirically given properties. It lacks such properties, not because it is not given in immediate experience, contra Hume, Ryle and others, but because it is of the same kind as the familiar hypothetical entities that are the referents of nominal expressions in deep physical theories. The mystery is resolved once one sees that the 'inner self' is in many ways like the 'gravitational field' invoked to express the structured properties of free fall as the products of an underlying ordered being. This innovation breaks the chain of McTaggart's argument in *The nature of existence*, given above. Just as I can ascribe properties to the gravitational field without experience of it, so too I can ascribe properties to myself without an empirical acquaintance with my 'inner being'. Persons are indexed (indicated) as speakers; selves are referred to as organizing principles of the psychological unities that confer subjective individuality. In a later chapter I shall associate these distinctions with the fact of personal identity germane to the individuality of persons and the sense of personal identity germane to the individuality of selves.

Since the dualism sketched in this section will play such a large role in the theory of personal being it is worth elaborating the theory of indexical expressions a little further. It is clear that the pronoun 'I' cannot be understood along the same lines as we understand proper names. Its referential function is dependent upon context and use. Ostensive functions of that kind are called indexical uses, that is, the pronoun is used to locate speech acts of various kinds, such as avowals, commitments etc. at a particular location in the array of persons. This feature can be brought out by comparing 'I' with other indexicals. 'I' is to Rom Harré as 'here and now' is to Binghamton. 'Here and now' is the space – time indexical I would use to refer to wherever I happen to be at the moment of speaking or writing, whereas Binghamton is the proper name of a location in space – time where I am only occasionally. 'I' is personal – indexical, locating the speech act where it is currently taking place, whereas Rom Harré is a proper name for a person by means of which speech acts can be located in the array of persons from any point within it. It is worth noticing that since the indexicals in the pronoun system are used by speakers in the first person, then the indexical system cannot function to refer reflexively to possible persons. These features of the use of pronouns are very well known and have been investigated in considerable detail.

However, there has been considerable controversy over the logical grammar of indexicals. On one account the pronouns have been treated as ambiguous proper names, terms without content whose function is just to refer or point to that which they currently name. But so far as my intuitions go 'I' is never ambiguous. It is not an ambiguous proper name because it is not a proper name at all. By turning to the way indexicals are used, a more plausible model emerges. To use a pronoun is to mark or label an utterance with a person location just as to use a space – time indexical is to mark an utterance with the space – time location of the act of utterance. Part of the temptation to treat 'I' as a kind of name is a misunderstanding about the metaphysical standing of people in the primary array. I have suggested that they are like locations, not like things. Indexicals are like marks of possession or origin. 'Me-spoken' is like 'British-made', a label that locates manufacture somewhere in space. It does not refer to that place as the proper name would in the exchange 'Where was that made?' 'In Delft'. 'I' does not refer to a speaker. It labels a speech as mine. It is like me spitting in my beer or the territorial defecations of hippopotami. By our acts of marking, the hippo and I lay claim to something as ours. We do not make an act of self-reference.

Metaphysical investigations

Both philosophers and psychologists, for instance Kant and Kelly, have seen the need for the concept of a self, a concept other than that of the socially defined 'person' who is the bearer of the indexical force of the pronoun 'I'. Each human being's conception of themselves is more elaborate than could be explained solely by invoking the hypothesis that he or she believes him or herself to be a person amongst an array of persons, each of whom is a publicly observable being. We are familiar in physics with concepts introduced to refer to transcendental, non-observable realities, belief in which enables us to order experience in various ways. For instance, a concept like gravitational field, or electric or magnetic potential, is of this kind. In learning to use the concept 'gravity', I acquire a way of organizing my experience of falling bodies, hot air balloons, earth satellites and so on into a single coherent framework.

The structure of the gravitational field enables us to understand the apparently unique and differentiated motions of bodies in proximity to the earth. The organizing power of the concept is independent of whether we treat gravitational potentials as real-world entities or mere fictions. I want to suggest that 'I', the first person pronoun, does have a referential force to a hypothetical entity 'the self', in much the same way that the gravitational term g refers to a hypothetical entity, the gravitational field. Possession of the theoretical concept 'self' permits just the kind of organization of a person's experience that Kant called 'synthetic unity'. If it is agreed that these are indeed the functions of 'I' and that this dual use of the language of self-reference enables us to locate speech acts in the array of persons and permits each person to organize his or her experience with the help of a powerful theoretical concept acquired by being taught and so coming to believe the theory that they are selves, that is, psychologically unitary beings, we must now ask how is the dual function of 'I' acquired by a speaker?

The concept of 'person' which I develop against that of 'self' does not need but does not run counter to the assumption that the being has experiences, but not necessarily the ability to know that those experiences are his or hers perhaps because of the lack of appropriate conceptual resources. The remark 'I am tired' could have force in the interpersonal conversation without the explicit reflection 'I know that I am tired' which might be used, say, to refute a suggestion that one was ill. In following Strawson (in *Individuals*) in identifying persons through capacities for self and other ascriptions of experiences, thoughts and feelings in *public* discourse, I do not want to exceed the public and collective contexts of avowals and expressive remarks; speech acts are part of the *expression* of feeling, opinion, intentions etc. It is to these uses that the Wittgenstein notion of criterion applies, and so too Strawson's notion of 'logically adequate criteria'.

For Strawson 'person' is: (a) a primitive concept; (b) such that a person can attribute experiences to him or herself in exactly the same sense as experiences are attributed to other persons. The same concept of 'tiredness' informs 'I am tired' and 'You are tired', though there are all sorts of differences between these statements. They are used in the same conversation for quite different speech acts. A use of the former could be an excuse, while an utterance of the latter could be an accusation. There are many other speech acts for which in context they might be used.

The grounds on which I make a public declaration of my condition (tiredness), my moral feelings (anger), my intentions and so on are systematically different from those upon which I describe, accuse or commiserate with you or you do the like with me. In order to maintain the identity of meaning of a basically constant psychological predicate in all of these diverse uses it is necessary to subscribe to a theory of the meaning of predicates which does not reduce meaning to the evidence or grounds, if any, upon which they are ascribed. Though I will not be defending any particular theory of the meaning of psychological or other predicates in this work, I shall be working with the presumption that any form of verificationist theory which reduces meaning to grounds of assertion must be rejected. It is widely agreed amongst philosophers that there are many psychological predicates which are properly self-ascribed without evidence.

Does it follow from this condition on the meaning of predicates that the referents of the 'person'-referring expressions in a conversation are just the publicly identifiable beings, persons in the sense I have marked out for the purposes of this discussion? Strawson (*Individuals*) makes a good deal of the central place that action predicates have in routine practices of ascriptions to persons. So for him and for Hampshire (*Thought and action*) 'digging the garden' in 'I'm digging the garden', 'You're digging the garden' and 'He's digging the garden' must have, indeed obviously just does have, the same meaning. And the three subjects of this attribution are severally publicly identified persons. As I hope to show, our local cultural and linguistic practices involve a secondary formation in the organization of belief and experience, so that these referring expressions are dual. Amongst these practices are a range of queries of the form 'Does he know he is digging the garden?', which we might ask of someone with a obsessive/compulsive neurosis, or who we thought was sleepwalking or under the influence of drugs.

Action predicates are centrally located in a spectrum of adjectives, verbs and adverbs appropriate for persons. There are the corporeal 'fat, red-faced and sweating', and then there are those used for intentional actions, such as 'running for the bus'; there are also 'natural compounds', such as 'flopping down feeling exhausted' and, finally, predicates used in private acts of self-description and self-admonition, for instance, 'I must try to control my irritation with him' or 'I really must lose some weight'. Notice that both 'irritation' and 'weight' appear in attributions in the primary structure, thus being guaranteed a public meaning.

Strawson's proposal (in *Individuals*) is presented as an analysis of the concept of person in everyday use. Whether this exercise in descriptive metaphysics is adequate as a study in psycholinguistics is a question needing research (*see* research menu 4). For my purposes, his analysis provides further support for my proposal to treat 'person' as an elementary 'location' in the primary structure, remarks emanating from which can be understood without reference to the truth or falsity of complementary descriptions of inner states. From the perspective of my study the concept of the simple unitary person is a hypothesis to be accepted or rejected in so far as the conceptual scheme, of which it is a part and which is developed in this work, advances our understanding of the nature and origins of personal being.

While Strawson's account is defensible for predication in the primary structure, I do not believe it is adequate for predication in the secondary structures appropriated from it. To appreciate this one needs to look more closely at first person predication. Consider again the remark 'I am tired'. It can be uttered as a complaint, as a move in the primary structure of persons in conversation. No particular organization of the speaker's experience and system of beliefs, memories etc. is required as a necessary condition for the effective production of that speech act. The speaker may treat his actions as done in obedience to the commands of the gods, as Jaynes has suggested in *The origin of consciousness*, was the case with the pre-Homeric Greeks. He may think of himself as an independent agent, but if the utterance is read as a report of an experience, then not only is it a move in the primary structure of the conversing group — say, an avowal — it is also a description of a condition located somehow in the secondary structure of that person. Tiredness as an experience is to be fitted in with other experiences, memories, beliefs, plans and so on.

The way the secondary structure is organized, and particularly the way it is unified by the theory of selfhood entertained by the being in question will, with the content of the experience, determine how that experience can be located within the secondary structure. There may be great differences in the way certain experiences — say, the realization that one has the solution to a problem — are fitted into the secondary structure. Those Greeks who believed in inspiration from the Muses would have taken no personal responsibility for thought. It would not have been theirs.

Moral considerations are strikingly absent from Strawson's account, but the emphasis on action at least provides a place for their natural introduction. If actions are ascribed to persons, the evaluation of actions can be transferred to persons if we can introduce the concept of 'responsibility'. To put it in psychological terms, persons are those beings who act intentionally. Much philosophical work needs to be done to link acting intentionally with the foundations for ascriptions of responsibility in the claim that a person on a particular occasion could have done other than they did. I believe that the link is conceptual rather than empirical but the establishing of this point must await the detailed analysis of the concept of agency. I hope to show that moral responsibility comes into being in a society by way of the people coming to believe that they are agents.

Anthropological and historical evidence will be presented to demonstrate that what every society recognizes as human individuality in the form of persons is the Strawsonian sense of embodied agent, that is, it has a common primary structure; there are very wide variations in secondary structure, that is, in the degree of singularity with which persons organize their experienced thoughts, feelings, premonitions and plans as their own. The most important evidence of all would be that of a tribe of persons without selves.

3 ANTHROPOLOGICAL EVIDENCE TO DEMONSTRATE THE ANALYTICAL SEPARABILITY OF INDEXICAL AND THEORETICAL ASPECTS OF SELF-REFERENCE

Though it would be hard to prove that there was a tribe quite without selves, there is enough diversity in the ways people conceive of themselves to support my case for a dualism between public – collective and private – individual concepts of human individuality. In this section I will sketch two case studies of 'psychologies' which are distinctive enough to support the tentative dualism of concepts of human individuality that is suggested by the philosophical analysis just attempted. If one could find cultures with well-established institutions of individual and reflexive personal reference as part of public discourse, but which have very different ways of organizing the structure of thought, emotion, consciousness, agency and so on, then one would have established in principle the distinctiveness of these two main aspects of reflexive reference that are sufficiently run together in our culture for it to be possible for schools of philosophy to form up around the one or the other.

To conceive of myself as a person, I must conceive of others as persons, a thought expressed by Strawson in terms of the capacity of a person to ascribe psychological and other attributes to self and others. But Strawson quite fails to explain how I come to conceive of myself as a self, an 'inner' unity. The idea that there is no such inner unity is a philosophical doctrine that can be dispelled by the anthropological case to be made in this section. I must remind the reader once again that the inner unity I am discussing is not an entity but a mode of organization.

The 'I' theory sketched in the last section requires a mode of reflexive reference to persons ubiquitous to all mankind, in so far as the fact of social responsibility is a feature necessary for the maintenance of any society whatever. In addition, there appear to be distinctive modes and degrees of private and individual self-reference dependent on concepts of psychological unity.

The first person pronouns in use in a culture could even all be plural, locating commitments at the obligated group. Such a culture might have no use for the concept of group-self and just have *no* organized unity for a consistent subject of psychological predication. If we could find or even imagine such a culture it would support the hypothesis of the logical independence of a theory of a real concept of the self, belief in which enables experience to be organized in a practical and satisfactory fashion, from the beliefs and conventions supporting public – collective indexical reference; this could be proved if different societies could be shown to use different self-theories, while capable of similar public acts of personal commitment such as promising or resigning. Anthropological research supports this conjecture. Our Western self-theory seems to be located somewhere towards a midpoint of a spectrum of self-theories, distinguished by the degree of emphasis on individual uniqueness and power. The anthropological material demonstrates the cultural relativity of the way in which European languages influence the construction of personal theories of self-reference. I want to illustrate this by taking two cases, one where the self-theory is weaker than the Western European, and one where it is stronger. Eskimos, though sharing a concept of social identity of persons with ourselves, have a weaker sense of personal identity, that is, they do not use a concept of 'inner' unity of self comparable to ours, by which each individual organizes his or her own experience, memory and so on. Maoris, on the other hand, seem to have a stronger sense of personal distinctiveness, inviolability and power of self-activation than we do. The evidence to be cited in this section is a mere sketch of what would be required for a fully conclusive demonstration. Nothing less than a series of psycholinguistically orientated ethnographic monographs would do (*see* research menu 4).

Eskimo psychology: grammar and the moral order

The fact of individual identity of each person as a social being is well recognized amongst the Eskimos. They deploy a system of personal names and make assessments of each other within a moral order, though in ways markedly different from ours. An economical way of revealing the differences in the personal centering of thought and feeling between the Eskimos and ourselves is to look at their indigenous psychology of the emotions and, by way of further evidence, their psychology of art and the premises of their moral theory.

The idea that linguistic forms determine psychological structures (the Sapir–Whorf hypothesis) is now widely agreed to be too simplistic Nevertheless, it seems reasonable to suppose that distinctive linguistic forms facilitate distinctive modes of psychological organization. Linguistic evidence can be telling only if it is accompanied by ethnographic reports describing the practices and setting out the theories of the folk which point to the same distinctive features that are hinted at in the way the language works.

Eskimo is a polysynthetic language with only minor variations over the vast area in which it is spoken. It is built up of complex word-sentences, by the addition of suffixes and infixes to bases. Qualification of a base continues until the utterance is disambiguated relative to context. There are strict positional rules governing the order of infixes and suffixes, both with respect to morphology and to sense. The system of personalizing suffixes should give us what linguistic evidence there might be for the resources available for expressing a sense of personal identity.

The personalizing suffixes form two groups. The '-ik' group locates something at the speaker, and these I take to be functionally equivalent to the indexical uses of 'I'. The '-tok' group locates matters at someone other than the speaker. Colin Irwin (personal correspondence) describes '-tok' as having a directive function, diverting attention away from speaker to some other. Thus 'indignation' is 'peu-gu-sungi-tok', not a feeling of the speaker, but annoyance directed at another. Further, where in English a referential form of the pronoun would be used as in 'I am', say, uttered in reply to 'Who (i.e. which person) is preparing dinner?'. Eskimo would render this with the possessive suffix '-nga', as in 'uva-nga', 'the being here mine'. These and other features of the language suggest very strongly that while the uses of English favour a theory of the person conceived not only as a location but as a substance, qualified by attributes, in Eskimo persons are rendered as qualifications (for instance, as locations) of substantialized qualities and relations. Similarly, according to Birkett-Smith in *The Eskimos*, the content of 'I hear him' would be expressed in Eskimo by 'tusarp-a-ra', literally 'his making of a sound with reference to me'.

In so far as vocabulary and grammatical form can be cited as evidence, Eskimos seem to be perfect Strawsonians, distinguishing the emotions of themselves and others by referring them to locations in the array of persons, the grammatical forms emphasizing the public display rather than the private feeling. For instance, anger, much disapproved of according to ethnographers, is almost always ascribed in the third person, 'ningaq-tok'. Virtues are similarly identified in terms of public display. Colin Irwin quotes an informant as explaining that wisdom is used to describe 'someone who has not said his or her thought for a long period of time'.

Languages radically defective in explicit vocabularies can usually be found to have the resources to convey a thought or express a feeling for which there is no specific lexical item. Conversely, it may even be, as Robert Heinlein once remarked, that English can describe emotions that the human organism is incapable of experiencing. To complete the case for Eskimo psychology as a counter-example to a strict universality thesis, one must turn to characteristic social patterns, to the social expression of emotions and to the patterns of moral judgement and the Eskimo conception of action.

Many travellers have reported the extraordinary degree to which Eskimos seem to be influenced by their fellows. When one weeps, they all weep; when one laughs, they all laugh. Jennes remarks in 'The Copper Eskimos' that, 'The Copper Eskimo, as a rule, displays very little independence in either thought or action . . . He follows the multitude, agrees to whatever is said, and reflects the emotions of those around him.' At least with respect to a large and varied catalogue of public performances, individual feelings, intentions and reasonings play a very minor role.

Important aspects of the Eskimo conception of action are revealed in the theory of art. Carpenter, *Eskimo realities*, has emphasized the degree to which Eskimos hold that 'man is the force that reveals form'. Riesman ('Eskimo discovery') says, 'a work of art is conceived of as the bringing forth, the releasing of a meaning, which was latent in the material itself.' First-hand description of Eskimo practices are alike in describing the trouble the artist takes in brooding on the question as to what form is latent in the material. According to Carpenter (*Eskimo realities*) there are no Eskimo equivalents for our concepts of 'making' and 'creating'; carving, for instance, is described in terms of releasing or revealing what is already there. The concept of active individual agency plays scarcely any role in their theory of art.

Eskimo morality is centred on a sharp distinction between communal matters and personal and private matters. Only the former are appraised as good or bad. The social virtues of cooperativeness, peacefulness and so on are highly praised. Fair dealing in an individualistic person-to-person sense or truth telling are at best secondary virtues. Theft from persons, as one might expect, is not conceived as a serious misdemeanour. According to Jennes ('The Copper Eskimos'), 'the majority of natives merely look foolish if caught in the act of stealing, and repent their clumsiness.' The overriding force of communal considerations in Eskimo ethics is emphasized by Jennes:

> To the Copper Eskimo goodness means social goodness, that and no more. Whatever affects the welfare of the community as a whole is morally good or bad . . . The foremost virtues therefore are peacefulness and good-nature, courage and energy, patience and endurance, honesty, hospitality, charity towards both the old and the young, loyal cooperation with one's kin and providence in all questions relating to the food supply.

Colin Irwin has taken this a step further to demonstrate that the practical virtues are based not on a concept of enlightened self-interest, but on a rational appreciation of the social conditions that will support the next generation. According to Irwin, 'the primary interest of the Inuit is the future generation. They use every part of their physical and intellectual abilities in the advancement of that end.'

Maori psychology of personal power

Maori psychological theory is centred on a system of active principles for which there are corresponding material representations. Their 'ways of thought' are dominated by a social psychological theory based on the concept of *tapu* which is embedded in their general psychology of active principles and powers. A parallel can be drawn between the Maori's injunction, 'Do not touch his head; it is *tapu*', and the contemporary injunction, 'Do not touch that bare wire; it is electrified.' Each apparently harmless and quiescent thing is charged: in our terms it has potential energy.

Maori psychological theory, according to Best, *Spiritual and mental concepts of the Maori*, is based on the hypothesis of three active principles:

(1) *Wairua*: a principle of being. Each particular has a distinctive *wairua*. Since the Maori system is non-Cartesian, mental and other functions of a particular human, say, are all within the scope of the *wairua* of that being. As a principle of being-in-general there are

wairua too for inanimate particulars. The *wairua* of a being is substantial. It can leave the body and travel in space and time. Its condition is variable. When *toi-ora*, it lends well-being to its proper particular, but if interfered with by magic, it can decline in tone, inducing *pawera*, a generalized condition of dread of impending evil. Each *wairua*, being particular, must have its own essence or *aiwe*.

(2) *Mauoi*: the physical life principle.

(3) *Hau*: vitality, zest or activity.

Both *mauoi* and *hau* are capable of material representation. An inanimate thing can represent the *hau* of an animate being. For my purpose, *mauoi* is the most important of these powers. As *mauoi* is not the abstract social expressive property of *amour propre*, dignity etc., but can be materially represented, it can be materially defiled. Threat to personal standing can come from insult and from violation. It is not violation as a bearer of insult (as it might be in Spain) but violation as a physical encroachment on the untouchable.

If the psychology of man is conceived in terms of active powers, it is easy to see how socially powerful people might be thought to be especially highly charged, and given the Maori view that powers are realized in material substrates, how dangerous it might be to touch such a being. The practices around the notion of *tapu*, such as *rahui* — putting some charged thing as a marker on some piece of property like a *kumera* (sweet potato) garden — has the same rationality as surrounding a prison or a storehouse of valuables with an electric fence. The obvious explanation of *tapu*, then, is reached by embedding an indigenous psychology of active powers in a cosmology or general theory of nature, which is based on a substantialization of energy potentials, the Western parallel being the ether theories of electricity. Charge, in this sense, is the property called *mana*, which, as a substantialized power, is present in varying degrees in different persons in different substances, depending upon the actual power which they have.

In sharp contrast to this is Freud's theory of *tapu*. In *Totem and Taboo*, Freud argued, in effect, that *tapu* is not a unique psychology but is a manifestation of the same psychological mechanisms as he observed in the genesis and maintenance of obsessional neuroses (pp. 21–22). In both the practices of *tapu* and the ways that obsessional neurotics behave, there is a displacement of the prohibition on touching, from one thing to another. On this view, *tapu* could not be an indigenous psychology since it is no more than a series of local manifestations of a universal psychological process. Freud bases his argument on the analogy that *tapu* is to obsessional behaviour what the indigenous practices of such as the Maori are to the behaviour of neurotics. In accordance with this line of reasoning he says, 'But one thing would certainly follow from the persistence of the taboo, namely that the original desire to do the prohibited thing must also still persist among the tribes concerned.' In short, they would like to do the thing but their fear is stronger. 'The desire is unconscious, however, in every individual member of the tribe, just as it is in neurotics.' To explain the transfer of *tapu* from one person or object to another, Freud says, 'Anyone who has violated a taboo becomes taboo himself, because he possesses the dangerous quality of tempting others to follow his example' (p. 32).

The weaknesses of this theory are apparent. First of all, as Freud himself is willing to concede, the argument from the personal history of an individual obsessional to the social history of a tribe would be unconvincing without the parallels that are presumed to be observed in the behaviour of members of a tribe practising *tapu* and an obsessional neurotic. The difficulty with Freud's view is revealed in this passage: 'Dead men, new born babies . . . stimulate desire by their special helplessness.' One might well ask how that sort of 'stimulation of desire' (whatever that might mean) can be compared with the desire to overthrow the king because of his special power, envied by lesser persons, the explanation Freud offers for the *tapu* character of the king's body. If, on the other hand, one were to treat Maori psychology as a unique theory, then a dead man would be a danger because of the likely presence of a malevolent power. Within the cosmology of the Maoris, as within the cosmology of many nineteenth century physicists, powers must be realized in material substances. Thus a dead man is highly charged with the material carrier of the malevolent power that killed him. It would be as unwise to touch a dead man as it is to touch a bare wire.

Relative to the collectivist psychology of the Eskimo, Maori culture exhibited as extreme a form of individualism as found in the courtly Middle Ages of Europe. Though social givens such as birth determine the scope for individual achievement, as indeed it did in Medieval Europe, *mana* were amplified by personal accomplishment. And it is individuals, who, above all, become so charged with power that their dignity-preserving sanctity is treated as something physical. A test for the degree of individualism within the ranks of an ordered collective is the treatment of proper names. So dear did a Maori hold his personal honour that elaborate games were devised to deal with the problems created by the arrival of a stranger. To ask a man for his honour-bearing name would have been to demonstrate publicly that his personal fame had not reached his hosts, and this would humiliate him. Nor could he directly reveal it without humiliating himself.

The next step will be to try to identify the source of self-concepts. To suggest ways of researching how they are acquired, we must first form some idea of the status of such concepts: are they empirical, theoretical, formal or what?

4   ANIMATE BEINGS TO SELVES: DYNAMIC RELATIONS BETWEEN QUADRANTS 1 AND 2

There are three main theories current to explain how people acquire minds. An organized belief system and a corpus of linguistic and practical skills are required as at least necessary conditions for·'mindedness'. Theories as to the acquisition of some or all of this foundation will qualify. The discussions of this chapter ought not to be thought of as restricted to the traditional infantile context of academic developmental psychology. It may be that there are other times in life when mindedness may be acquired or amplified.

Contemporary innateness theorists are careful to avoid any claims involving innate cognitive contents. Chomsky's well-known theory of an inborn language acquisition device proposes an organ preprogrammed to pick out language from all other environing happenings. Much recent work in the study of very young children suggests a pre-programming of actions that provoke from the mother the kind of performances and displays that are 'just right' as a foundation for acquisition of person-engendering beliefs and skills. While it is fair to say that the language acquisition device is not held in much favour by developmental psycholinguistics, the preprogrammed prompting theory is becoming well grounded empirically.

Two rather different brigades make up the non-innateness or early experience camp. Freudian developmentalists look for, at the very least, the structuring of mind into the familiar Freudian form as a product of inevitable interactions with and relations to the mother and father in Lacan's 'mirror phase' for instance. Since I believe it can be fairly easily shown that the Freudian structures of mind, while of great importance locally, are of limited universality, I shall treat them as a species of the third main theory. That theory appears as an outgrowth of critical attention to Piaget's staged development conception, contributed to by various hands, notably Bruner ('Early rule structure') and the Shotter—Newson partnership ('How babies communicate'). Like the Freudian theory, it directs attention to the social processes and relations in which an infant is engaged. That attention is focused particularly on the linguistic environment, which appears in the form of speech-in-a-situated-practice, the type of episode Wittgenstein called a language game. Various such games have been seen to be involved in the acquisition of the wherewithal for acquiring personal being, but those in which psychological symbiosis occurs, that is, routine supplementation of the incomplete cognitive, emotional and intentional repertoire of one being by another through speech, are the most potent. It is in the language games of psychological symbiosis that the transformation of animate beings into persons is accomplished. Those principles that Wittgenstein called the grammar of such ways of talk become the metaphysics of distinctive ways of personal being.

Some measure of preprogramming can be accommodated in the psychological symbiosis theory in that the infant prompts the mother to produce the kind of performances that supplement the infant's current deficits. Furthermore, if the particular forms that the belief systems take are determined by the language games thus played, local differences in such mutual activities could be cited to explain the actual distribution of structures approximating those identified by Freudians, neo-Freudians and others (*see* research menu 4).

I now take up the problem of how to represent the transformation of animate beings into persons. The basic thesis of this work is that animate beings are persons if they are in possession of a theory — a theory about themselves. It is a theory in terms of which a being orders, partitions and reflects on its own experience and becomes capable of self-intervention and control. In the span of human kind there may be many such person-engendering theories. The ordering and partitioning as it is carried on in our social and historical conditions is dependent on a belief that the three unities involved in the structuring of consciousness, agency and history, namely point of view, point of action and life trajectory, are manifestations of a more fundamental unity. The theory of the unity of unities, so to speak, should appear in characteristic ways, in particular how a person talks and is talked to by those who take him or her to be a person, and in the degree to which a person believes him or herself to be autonomous. This is not just a philosophical theory about the necessary conditions for personhood as we live it and conceive it. Since I have offered a hypothesis about how these conditions are met in a particular culture, namely ours, there are empirical consequences. For instance, the relation of the theory to actual occasions of talk suggests a project in developmental psychology. It would make sense to look for conversational practices in which a theory of the appropriate kind could be acquired by an animate being who is thereby transformed into a person.

Why should this account of the transformation of an animate being to a person be taken seriously? Might it not be that by a process of biological maturation an individual develops in such a way that it can discover empirically, by a certain kind of observation, prompted perhaps by others, that it is a person; that there is an 'I' and a 'Thou'; that there are some states of affairs (and so a world) which are independent of any of his or her plans and best attempts to realize them and some that are not; that, by and large, human sensibility extends roughly as far as the bodily envelope, and so on. Why could these not be empirical discoveries made by virtue of growing powers of discernment as a result of the natural process of maturation? Two objections can be made to a maturation theory. First, one could try to specify the kind of experience which would have to be possible if the 'inner' unity of one's own personhood were to be a possible object of empirical discovery. Even the most dedicated of all the many explorers of the psyche, Husserl, failed to find an entity at the centre of experience (see *Cartesian meditations*). In developing his idea of the transcendental reduction of experience, in what he calls the first and second 'epochés', he takes us through an intellectual exercise in which each progressively examines his or her experience, looking for the characteristics, labels or markings which would identify items in that experience as belonging to this or that person. He claimed that there is an ultimate stage of transcendental reduction, where experience is reduced to a 'primordial sphere' of phenomena, in which no labels of ownership remain. It cannot be through an empirical discovery that experiences are marked as mine that I become aware of my own 'objectivity'. Somehow I must perform the act of labelling and so create the self I can thereby experience. Even if one is obliged to concede that the 'primordial sphere' is organized from 'here and now', that the sphere has a centre, so to speak, there is no way of partitioning the primordial experience of the world into 'mine' and 'other than mine' by reference to given empirically distinguishable features of that experience. According to Husserl such distinction must be *constituted*. I will return to a more detailed account of Husserl's view and its rivals within phenomenology in a later section. Interestingly, yoga psychology, with its emphasis on techniques of self-discovery, is based on the thesis that the 'self' to be discovered is without content.

A different but complementary argument starts with Hume's sceptical doubts about the self. He pointed out that 'the self' itself can never be presented in experience. 'When I turn my reflection on *myself*, I never can perceive this *self* without some one or more perceptions; nor can I ever perceive anything but perceptions. It is the composition of these, therefore, which forms the self' (*A treatise of human nature*, book I, appendix). Ryle, *The concept of mind*, has offered a very similar argument as a glaringly obvious truth. Instances of thinking, feeling and so on are not related to a central being experienced in just the same way as they are, and to which they could thereby be seen to be related. That which unifies them as *my* thoughts, processes of reasoning etc. is not an empirically manifested individual substance. According to Hume, the mere composition of thoughts and feelings into sequences is the real referent of the concept of self.

5 KANT: CREATION OF THE SELF IN THE SYNTHESES OF EXPERIENCE

Personal unity

Kant's introduction of the concept of the transcendental unity of apperception could be thought of as filling the gap Hume drove between the apparent substantial referent of the cogito of Descartes and the 'plain facts of experience'. It suggests a non-empirical referent for 'I' which is not a mere composition. For Kant, the unity of experience that is given in experience is an orderliness which is the product of a synthesis. As he says in the *Critique of pure reason*, 'I am conscious of myself not as I am in myself, but only that I am. The *representation* is a *thought* that is, has the status of a theory not an intuition that is, it is not an experience' (B157).

To formulate a theory one requires not only the thought of an object in general but an intuition to determine it, to make the representation concrete, that is, thinkable, so 'I require . . . besides the thought of myself [which I shall be arguing is a socially engendered theory] an intuition of the manifold in me, the unified field of consciousness, in time etc. by which I determine the thought' (*Critique of pure reason*). So Kantian synthetic unities in experience are not to be treated as inductive evidence for the theory of transcendental self (and unity of apperception) but as concrete manifestations of personhood, that is, as representations of a theoretical concept they provide the grounding for the sense of self.

Kant's account of determination of this kind is by reference to the temporal properties of inner experience. In another passage from *Critique of pure reason*, Kant elaborates this idea: 'But it [the 'I think'] can have no special designation, because it serves only to introduce all our thought, as belonging to consciousness' (p. 329). In short, the 'I' in 'I think' is not a referring expression in the demonstrative sense, that is, it does not denote a possible object of experience, but identifies (indexically) or labels a collection of expressions of thought as belonging to one person. Unlike the constructivist position which takes the basic role of 'cogito'-type expressions to be in the primary structure, that is, the public conversation, anchoring expression of opinion to their proper persons, Kant asks us to think of the 'cogito' as a label by the use of which both public and private discourse about experience becomes an expression of the unified experience of a being. But the experience of that being as to its form(s) of order is just the awareness of that unity.

Three syntheses of mind and how they make possible a sense of self

By its synthesizing powers, the human creates order and unity both in the flux of sensations engendering an empirical world as experienced *and* in the experiences which are of that world. Both 'outer sense' and 'inner sense' are unified by an active synthesizing of experiential fragments. The self emerges for each of us in a complex interweaving of complementary syntheses, which are necessary, Kant believes, to give form to experience as we have it. Our experience has three prominent structural features: it is organized as a spatiotemporal manifold; it presents a world of causally interacting objects; and it is unified as a field of consciousness. The self-unity appears in the syntheses which produce the two latter. To produce the given unities three syntheses are required.

(1) To show that the unity of apperception, that is, conscious awareness as a unified field is the product of a synthesis: according to Kant there is '. . . the necessity of a synthesis of the manifold given in intuition, without which the thoroughgoing identity of self-consciousness cannot be thought' (B135). The argument has the form: 'The identity of self-consciousness is given. What makes it possible?' The answer: 'Only a synthesis'. According to Walker, in his book *Kant*, this argument is successful because the synthesis involved in self-descriptions must be transcendental that is, involving the application of a concept. 'It could hardly be held to be governed by an empirical concept, learned by abstraction from experience'; hence it must involve an a priori category.

(2) To show that the transcendental affinity of appearances, that is, the physical world of which I am aware, must be a unity because consciousness is a unified field:

> I must think of myself as a unity
> therefore
> I must think of my experience as a unity
> therefore
> I must see them as forming a unified objective world.

to paraphrase the argument of A113f.

Even if these arguments were successful (and (2) looks quite implausible), neither goes to show that conscious experience must have the particular form of unity that we mean when we talk of 'self', that is, an asymmetrical centralized structure.

(3) To show that inner sense must be synthesized according to a concept, the same line of argument is brought to bear on the explication of a person's subjective sense of self, as the nodal point of his or her structured mode of experience. According to Kant, whatever concept it is must be the application of some a priori category. The arguments of the transcendental deduction take the personal unities as given. Can we find in Kant any further observations on how they emerge?

I believe Kant's view to be that the personal unities as experienced do not emerge in a special synthetic act, but are engendered in the course of synthesizing the sensory flux into the spatiotemporally ordered dualistic world of things (outer sense) and thoughts (inner sense). To see this, I examine one of the syntheses, that involved in engendering the 'transcendental unity of apperception'. In B133, Kant says:

> Only in so far, therefore, as I can unite a manifold of given representations in *one consciousness*, is it possible for me to represent to myself the *identity of the consciousness in (that is throughout) these representations*. In other words, the *analytic* unity of apperception is possible only under the presupposition of a certain *synthetic* unity.

This is second-order synthesis, so to speak, operating upon the groundwork of primary synthesis in which space, time and objects are created. One could look on Kant's observation in B133 as a statement of a key feature of the deep grammar of expressions like 'I think'. The proper use of this expression to mark the contents of one consciousness does not require that a substantial referent be secured for the 'I'. To suppose that it does is to be guilty of the fallacious reasoning Kant exposes in the Paralogisms.

Strawson in *The bounds of sense*, takes the central Kantian point to be 'the duplicity of aspects' of experience. 'On the one hand, it cumulatively builds up a picture of the world' in which things and events are presented as having an objective order. 'On the other hand, it possesses its own order as a series of experiences' (p. 106). This duality is related to self-consciousness, according to Strawson, by the fact that Kant expresses the important feature of the possibility of self-description of states in terms of the notion of self-consciousness. The duality does not provide the ground for the full conditions for personal self-awareness as we experience it, but just the essential core: 'It provides room on the one hand for "Thus and so is how things objectively are" and, on the other, for "This is how things are experienced as being"; and provides room for the second thought *because* it provides room for the first' (p. 107).

Strawson arrives at this 'minimal interpretation' by examining certain difficulties with Kant's requirement of synthesis. The above account is notable for the absence of reference to unities. Yet it is just to the exposition of the conditions of unification of the world *in* experience that Kant's account of experience is directed. In Strawson's rather 'cavalier' treatment of the syntheses in which Kant finds the ground for the unities of self and the world, he considers three ways in which 'synthesis' could engender 'consciousness of unity': by awareness of a synthesizing activity; by awareness of the power to perform a synthesizing activity; and by awareness of the synthesized product of the exercise of such power (*The bounds of sense*, p. 94). Kant is clear enough that it is not by awareness of the *synthesizing being* that we can grasp the unity of experience.

In commentary on a brief sketch of the theory of synthesis, that 'all combination, all connection, is produced by' the activity of the mind, Strawson says 'It is useless to puzzle over the status of these propositions. They belong neither to empirical psychology . . . nor to an analytical philosophy of mind (*The bounds of sense*, p. 97). On the basis of this remark, Strawson moves on to 'bypass the doctrine of synthesis altogether', but in so doing and on such flimsy grounds, we arrive at the treatment sketched above. A glance at that treatment reveals that, far from bypassing the doctrine of synthesis, it presupposes it. In the duality of world and experience 'it [experience] possesses its own order as *a* series of experiences' (perhaps ultimately as a series of judgements). But only if that series is as *a* series could it serve as a basis for self-ascription since it is just by virtue of the unity of the sequence of experiences as a series that the singularity of an experiencing self is presented since we are all agreed that it is not presented *in* itself. Admittedly Kant does not give an account of what sort of intellectual activity synthesizing might be, but the clue lies in the passage in which the synthetic unity of apperception is presented as a *thought*. By this remark Kant means what I believe we would mean by saying that it is a theoretical concept. Kant's theses concerning syntheses are the essential core of a psychological theory.

The treatment I offer differs from Kant's in two important respects. Kant thinks that the investigation of a transcendental object 'can contain nothing but transcendental properties', but this is so only if we stick to inner sense. One way of putting the great advance made by social constructivists is that they see that *social* predicates can serve in discussion of the transcendental conditions and forms of mind. Kant also thinks that the ultimate referent of the concept of 'active self' is a real, singular but necessarily hidden being, the final source of the activity by which minds and empirical worlds are created in complementary synthetic acts. I hope to show that the latter proposal multiplies entities beyond necessity.

The outcome of this is the conclusion that, for example, to know that *I* am is not to have a special reflexive experience in which I am presented to myself as an object, contrary to Hume's observation. Rather, it is to have accepted a special kind of theory in terms of which experiences are categorized as 'of myself' and 'not of myself', and actions are taken as 'mine' and 'not as mine', the central theoretical concept being that of an organizing, experiencing and active self, the hypothetical entity corresponding to which is the putative referent of 'I' ('my', 'mine' etc.). The same theory allows us to categorize some reflections as memories, i.e. as representations of incidents in *my* life, and so create the possibility of an autobiography. In short, to be a person is to entertain a special kind of theory, not to have had a special kind of experience. Of course, being in possession of the theory as a working hypothesis for categorizing and ordering experience does indeed make available to a human being the possibility of new kinds of experience, i.e. the experiences *as of* being in the world as a person, that is, a being not only defined as singular by the social practices of others of this collective, but as conceiving of itself as a self and so organizing its experience in certain ways. The question of whether there is a referent for the theoretical concept of 'the self' other than the unity of the unities of experience need never be raised in psychology. Since I shall be arguing that its aetiology begins for each of us with the public concept of a person any metaphysical or noumenal self, pulsing away beyond all possible experience, is quite redundant. But this I have yet to prove.

6   STATUS OF THE HYPOTHETICAL ENTITY TO WHICH 'I' AS A THEORETICAL CONCEPT MIGHT BE TAKEN TO REFER

Some transcendental concepts in the physical sciences are strongly referential and most right-thinking persons believe that their referents are real, even though they are ordinarily not observable with the unaided senses. Most chemists believe, I suppose, in the reality of ions. Some theoretical concepts do not refer to real things. The skin of a falling drop is not a real entity, although there are pseudo-referential concepts in the theory of droplet formation which seem to refer to it. The referential aspects of the use of 'I' as a theoretical term must be examined as seriously as one would the putative reference of important concepts in physics or chemistry. There are three obvious possibilities: the 'self' has no referent; its referent is the same as that of the public—collective concept 'person'; or it refers to structural and dynamic features of experienced organization.

One might treat 'gravitational potential' as a convenient fiction, that is, as a theoretical concept which serves to order our experience of falling bodies and planetary systems. Taking this case as a model would suggest that by the use of 'I', 'my' etc. each of us can order our experience into mine and not mine, into a public and private sphere, into present experience and memories of the past by reference to a fictitious psychic unity. In Kantian terms, one could say that provided we can schematize (synthesize) our experience into a unified structure, we do not need the hypothesis of a noumenal self, a unity beyond experience (cf. Strawson, *The bounds of sense*). Recognizing the dual role of 'I' would allow one to say that expressions like 'I think . . .', 'I believe . . .', 'I undertake to . . .' and 'I'm sorry . . .' etc. need not be read as predications of properties to an individual psychic substance, some mysterious self, but social acts proper for a *person* of my sort. In its social use 'I' would have the major self-referential function of indexically locating the speaker in the array of persons. However, there are two further possibilities.

Perhaps persons are the referents of both indexical and theoretical aspects of reflexive reference. Thus construed persons would be exhaustively accounted for as social beings. However, although I want to emphasize that the most plausible account of the origins of the theoretical concept of myself that I use in ordering my experience is to be found in social practices in which persons as social beings are referred to, it would be a genetic fallacy to identify 'self' as an organizing concept with the public—collective or social concept of person without further ado. As I argued, the theoretical concept of the self is required to give an account of the synthetic unities in experience, the organization of our fields of consciousness, the hierarchical organization of our mastery of lower desires in the service of higher aspirations, and all the other features of our mental life that in Kant's phase 'determine the thought I am a transcendental ego'.

Perhaps the theoretical aspect does have a referent distinct from that of the person as social being, but the entity so picked out is not what it seems. It could be that there are certain open systems features of the cyborg in our heads that lie behind the experiences that I cited at the beginning of this section, that seem to call for a theoretical concept like the self. The empirical referent is not then some thing, but a structured and hierarchical system of capacities: I mean such matters as to be able to act at the top level of a decision-making hierarchy when the final alternatives are equally weighted, to be able to turn one's attention to subordinate moments of awareness, to attend to an awareness of being aware of something. I call this a structured system of abilities since, for example, in achieving reflexive consciousness we may need to force ourselves to attend to or away from certain interesting or attractive objects. And this is a capacity or power necessary to this kind of achievement. For the philosophical foundation of personal psychology the third possibility is to be preferred. I am inclined to think it is to be preferred in general, though I do not propose to argue the more general case here.

However, the variations in the 'I' theories, some of which I have used to illustrate the argument and which are typical of different cultures, leave room for more specific distinctions within each culture, in the form in which individuality of personhood is displayed in the public – collective sense that I have identified as the referent of indexical uses of personal pronouns. These can be understood in terms of the Durkheimian conception of *représentation sociale*, collective representation. The general, culturally relative and social concept of a person can become more highly differentiated within a culture by the spread of conceptions about what it is to be a proper or fashionable kind of person, and what sort of capacities are needed to be able to illustrate that one is such a being. Nicknaming systems provide a nice example. Social norms are represented by pejorative uses of nicknames which highlight ways in which proper persons in closed societies are *not* meant to be. For example, 'Dumbo' and 'Brainbox' identify levels of intelligence which are either too low or too high for the norm sustained in that group. 'Piggy' identifies a bodily form that is generally unacceptable. The effect of a nicknaming system is not merely to describe the existing range of ways of social being in that society; it also creates distinctive persons. A person is given a nickname primarily to illustrate a social norm. The individual whose idiosyncracies have marked him or her out may not violate the norm very much, but the behaviour and even the appearance of the bearer are often pushed further along the dimension in which that nickname lies. Someone who is only a bit grubby but is stigmatized as 'Stinker' can be required to exemplify the sin of uncleanliness in a more florid fashion than he did originally. The Brainboxes are required to be cleverer, the Dumbos more stupid than their natural endowment would demand. The system of nicknames is a *représentation sociale* which actively creates distinctions among persons in the real world. It is not confined to the autonomous worlds of childhood for wherever nicknaming flourishes, in prisons, in jazzbands and so on, this phenomenon is clearly identifiable.

In like manner a person's self- (the supposed private – individual referent of the 'I' by which experience is organized as mine) is a conjunction of a generic element, that determined by the rules for using 'I' and its cognates, and a specific element, local folk theories of how a self is supposed to be. For example, Western societies differ greatly in the amount of self-attention regarded as proper. What a person will be capable of will depend in part on the particular form of generic self-theory they acquire, because it is in terms of that theory that they will construe themselves as more or less autonomous, determined and so on. These more specific theories are, I believe, also encapsulated in the *représentation sociales* and the associated linguistic practices in terms of which cognitive capacities are legitimately displayed, just as variants of public – collective ways of being a person are determined.

To illustrate the power of a *représentation sociale*, let me quote from David Ingleby's influential paper, 'Ideology and the human sciences':

> reifying model of human nature, by definition, presents men as less than they really are or could be. To the extent that society requires men, or a certain proportion of them, to be thing-like in their work, orientation and experiencing, such a model will constitute both a reflection and a reinforcement of that society, reinforcing because men tend to become what they are told they are. . . Above all, he is confronted in the possibility of being understood as a species of thing with the threat of ultimate finality, denied the facility to transcend in any way the material out of which he is made; all value must lose value for him.

I do not think we have much idea yet of the language games which, as bearers of social representations of exemplars of personhood and theories of the self, teach us how we are to operate (work) as personal beings, with an organized psychic life. Freudian psychology (*see* Moscovici, *La psychoanalyse*) is surely one of them, but there are probably many others (*see* research menu 4).

7   SOURCES OF OUR PERSON THEORIES

There are a great many different ways in which a local 'I am a self' theory could be acquired, and no doubt several are involved in its actual acquisition in the course of human development. I shall concentrate on only one by examining the possibility that learning the pronoun system and, in particular, the rules for the use of 'I', is in part the learning of a theory. Bruner's work ('Early rule structure') suggests that the rules for the use of personal pronouns are learned through a sequence of language games. Midway in the sequence is the language game of indexicality, that is the use of 'I' to locate all sorts of matters at a certain point (individual) within the array of persons. These include the point of view from which the world is being perceived, which person has made a commitment, who wishes to be seen as contrite, who has performed some action and so on. Since social practices such as blame, commitment, describing from a point of view etc. essentially involve both speech and action, it would be reasonable to look for the key occasions in Wittgensteinian language games. I believe that only some of these key occasions and their typical practices have been described. Some psychologists have yet to grasp the role of linguistic competence in psychological growth. In a well-known work on human development by Mahler (*The psychological birth of the human infant*) no reference whatever to the kind of social event Wittgenstein called language games is made. Psychodynamic 'processes' are supposed to provide all. In Mahler's world, as she describes it, there is only speechless action. That is not the human world. Bruner, as I have already pointed out, has begun in a very prescient way to identify the key language games involved in the acquisition of linguistic competence. I want to show, from the theoretical point of view, where his researches fit into the investigation of how we each acquire the theory that we are persons like the others.

Learning to think as a self

What sociolinguistic practices (language games) are there in the course of which competence in the use of personal pronouns is acquired? If we follow this programme we can control our researches with the help of the following hypotheses.

Point of view

We might look for occasions of address which imply a standpoint other than that of another person. Contrary to the mythology of 'moral development' psychology, the idea of multiple points of view is grasped very early. In 'Early rule structure', Bruner's pioneering analysis (with Sherwood) of the peek-a-boo game, we find a study of one of the many sociolinguistic practices in the course of which the connection between personhood and point of view is established. Two ideas are acquired in playing this game: (a) that there are distinct points of view from which the world takes on a different cast; and (b) that those points of view are located at persons. It now seems likely that all this comes to pass in the course of six or seven months. From a developmental psycholinguistic viewpoint it could be said that in mastering this language game a child begins to grasp the indexicality of speech. In such practices we learn to locate our speech acts in the array of persons *including ourselves*. This is all part of the foundation of deixis, the capacity to direct attention to one thing from the standpoint of a point of view in an array of other things. A number of psychologists have studied the development of deixis, in infants, in particular E. V. Clark. However, her work merely catalogues ascending degrees of mastery of the deitic and indexical referential uses of referring expressions, including pronouns. So far as I have followed her studies, she has paid little attention to the language-game features of deictic activities, and none at all to the kind of talk in which a mother embeds the whole business of making requests, a crucial step in creating a person by treating a merely animate being as such. Bruner's investigations of deixis have been much more sophisticated. He has spoken of 'request formats' as part of the development of reaching, following line of sight and so on, and such formats are indeed language games.

Point of action
Our second hypothesis draws attention to the effects of those occasions in the practical and moral orders in which speech acts of accusations, praise, blame, justification, excuse, attribution of intentions, wants and so on are involved. It is in these language games that the child is introduced to the idea of itself as an autonomous actor. Believing itself to be the author of many of its actions permits a consequential expansion in its capacity to order its experience and control its actions. A research programme parallel to Bruner's on deixis should be undertaken to explore the *sequence* of language games in the course of which the acquisition of the full sense of self-activation is acquired (*see* research menu 4).

The argument so far suggests that the process of transformation from animate being to person follows two steps. In one the concepts of point of view and point of action are acquired. In the second, the capacity to contemplate oneself reflexively as the unifying principle of these 'origins' implies the separation of the use of indexicals from the deployment of a theoretical concept of the self. Only thus, it will emerge, can one explain how it is that self-consciousness, self-intervention and autobiography are possible. Self-consciousness on this view is not a new kind of consciousness but rather a new way of partitioning that of which one is aware by reference to a theory, one's theory of oneself.

Psychological symbiosis
If selfhood is learned, how is it learned? I have already introduced the idea of cognitive psychology as the study of some of the attributes of public performances, particularly talk. Further, any investigation of cognitive development must take into account that human beings treat each other as persons within a moral order, for instance, as responsible

actors. The processes by which merely animate beings become self-conscious agents must be looked for in social episodes in which certain kinds of language games are played, engendering talk with appropriate cognitive properties, for instance self-expression of feelings and intentions. All this is to be found in the phenomenon of psychological symbiosis. The idea of psychological symbiosis arose with Spitz in his *The first year of life*, but has been developed by Shotter and Newson in 'How babies communicate' in the study of the kind of talk in which mothers embed their infant offspring. Psychological symbiosis is a permanent interactive relation between two persons, in the course of which one supplements the psychological attributes of the other as they are displayed in social performances, so that the other appears as a complete and competent social and psychological being. The general definition does not specify the relationship between the two persons who form a symbiotic dyad. There are many possibilities. For example, there are cases of considerable practical importance where, though the supplementations are mutual, the power relations in the dyad are asymmetrical. The symbiotic dyad is to be conceived as a single social being. There is plenty of evidence from the work of Richards (*A child's entry into a social world*) that the dyad as a social being may interact socially with one of its own constituent persons, who displays individually proper attributes and powers.

The relevant characteristics of mother-talk have been noticed by psychologists other than Richards and Shotter and Newson, but not correctly described. Snow is reported in Bruner and Garton (*Human growth and development*, p. 76) as saying 'Mothers constantly talked about the child's wishes, needs and intentions.' The use of 'about' in this sentence misconstrues the relationship as it is seen from the standpoint of psychological symbiosis. In psychological symbiosis mothers do not talk *about* the child's wishes and emotions; they *supply* the child with wishes, needs, intentions, wants and the like, and interact with the child as if it had them. Psychological symbiosis is a supplementation by one person of another person's public display in order to satisfy the criteria of personhood with respect to psychological competencies and attributes in day-to-day use in a particular society in this or that specific social milieu. A mother may undertake to supplement her daughter's psychology differently in a medical consultation from the way she does it for a visiting relative. I want to extend the idea of psychological symbiosis far beyond the context for which it was originally introduced, namely for the ways mothers publicly supplement the psychology of their children. I shall use the term for every case in which a group of people complete through public symbiotic activity, particularly in talking for each other, inadequate social and psychological beings. There may be several persons involved in the supplementation process.

Why do these practices exist? I believe that the answer can be found by reference to the requirements of moral orders, as they are defined and sustained in particular collectives. By a 'moral order' I understand a collectively maintained system of public criteria for holding persons in respect or contempt and the rituals for ratification of judgements in accordance with these criteria. The moral value of persons and their actions are publicly displayed by such a system. It is realized in practices such as being deferential to someone or censuring someone, by trials, by punishments, by insults, by apologies and so on. Psychological supplementation of another may be required if a display of personal incompetence or deficit is routinely taken as a reason for unfavourable moral assessment. Goffman adds the thought (in 'Facework') that support of this sort may be forthcoming not so much on behalf of the moral standing of the one who is supplemented, as in defence of the reputations of those with whom he or she is seen to be consorting.

The term psychological symbiosis has also been used by Mahler in her book *The psychological birth of a human infant*. For her the term refers to an emotional dependence of the infant on its caretakers somewhat similar to the emotional bonds of attachment and loss so vividly described by Bowlby (*Attachment and loss*). Psychological symbiosis in my sense has nothing much to do with emotional ties, though as a cognitive process it is important in processes such as those by which mere feeling is publicly and collectively defined as emotion. It is an act of psychological symbiosis to define someone else's display of feeling as anger, hunger, frustration, misery etc. The definienda, of course, are the referents of concepts of a very high order of sophistication and are properly applied only in the dyad or other group created by the symbiotic relationship.

The crucial person-engendering language games involving the indexical and referential features of the uses of pronouns, and all sorts of other devices by which concept pairs like 'self and other', 'agent and patient', complementary points of view, continuity and discontinuity of experience etc. are shared with an infant, take place in conditions of psychological symbiosis. One who is always presented as a person, by taking over the conventions through which this social act is achieved, becomes organized as a self. That is the main empirical hypothesis which I believe to be a consequence of the considerations so far advanced, and in the testing of which the limits of the conceptual system from which it springs can be discovered.

Profound consequences follow for developmental cognitive psychology from admitting the existence and central place of psychological symbiosis. They will be taken up as the relevant issues arise. I turn now to an analysis of those features of personal psychology for which neither psychodynamics nor traditional cognitive psychology have provided adequate treatments. Those which depend on Kantian syntheses I call the 'unities', while those which cannot exist without a public−collective dimension, even in a mature being, I call the 'dualities'. Since the very possibility of personal being depends on the existence of selves as the modes of organization of experience that I have called the unities, the examination of these features of human experience will occupy us in the second part of this work. To complete the working out of the relations between quadrants 1 and 2 of the psychological space I have presented, I shall develop, as an example, a conceptual system for the study of emotions, in which they are conceived as typical dualities.

8   SUMMARY OF THE ARGUMENT

In terms of the basic conceptual scheme of psychological dimensions introduced in chapter 2, the argument of this chapter is aimed at showing that at least it makes sense to consider the possibility of an individual private or personal concept of 'self' derived by Vygotskian appropriation from the social, public−collective concept of 'person' (figure 4.1).

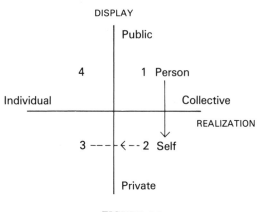

FIGURE 4.1

In this chapter I have described the processes by which I believe the concept achieves its passage from quadrant 1 to quadrant 2. Further development of the sense of self, from quadrant 2 to quadrant 3, must await the study of the idea of personal development.

We learn to conceive of ourselves as personal beings by the appropriation of the concept of social being from our public–collective activities for the purposes of organizing our experience as the mental life of a self-conscious agent. But that may be only one of the ways experience can be organized. It remains possible that there may be human beings who do not organize their experience as a 'mental life' at all. It would follow that the logical grammar of 'self'-concepts would closely resemble that for person-concepts, in particular the concept of 'self' would be treated as having referential force. Thus we are *driven* to look for substantial centres for our acts and experiences conceived as mental, which reflects the ways we as persons are the centre of public–collective spheres of perception and action. The 'centred' model of experience is not a dispensable option in *our* psychology. It is a permanent feature providing a perennial temptation to believe in an extra being, a noumenal self deeply embedded within our persons. Paradoxically, it is only by believing in such an inner active core of self that *our* psychological attributes and *our* moral order can be realized.

RESEARCH MENU 4

The suggestion that anthropological evidence could be used to back up a separation between the concept of 'person' and that of 'self' opens up a wide field of further research. Though there are several very interesting discussions of 'self' in Heelas and Lock's *Indigenous psychologies*, a deeper test of the Bruner language-game theory of self-discovery could be made by sharpening up the linguistic part of the research. The languages of West Irian differ very widely in their pronominal systems and so in their powers of grammatically easy self-reference. Laycock's 'Me and you versus the rest' and his 1965 *The NDU language family* provide enough linguistic material to open up the possibility of a detailed comparison between weak self-referential languages and local cultural practices, belief systems, infant–mother language games and the like.

Much of the developmental work in our own culture has either ignored the pronominal development sequence or simply catalogued it, without recording the language games (in Wittgenstein's sense) then going on. For instance, notice the incompleteness of the work of E. V. Clark on deixis. If the theory of grammatical models for mind is correct, then it should be possible to link up sequences of models with other self-referential practices like accepting responsibility (*see* research menu 9).

A note on method of cross cultural studies: much of the argument of this chapter would be undermined if the anthropological material were seriously faulted. Even though only a sketch has been offered here the method is distinctive. Careful consultation of the monumental Triandis, *Handbook of cross cultural psychology* particularly Vol 2, reveals a failure to bring linguistic and ethnographic studies *together*. Triandis has made some headway with the problem of emics and translation with his idea of retranslation and decentering, but so far as I can see the putative translations are not relocated in Wittgensteinian language-games from which the exemplary sentences must have originally come. The contributions by Berry on 'measuring behaviour' and by Irvine and Carroll fulfil one's worst forebodings. The kind of research they describe must inevitably bring out just those aspects of the ever biddable human being that flourish in the United States.

The collectivist way Eskimos seem to experience emotion raises further theoretical questions as to the kind of psychological attributes that can be collectivised. Even such an apparently individual experience as pain can take on a social dimension as in the *couvarde*. Further research into the limits of the possibility of collectivisation should prove illuminating. This could have a conceptual aspect, but it could also be studied empirically. For example the fascinating discoveries recorded by H. S. Becker in his *Outsiders* (Chapter 3) on the extent to which the experiences induced by smoking marijuana are socially created and sustained. The problem of how we learn how to be ill has been just touched upon, but so far as I know nothing has been done on how we learn to taste and smell.

BIBLIOGRAPHICAL NOTES 4

The volume of writings on the person and the self in philosophy, psychology and anthropology is quite enormous. This set of notes is restricted to a tiny sample of the literature, simply to illustrate how the line of argument of this chapter can be supported and might be qualified. The way psychologists deal with and to some extent avoid the interesting problems of the self can be seen in D. M. WAGNER and R. R. VALLACHER, *The self in social psychology* (Oxford: Oxford University Press, 1979). Social learning theory has contributed a good deal to a socially powered developmental perspective, see A. BANDURA, *Social learning theory* (Englewood Cliffs (NJ): Prentice Hall, 1977).

From the vast literature on the logic of self-reference, I pick just enough items to illustrate the main lines of discussion. There is an excellent review of the issues by G. MANDELL, *The identity of self* (Edinburgh: The University Press, 1981). The discussion of the first person and its uses and abuses can be sampled with J. M. E. MCTAGGART, *The nature of existence* (Cambridge: Cambridge University Press, 1927, vol. 2, p. 36), S. COVAL, *Scepticism and the first person* (London: Methuen, 1966), G. VESEY, *Personal identity* (Milton Keynes: Open University Press, 1973) and G. E. M. ANSCOMBE, 'The first person' (in *Mind and language*, ed. S. Guttenplan, Oxford: Clarendon Press, 1975, pp. 45–66). For a formal analysis see Y. BAR-HILLEL, 'Indexical expressions' (*Mind*, 63, 1954, 359–79).

P. F. STRAWSON, *Individuals* (London: Methuen, 1959) has proved perenially influential. The idea of self as a cultural discovery is implicit in J. JAYNES, *The origin of consciousness in the breakdown of the bicameral mind* (London: Allen Lane, 1979). In psychology 'self' often means a system of beliefs about self, see C. R. ROGERS, 'A theory of therapy, personality, etc' (in *Psychology: A study of a science*, ed. S. Koch, New York: McGraw-Hill, 1959) and, for example, R. M. LIEBERT and M. D. SPIEGLER, *Personality* (London: Irwin Dorsey, 1974).

My position depends rather heavily on the demonstration of actual cross-cultural differences in the organization of mind as self. The Eskimo material is drawn from R. C. SOLOMON, *The passions* (New York: Doubleday, 1976), E. E. CARPENTER, *Eskimo realities* (New York: Holt, Rinehart and Winston, 1966), L. R. SMITH, *Some grammatical aspects of Labrador Inuttut* (Ottawa: Eskimo Museum of Canada, 1977), R. RIESMAN, 'Eskimo discovery of man's place in the universe' (in *Sign, image, and symbol*, ed. S. Kepes, London: Studio Vista, 1966) and D. JENNES, 'The Copper Eskimos' (*Report of the Canadian Arctic Expedition 1913–18*, Ottawa: The Government Printer, 1922). I owe a great deal of my still limited understanding of the language and customs of the Eskimo to Colin Irwin of Syracuse University.

Similar issues arise in rather different ways in other cultures, see for instance, S. COLLINS, *Selfless persons: imagery and thought in Theravada Buddhism* (London: Cambridge University Press, 1982). For the Polynesian concept of personal being see E. BEST, *Spiritual and mental concepts of the Maori* (Wellington (NZ): Dominion Museum, 1922).

Bruner's search for a Wittgensteinian 'language game' foundation for linguistic universals begins with J. BRUNER, 'Early rule structure: the case of peek-a-boo' (in *Life sentences*, ed. R. Harré, London: John Wiley & Sons, 1976). It is developed further in his 'Learning how to do things with words' (in *Human growth and development*, eds J. Bruner and A. Garton, Oxford: Clarendon Press, 1978, ch. 3). The contribution of J. SHOTTER and J. NEWSON can be found in 'How babies communicate' (*New Society*, 29, 1974, 345–7). The idea of psychological symbiosis comes from R. A. SPITZ, *The first year of life* (New York: International Universities Press, 1965), while the power of the infant to draw forth appropriate activities from the mother has been demonstrated by C. TREVARTHEN, 'Communication and cooperation in early infancy: a description of primary intersubjectivity' (in *Before speech: the beginning of interpersonal communication*, ed. M. Bullows, Cambridge: Cambridge University Press, 1979). In stark contrast is the silent world of M. MAHLER, F. PINE and A. BERGMAN, *The psychological birth of the human infant* (London: Hutchinson, 1975).

Discussion of philosophers' theories of the self is confined to D. HUME, *A treatise of human nature* (1739, edn by D. G. C. Macnabb, London: Fontana, Collins, 1962) and I. KANT, *Critique of pure reason* (1781, edn trans. N. Kemp-Smith, London: Macmillan, 1929) and P. F. STRAWSON, *The bounds of sense* (London: Methuen, 1966), exemplifying main themes.

For the theory of *représentations sociales* put to use, see J. MORGAN, C. O'NEILL and R. HARRÉ, *Nicknames* (London: Routledge and Kegan Paul,

1979) and S. MOSCOVICI, *La psychoanalyse: son image et son publique* (Paris: Presses Universitaires de France, 1961).

The quotations from Kant are taken from I. KANT, *Critique of pure reason* (1781, edn trans. N. Kemp-Smith, London: Macmillan, 1929). There are a great many commentaries on Kant's great work, but for my purposes the tension I detect between the treatments of P. F. STRAWSON, *The bounds of sense* (London: Methuen, 1966) and R. C. S. WALKER, *Kant* (London: Routledge and Kegan Paul, 1978) brings out the issue I want to address.

Additional works cited in text are A. BANDURA, *Social learning theory* (Englewood Cliffs (NJ): Prentice-Hall, 1977); H. S. BECKER, *Outsiders* (New York: Free Press; London: Collier-Macmillan, 1963); J. BOWLBY, *Attachment and loss, Volume I: Attachment* (London: Hogarth Press, 1969); E. V. CLARK, 'From gesture to word' in *Human growth and development*, ed. J. Bruner and A. Garton (Oxford: Clarendon Press, 1978); S. FREUD, *Totem and taboo: The standard edition of the complete psychological works of Sigmund Freud*, 13 (London: Hogarth Press, 1955); E. GOFFMAN, 'On facework' (in *Where the action is*, London: Allen Lane, 1969); S. HAMPSHIRE, *Thought and action* (London: Chatto and Windus, 1959); P. HEELAS and A. LOCK, *Indigenous psychologies* (London: Academic Press, 1981); E. HUSSERL, *Cartesian meditations* (trans. D. Cairns, The Hague: Martinus Nijhoff, 1973); D. INGLEBY 'Ideology and the human sciences' (*Human Context*, 2, 1970, 159−80); D. LAYCOCK, *The NDU language family* (Canberra: Australian National University, 1965); M. P. M. RICHARDS (ed.), *A child's entry into a social world* (Cambridge: Cambridge University Press, 1973); G. RYLE, *The concept of mind* (London: Hutchinson, 1949); H. C. TRIANDIS (ed.), *Handbook of cross cultural psychology* (Boston: Allyn and Bacon, 1980, 6 vols).

The Piagetian thesis that 'decentering', the capacity to adopt the points of view of others, is a late development, has been refuted by the studies reported in M. Donaldson, *Children's minds* (London: Croom Helm, 1978), see particularly the 'policeman' version of the 'three mountains' game. (See also Bibliographical notes to Chapter 9).

CHAPTER 5

DUALITY TWO:
THE SOCIAL STRUCTURE OF
COGNITION AND EMOTION

Theme: Freed from the Cartesian restrictions, we can now do justice to the way that social considerations, influences and structures enter in various ways into many personal attributes that have hitherto been taken to be personally realized. I illustrate this with intentions and intentionality, rationality and the emotions.

Contents
1 The social in the psychological
2 Intentions and intentionality
3 Rationality
4 Emotion
5 Obsolete emotions and moods
    Accidie: an extinct emotion
    Melancholy: an obsolete mood
6 Basic emotions

1 THE SOCIAL IN THE PSYCHOLOGICAL

In chapter 4 on 'duality one' I explored some of the consequences of adopting the scheme represented in the two-dimensional display — location space. The topics of this chapter, 'duality two', are created by the construction of a scheme deriving from the main diagonal distinction of the first space, the distinction I have labelled personal — social. We can ask whether a state, condition or process is personally or socially defined, and whether as so defined it is individually or collectively realized (*see* figure 5.1).

This space permits the consideration of matters which are individually realized but socially, that is, public — collectively defined. I shall try to show that emotions are to be found in quadrant D. Certain sorts of religious enthusiasm could be found in quadrant B. The condition of the followers of the Reverend Jones was defined by him but collectively realized in their mass suicide in Guiana. Rationality and intentionality have realizations in both quadrants D and A. It is the priority of these realizations both conceptually and developmentally that can be in question.

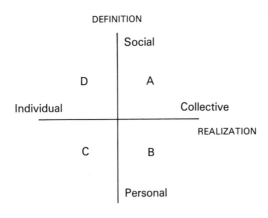

FIGURE 5.1

The argument of chapter 4 on 'duality one' establishes human life, in our local cultural and historical context, as ordered in two domains; I have called them quadrant 1 and quadrant 3. The order is created by the use of a concept pair 'person' and 'self', the latter coming into being as a reflection of the former, in a process involving a transition through quadrant 2. I take the transition through quadrant 2 to have been adequately described by Vygotsky in his reconstruction of the kind of speech that Piaget called 'egocentric'. At about the age of two years 'thought becomes verbal and speech rational'. Egocentric speech *is* thought, now in characteristic human form. That is why it is *ego-*centric. It represents the child's commentary upon its own states, plans and so forth. The expressive function of speech is public conversation (built around the indexical 'I'), while the cognitive function of speech is private conversation (structured by the self-referential 'I'). These functions are distinguished only towards the sixth and seventh years when egocentric speech becomes more and more different from publicly directed speech. 'Person' and 'self' are the expressions for forms of order, of public — collective discourse on the one hand and of private — individual discourse on the other. But what of the content of these discourses? I hope to make a case for the view that just as human individuality is distributed over quadrants 1 and 3 so is the most characteristic content of the domain of the psychological.

In proposing a multidimensional space for representing the subject matter of psychology, I took the individual — collective dimension simply as representing the location of the entity, property, process etc. in question. Given this dimension, we can now formulate such questions as: 'Are intentions private — individual entities, pre-existing actions, occupying a crucial place in a causal chain, from ''inner resolution'' to ''outer performance''?' 'Is rationality a property of cognitive processes occurring in an individual?' 'Are emotions just interpreted personal feelings?' Even to formulate such questions invites one to doubt the assumed individualism which has had considerable influence on the way these matters have been dealt with in psychology, tending to make intentions unresearchable, rationality an attribute of AI analogues of individual information processing and emotions individual responses to accidents like frustration, bereavement, the appearance of wild bulls and so on. I hope to be able demonstrate an essential duality in all three cases, and to provide at least the outline sketches for arguments for the ontological, conceptual and temporal priority of the public — collective realm for each. Realigning these matters, so to speak, will have a dramatic effect on the design of research programmes.

The idea of 'personal psychology' traditionally conjures up the idea of an investigation into an 'inner world' of bodily feelings, sensory responses and a vain search for an elusive but essential noumenal self. Such a world is wholly mysterious for other people, but wholly transparent and given for the individual whose mental life it is. Metaphors proliferate: 'inner world', 'mental life' etc. I hope to show in some exemplary cases that the *concepts*, that is, the linguistic apparatus by which mental phenomena are characterized, identified and talked about, are such that social (i.e. public — collective) matters enter into the very conditions for their application.

To begin with a very simple but dramatic case: the persistent attempt to treat perception as a processing of individual and private sensations known only to the perceiver, as if the experience of the world revealed to us by our sensory systems should have a structure like that of the neurological apparatus by which we perceive it. The case against such a view can be made in a few words, elegantly uttered by Coulter in *The social construction of mind*:

> When we have learned to guard our declarations about colours, e.g. by saying 'This *looks* red', we have not learned a way of describing something in a phenomenal inner realm, but a way of *limiting our*

responsibilities for our perceptual judgements, a way of justifying or excusing our perceptual claims when confronted with disagreement. (My italics)

The claiming and disclaiming of responsibilities places the language of perceptual declarations at least partly in the moral order of the society within which the practice of declarations and limitation of responsibilities is commonplace. Coulter's argument is an application of Wittgenstein's strategy: look to see how the psychological vocabulary is actually used — then we will know of what it is used!

2 INTENTIONS AND INTENTIONALITY

Of all the ways by which the realm of the mental, and so the subject matter of psychology, as a non-positivistic science is to be identified (subjectivity, private access, non-corporeality etc.) one stands out — Brentano's notion of intentionality. In this section I shall put forward some concrete forms taken by intentionality, and try to show that most of these have their origin (both conceptually in a culture and developmentally in a person) in the public—collective conversation among persons I have called the 'primary structure'.

The concept of 'intentionality' has often been presented in an unnecessarily mysterious way. One can start with the metaphor of 'pointing to'. An intentional entity is one which 'points to' something other than itself. A sign on a forest path can be seen as 'pointing to' a distant lake, a belief in fairies as 'pointing to' some minute, elusive but attractive beings. Brentano's root idea was that intentional entities are taken as 'pointing to' something whether or not the putative target exists. Intentionality is not a relation between one entity (as sign) and another (as signified), but a feature or property of one entity. Though 'meaning' is an obvious gloss on 'intentionality', the opacity of that notion makes it an unsuitable device for explicating Brentano's idea.

Of all the applications of the idea of intentionality, two are of special interest to this study. There are entities which represent or indicate something other than themselves. I shall call this the 'sign-function'. Representing and represented entity are not causally or otherwise productively related. Then there are entities (amongst others movements and utterances) which contribute towards an outcome, sometimes causally (when the outcome is an effect mediated by physical processes) and sometimes by virtue of conventions (when the outcome is an act mediated by cultural interpretations).

The ordinary notion of 'intention' as the conceived, proposed or declared outcome of an action, that which an action is taken to be aimed at, can now be introduced. But only if there is some entity which can stand for the as-yet-unrealized outcome of an action (whether the particular result is represented in its singularity or merely as a type of outcome) can a person entertain or display an intention by entertaining or displaying a representation of that outcome from which that result can be 'read off'. For there to be the display of intentions there must be entities with intentionality.

An outcome aimed at can be variously described or represented. Since the intentionality of an entity will depend on just how the intentional object is represented (or described) the intended act, for instance, can be taken only as it is actually represented or described. A person may not know that what they intend can be otherwise described, with perhaps a very different moral quality. This point has been especially stressed by Anscombe in 'The intentionality of sensation'. It follows that a person can only be said to have an (the) intention to perform (bring about) the result in question under the description by which it was actually represented. This is of central importance in the psychology of action considered within a moral order, since a grasp of the further consequences of an action may be facilitated or inhibited by the way the action is described by the actor either to others or sometimes to him or herself alone. The choice of description determines, to some extent, the range of premises available to the actor from which to infer possible outcomes.

I have argued elsewhere (*Social being*, ch. 12) that the action function can be achieved by a display of intentions, for instance, by the performance of a metonymic action fragment (say a clenched fist) or in declarations like 'I intend (am going to) visit the town today', in public–collective 'space', without there being any private–individual counterparts in thought. An actor may be kept up to the mark by the expectations of his fellows rather than by any personal resolution not to be foresworn. Since gestures and declarations 'point beyond themselves' Brentano's conception of the mental as the intentional must include public–collective entities. The 'pointing to' property of a significant thing or gesture or remark must be created in the interpretative procedures of the collective within which it is displayed and to which the actor must belong, sharing the conventions of that collective as to the interpretations and constructions placed on his or her public performance. Without this sharing, nothing an actor does could count as displaying or declaring an intention.

The general principle of this work — 'Nothing in the mind that was not first in the conversation' — would suggest that both sign function and action function should have their primary realization in the public–collective space of quadrant 1, from which they can be borrowed by individuals for private and personal use. This suggests a re-working of developmental research on deixis, the capacity to point, to see how far the capacity to point to what is wanted is involved in the display of a want as the ground for a later private—individual formulation of a want as an 'inner', that is undisclosed, state (*see* research menu 5).

To defend the public—collective priority of the sign function needs no more than a reference to the arguments of Wittgenstein (and more recently Lewis, *Convention*) for the essential role that stability of conventions plays in the maintenance of meaning and so the possibility of there being a sign function, coupled with the observation that that stability is possible only if there are collective or consensual constraints on conventions. This issue will recur when I take up the question of the possibility of 'personal meaning' and whether such an apparently paradoxical notion may not be needed in certain kinds of research projects.

To prove the point for the action function of an intentional display, one must notice that a recognition of a 'pointing to' in the public domain involves a collective interpretation as to the expected outcome of the action. In our culture, unless the display is qualified as non-serious in some way, it licenses an expectation in all members of the collective, including the actor, that the intended outcome will be realized *ceteris paribus*, by the performance of an action of the type displayed. I have emphasized that the public—collective or primary structure is always in a moral order. In many moral orders, but not in all, the psychological complex of display, interpretation and expectation just described is completed by a commitment on the part of the initiator to act. In the Indian subcontinent the institution of making a date is not bound up with the counter-institution of keeping appointments. But in many moral orders failure to realize declared or displayed intentions can lead to ac-cusations ranging from 'You've disappointed me' to 'Foul cur, you are foresworn!'.

The structure of commitment is essentially interpersonal. In those moral orders in which commitment and intention are related by a moral norm priority must lie not with private and individual resolutions or reservations about the fulfilment of displayed intentions, but with declarations in the public—collective domain. Commitment in the public—collective domain is ontologically prior so private reservations and *sotto voce* nay-sayings do not count against accusations of moral turpitude or moral weakness levelled against those who, having declared or displayed an intention, fail to realize it in action.

If we follow Brentano in taking intentionality to be at least a sufficient condition for an entity to be 'psychological', then the necessary involvement of public – collective matters in the important intentional properties of linguistic meaning and declarations and proposals to act supports the general thesis of the 'social construction of mind'.

In this account the property of 'intentionality' has remained un-explicated save for the observation that it is not a relational property be-tween, for instance, sign and thing signified. The illustrative metaphor of 'pointing to' cannot serve as an undefined primitive with which to build up an account of intentionality. How can I know that something, say a signpost, points to the lake (of all the myriad things there are in the forest in that direction) unless it includes a representation or symbol of that to which it points? That symbol can only serve to display the in-tentionality of the signpost if it can be understood as 'pointing to', say, a lake. And so on.

In an attempt to make the notion of the psychological more clear cut there has been an attempt to reconstruct the notion of 'intentionality' in terms of the truth properties of statements and the denotative or re-ferring function of nominal expressions.

A simple test for intentional concepts has been devised by logicians. We have noticed that the intentionality of a psychological state or act, or even interpreted bodily action, does not depend on the truth or even the existence of what is 'pointed to'. I can be seen as reaching for a jar of jam when there is no jar on the top shelf of the cupboard. Compare the following sentences:

> I believe that fish have fins.
> I believe that fish have lungs.

Both may be true of someone pretty ignorant of icthyology. In the first case the embedded sentence is true, in the second false. So the truth of the whole structure is independent of the truth value of its components. On this criterion, 'I believe . . .' is an intentional operator, and belief a mental state or condition or, perhaps, disposition. The same sort of test brings hope into the mental realm — 'I hope for rebirth as a higher form of life' — and into some actions as well — 'I am looking for Shangri La'. Both exemplary statements may be true even if the object of hope is impossible and the goal of the search does not exist. The status of the intentional objects may trouble us, that is, of false beliefs, impossible events and non-existent objects. To cope with these sorts of things, Brentano introduced the category of 'intentional inexistence', a characteristically mental mode of being.

An unproblematic understanding of 'intentional inexistence' could perhaps be found in the idea of lexical items which obey the logical grammar of those from a certain ontological category, of which ex-amples do exist, coupled with a treatment of the creative use of images.

I will not offer to develop this here. Rather I want to point out something paradoxical about this test. According to the test neither 'I know . . .' nor 'I have found . . .' can be intentional operators so that neither items of knowledge nor things found can be intentional objects. If what I claim to know is false, it is not true that I know it, and if I have found something other than that which I have claimed to have found, I have not found it. But one might well want to say that if belief is psychological so is knowledge, and if looking for is intentional, so should finding be. For this and other reasons, the attempt to tighten up the intuitive notion of the psychological as the intentional by finding a logicogrammatical representation of it seems to be partially unsuccessful. In this work I am obliged to take the general notion of intentionality as an intuitively given primitive to be understood through the assembly of a variety of illustrative cases. The crucial intuition, upon which this phase of my argument depends, is that the property of intentionality, however ultimately analysed, is as much a property of publicly displayed and collectively interpreted entities as it is of those which are private and individual.

3 RATIONALITY

The cluster of concepts comprehended under the terms 'rationality' and 'irrationality' also typically display public–collective and private–individual duality. Rationality is certainly a feature of public–collective discourse to which there may have been several individual contributors. Recent studies have shown that the rationality of individual cognitive processes (private–individual discourse) is not a necessary condition for the rationality of the public–collective discourse to which those individuals contribute. It may often be that social conventions for the proper structure, topic distribution and order of contributions to conversations or collectively produced documents impose rational properties on public discourse, such as consistency, deductive validity and the like. To say that someone is rational is not to congratulate them on their private cognitive processes but to praise them for their contributions to the collective discourse. The quality of the contribution may be assessed wholly by reference to the rest of the public conversation or the collectively produced document. To be rational is to meet, publicly, the relevant standards of the local collective. Just as one can publicly commit oneself to a line of action by raising legitimate expectations in others who hear one's declaration of intent without there having to be any privately formulated explicit personal representation of the outcome of the action proposed, so one can display rationality and irrationality in collective activities without there having to have been a matching 'inner' rational or irrational process by means of which the contribution was generated (*see* for example, Pearce and Cronen, *Communication, action and meaning*). Contributions which are rational relative to the flow of the public discourse may issue from private discourses, which, if they were made public, would unhesitatingly be judged irrational.

The truism that public discourse must antedate each individual's personal discourse does not establish the logical priority of public over private rationality. The case for the logical priority of the public – collective applications of this cluster of psychological concepts would be strengthened if we were able to explain, in terms of social constraints, why it is that public discourse is created in such a way as to display the appropriate properties. One can look into this by trying to answer an apparently bizarre question: 'What is the point of putting 'logic', that is, consistency, deductive order and so on, into public discussion, or for that matter their opposites to create an irrational discourse?'. In recent work in the sociology of science this sort of question has been answered by proposing that people can use a discourse to display personal qualities publicly. By putting in the 'logic' or the 'illogic', if that is appropriate, a person can present themselves to others as one of good standing, acquainted with social norms, and encourage the inference that they are someone whose contributions to the discourse are so nicely adjusted that they must have socially valued capacities. (The conditions for inferences to Machiavellianism have been studied but it is significant that Machiavellians are rarely the targets of accusations of overt rationality.)

That a sociological account of some paradigmatically rational discourses is essentially correct has been supported by the recent work of Latour and Woolgar, *Laboratory life*, and that of Knorr-Cetina, *The manufacture of knowledge*, on the way that the messy results of scientific research are brought together with fragments of the existing recognized corpus of scientific knowledge to create a scientific paper. These authors make a good case for the idea that 'logic' is an artful insertion into a discourse through the effect of a collective criticism and evaluation of the structure of the paper during its composition. Its presence is called for by the practical necessity to cope with debates and disputes with other scientists, who will use accusations of 'illogicality' to denigrate the contributions of their rivals. It is suggested that 'logic' is not involved in the primary cognitive activity of 'doing science'.

It might be argued that it is possible to read back a kind of rationality into the personal thinking and planning of an individual, say, of the one giving the advice that appears as a public suggestion to the writer. If rationality is injected as a strategy to win a debate, is not that act rational with respect to social means—end reasoning apropos the agonistic engagement which both parties have in mind? For instance:

> Belief: All coherent arguments are defensible
> Project: I want my argument to be defensible
> therefore
> Intention: I will make my argument coherent

and all this is itself a coherent argument!

Knorr-Cetina, *The manufacture of knowledge*, argues that though such reasoning does go on and that there are sometimes regresses of rationality, there is never any need to hypothesize individual rational processes to account for the production of rational scientific discourse. The social processes involved in its mutual production are always sufficient to account for its logical properties. If someone were to produce an irrational discourse and to defend it by reference to a superior faculty of 'intuition', he or she would not only lose the attention of the audience but their respect as well.

To clinch the argument, we ought to be able to find cases where illogicality has been inserted into a discourse in pursuit of similar social goals and under similar social constraints and promptings. There have indeed been people who have made an effort to display intuition rather than logical reasoning, inconsequentiality rather than consistency, sensibility rather than sense. Most of these people have, until recently, been women.

One can study the conventions for women's speech quite successfully by analysing certain properties of the speech of women that is displayed in novels and plays. The property to look for is accountability. If a discourse is accountable an individual can be called upon to justify his or her contribution, on a number of dimensions, such as content, emotional tone, performative force and, of course, logical relevance and coherence. Typically, the last of these would be achieved by organizing a defence by the giving of reasons for what had been said. (Of course, there ought to be no scientific inference that the offered reasons were indeed the premises which engendered the contribution, but the expressive force of the giving of such reasons encourages a social inference of that rough sort.) An examination of the literary material shows a cyclical swing in the accountability of women's speech.

The speech of Shakespeare's heroines is mostly represented as accountable, though it ought to be noted that those who display high levels of rationality are usually got up in men's clothes at the time (e.g. Portia and Rosalind). However, by the end of the eighteenth century conventions of public accountability seem to have changed. There is a telling passage in Jane Austen's *Pride and prejudice*. Elizabeth Bennett is staying with the Bingleys and conversing with Mr D'Arcy. He congratulates her on her accomplishments both musical and conversational. She realizes that she has been displaying altogether too much rationality for the local conventions of feminine charm and hastens to repair the damage by declaring that she prefers girlish chit-chat. There are other examples in *Kilvert's diary* in which one can infer the kind of feminine conversation that the good vicar found most attractive. A beautiful description of this phenomenon as a convention can be found in Flora Thompson's, *A country calendar and other writings*, dealing with village life before the First World War: 'As Laura came to know the girls better she found that much of their frivolity and brainlessness was a pose, an unconscious pose, due to their determination to appear wholly feminine. They had been told, and believed, that serious thought was the prerogative of man; women's part in the scheme of creation was to be charming'. I will return to the question of the effect of the existence of such conventions on individual cognitive processes and private discourse when we look at the developmental implications of the social constructivist view.

An intriguing historical problem is raised by this example. The women that appear in sixteenth and early seventeenth century literature display a striking bouquet of psychological attributes including great strength of character. Shakespeare tends to represent women as more decisive and determined than men. *Love's labour's lost* portrays, in detail, the psychological differences thought to characterize men and women in the fifteenth century (*see* Yates' *Love's labour's lost*). Despite swearing a binding oath, the four young men are quite unable to maintain their resolution when confronted by the power of will of the four young women who are determined to overcome them. Portia, Lady Macbeth and many others exemplify the power of will. However, in eighteenth and nineteenth century works, for instance the plays of Sheridan and later the novels of Dickens, a more complex feminine psychology is portrayed: the norm is easily seen to have shifted towards the fickle, inconstant and irrational. Does this change in literary conventions represent a change in the cognitive processes of half the human race or are we seeing a reflection of one set of conventions in another?

One way of trying to decide this question is to examine the plausibility of the transfer of a conventional attribute of speech, essentially something public – collective, to individuals as a personal cognitive attribute. In this case there is the folk theory that the social conventions governing accountability merely reflect the existence of a special feminine mode of reaching conclusions 'women's intuition'. It seems likely that thoughts pop up in the minds of men and women in much the same way. Traditionally, men were liable to called to account for the public expression of such thoughts, while women (and poets) were not. It would not be surprising if men prepared for such demands by pre-empting the request for reasons, by embedding their contributions in a discourse which already exhibited the socially favoured property of rationality. Women, until recently, have been under no such constraint. It might be that in working towards a thought in *sotto voce* discourse men appropriate the conventions under which they are required to speak publicly, thus actually prefacing speech with rational thought. Since a woman could legitimately produce a contribution without being called upon to display it as a conclusion drawn from suitable premises there would no pressure towards this private cognitive elaboration.

An extreme form of the dissociation between private thinking and public rationality is to be found in the 'Delphi' method for making business decisions. A random collection of sentences is offered to a group. The public — collective convention that such a group should pro-duce a rational discourse leads them to construct a formal basis of de-cision even from unpromising material.

4 EMOTION

The second type of public — collective/private — individual duality arises from the involvement of moral judgements in the identification of what one is experiencing as a particular emotion. By this I mean that to use the concept, say, of anger, either of oneself or in the assessment of what another person is doing or feeling or both, requires the grasp of a quite definite social fact, for instance, a specific social relation be-tween persons, assessed within the local moral order. Anger requires the assessment of an interference with oneself or some other with whom one has bonds of care or responsibility as a transgression. Aristotle defined anger (a typical 'red' emotion) in terms of the perception of transgression and an impulse to revenge, but there are typical physiological and ethological accompaniments of these moral assessments and justified intentions, for instance, adrenalin flows and threatening postures are adopted. The feelings occasioned by the physiological changes were fastened on by James ('our feeling of the same changes as they occur *is* the emotion') and the gestures, postures and facial expressions typical of a display were emphasized by Darwin.

In restoring judgement to a place in the theory of the emotions subse-quent to the decline in popularity of James's reductive account, Schachter and Singer, following Maranon, demonstrated how, for emotions in which adrenalin is heavily involved, such as fear, anxiety and jollity, the identification of a specific emotion depends on how a person explains their felt state of arousal. Subsequent developments in emotion theory have led to closer study of the physiological states involved with some refinement in discrimination, and the realization of the importance of the ethological aspect. This development has been summed up in Leventhal's 'network' theory in 'Towards a comprehensive theory of emotion' in which physiological, ethological and cognitive factors are integrated as severally necessary conditions, differently weighted in different cases. (The ethological theory of emotions was closely tied to the physiology of the accompanying feelings in early work on displays. Bell's classic text on the influence that anatomical and physiological bases of expression determined the way an emotion could be displayed was an essential text in the training of artists throughout the nineteenth century.)

According to the ethological view, the anatomical requirements for performing smiling, eye-widening, adopting threatening postures, weeping and so on involve specific muscle systems, physiological pathways and consequent somatic tensions, distributed in quite definite ways amongst the major emotions. In short, the phenomenal quality of grief is partly determined by the physiological requirements for its typical expression. This is not incompatible with Schachter's discoveries, since he was concerned with the transformation of fairly generalized feelings of arousal into emotions. And, too, there are many emotions in which adrenalin plays no part, for instance, ruefulness.

Averill, in 'A constructivist theory of emotion', has recently drawn on the Aristotelian point that at least some emotions are identified by and consequent upon assessments within a moral order. The most interesting recent elaboration of a fourth 'factor' in the network of conditions supporting the construction of an emotion is Sabini and Silver's analysis of envy in *Moralities of everyday life*. Envy and jealousy are typical 'green' emotions. Both involve a moral order incorporating assessments of rights and worth.

B is *envious* of *A* if the following conditions obtain: (a) *A* has acquired or achieved something, *X*, to which he has a right or which he deserves; (b) *B* feels belittled or demeaned by *A*'s possession of *X*, since *B*'s lack of *X* is presumptive evidence of a lack of worth or desert. Since *B* knows *A* has a right to *X*, his defensive strategy must be to undermine that right by belittling A.

B is *jealous* of *A* if the following conditions obtain: (a) *A* has acquired or achieved something, *X*, to which he has no better right than *B*; (b) *B* wants *X*. Since *B* believes he has as good a right to *X* as *A* his defensive strategy must be to deprive *A* of *X*. Sabini and Silver point out that *B* feels righteous indignation if he thinks *A* does not deserve or has no right to *X*, even if he himself has none either.

Moral assessments enter too into the 'blue' emotions. Declarations of 'I am lonely' may serve as invitations, but are often avowals. On what are they based? So far as I can determine, there has never been shown to be any specific bodily feeling of loneliness. According to Linda Wood (personal communication) such avowals are typical of people who believe themselves to be solitary or isolated more than they think they should be, that is, more than they think is normal or proper. For instance, some of the complaints of old people are based on the assessment of normal isolation as improper. Loneliness has no characteristic bodily manifestation which would enable a sufferer to distinguish it Darwin-fashion from sadness, melancholy, depression, boredom and a host of other 'blue' emotions.

Suppose we call the four-component theory of the emotions, sketched in this chapter, the neo-Leventhal theory. In Leventhal's own three-component theory the elementary conditions are severally necessary and jointly sufficient for a person to experience (sincerely avow) an emotion of a quite specific type. If the issue of necessity and sufficiency is raised for the four-component network, some intriguing possibilities emerge. Two of the four components are social. The assessment of moral issues in some local moral order is overtly so, and the Schachter-type interpretation involves a process of at least a socially influence through the conventions that govern the kind of causal story that is admissable in some particular society.

It is conceivable that though we are accustomed to deal with our bodily feelings by the use of the four-fold scheme described in the neo-Leventhal theory, there could be cultures whose ways of dealing with the 'passions' are different. There are cultures at least who use a somewhat different scheme. The moral and causal components are replaced by a fanciful anatomical attribution. Paul Heelas has reported (*Indigenous psychologies*) that the Chempoy use such a scheme, leading to such reports as 'My liver is tiny' when dealing with somatic passions in situations when our four-component theory would require 'I am sad'.

The main structure of the Maori vocabulary of the emotions is as follows:

    (1) *Heart emotions*

manawa-kino	uneasy
manawa-pa	grudging
manawa-reka	gratified
manawa-rera	excited

    (2) *Bowel emotions*

nga kau-nui	eager
nga kau-rua	uncertain
nga kau-kine	disinclined

(3) *Stomach emotions*

puku-takaro	playful
puku-mahara	cautious
puka-riri	quarrelsome

If we compare the Maori terms with the best English equivalents one is struck by the persistence of an explicit reference to the associated bodily organ. We have such phrases as 'heart-felt', 'his bowels turned to water', 'my stomach turned over', but these express the feelings and the emotions have to be inferred from context. The Maori nomenclature seems to reflect a way of treating bodily passions much closer to the James – Lange conception of differential bodily feelings than current research will admit for ourselves. We do not know what role avowals and declarations of emotional states played in the social life of the Maori, but one ought not to be too reckless in concluding that it was radically different from ours. The linguistic forms do suggest that the social – moral component is of lesser importance in the identification of the emotions than the phenomenal. Taking this line of thought a step further, Heelas has suggested that there may be tribes whose ways of conceptually managing the passions may involve no social – causal element at all. Under such circumstances I would be prepared to follow his thought that we should say that such people do not have emotions.

Even within the four-component theory there are possibilities for cross-cultural variation of some moment and interest. Aristotle's conception of friendship involves a greater emphasis on the moral structure of the relationship than does ours, so one would expect a richer and touchier emotional complex to arise around it. The emotion of romantic love seems to be a fairly recent increment to our cultural repertoire, the advent of which can be dated fairly precisely. On the other hand, some emotions and moods which once had great importance for us have become extinct or obsolete. I shall illustrate this with a brief history of the extinct emotion 'accidie' and the obsolete mood 'melancholy'. By comparing melancholy with one of its modern descendants, clinical depression, I hope to illustrate the power of shared and culturally affirmed theory to determine our mental life by providing us with emotions and their more persistent siblings, moods.

5 OBSOLETE EMOTIONS AND MOODS

At least a necessary step towards establishing the social relativity of forms of mentation (itself a step to proving the social engendering of forms of thought) would be to show the cultural relativity of some important psychological matter. I have sketched a cultural distinction in the case of Eskimo and Maori ways of dealing with feelings as emotions and moods. It would carry even more weight if I could establish, in detail, the historical relativity of emotions in ways of thought temporally continuous with ours. I hope to show that certain emotions became obsolete that is, neither exotic nor extinct, but with recognizable though different descendants. By making use of the conceptual system within which they were defined, men and women came to have a certain kind of personal being different from ours. I shall compare these emotions and moods with their nearest contemporary equivalents or counterparts to establish their difference. I take as my examples, melancholy and accidie, both emotional conditions with which our ancestors were much concerned.

Medieval psychology was, I believe, right to treat emotions and moods together as the passions. I shall try to show that emotions, for example, anger, grief and elation, require the same kind of treatment in a proper psychological study, as do moods, such as sadness, depression and happiness. White, in his venerable but admirable *The philosophy of mind* (which one could treat as a study of the psychology implicit in contemporary commonsense) sets off a category of feelings which he calls those of 'general conditions'. He distinguishes bodily feelings such as seasickness from moods such as depression or frivolity, from emotions such as admiration or indignation, from agitations such as amazement or hilarity, and from 'completions', an ill-chosen expression for states such as tranquillity or boredom.

For my purpose the distinction that matters is that between moods and emotions. They are marked out from each other by two main features.

(1) *Degree*. Moods are longer lasting than emotions and they colour everything one does or thinks. To be disappointed is to experience an emotion; to be embittered is to succumb to a mood. If this distinction is one of degree, one might expect indeterminate cases; 'sadness' I think, is one.

(2) *Kind*. Emotions, for instance, grief, and what White calls agitations, such as amazement, have intentional objects, e.g. 'grieving over . . .', 'amazed at . . .' etc. Moods do not generally take objects. It makes no sense to ask what one is jovial about. Sadness, on this criterion, can be ambiguous. We can be 'sad about . . .', or just plain sad. The medieval ancestor of this mood/emotion, *tristitia*, seems to have had the same double use.

Moods and emotions, whether contemporary or obsolete, are to be tackled with the same four-fold scheme I have set out for bringing together the work of Leventhal, Schachter and Sabini and Silver, into a unified scheme. There is (a) a bodily feeling; (b) a characteristic way of expressing that feeling; (c) an interpretation, locating the feeling in some presumed causal order; and (d) a supervening interpretation by which these subordinate features are located in a moral order.

With respect of the causal component, moods tend to be related to endogenous conditions (an excess of black bile, 5-hydroxy-tryptomine etc.), while emotions seem to be related to exogenous conditions (an insult, a failure, a bull, etc.). This accounts for, and is a reflexion of, the 'deep grammar' rule that emotions, not moods, take intentional objects.

Each of the four components may be lost when an emotion becomes obsolete. The feelings may come and go unattended (e.g. hubris); a characteristic form of expression may disappear from the socially accepted repertoire of grimaces, postures and gestures (e.g. hauteur), which is not the emotion of contempt, but a feeling of natural superiority; certain causal laws may be dropped as false; and a moral order may be abandoned, e.g. accidie. The two former hardly need comment. For the purposes of my argument I will concentrate on the third and fourth case.

Accidie: an extinct emotion

Accidie is an emotional state; *negligentia*, *pigritia* and *otiositas* (negligence, laziness and idleness) were amongst its typical manifestations, while *taedium*, *desperatio* and *tristitia* were associated or consequential emotions. Medieval moral psychologists analysed accidie in detail, since for many it was not just the major spiritual failing to which those who should have been dutiful succumbed, but to feel it at all was a sin. By the fifteenth century the popular conception of 'the sin of sloth' had ceased to be a state of mind and had shifted to manifest behaviour (or lack of it). 'Sloth' had taken on its modern connotation.

I offer accidie as an example of an obsolete emotion, since I think modern people do not associate any specific emotion with laziness or procrastination in the carrying out of tasks duty demands. Rather, emotions cluster around occasions of reprimand, real or imagined, and urging. They can range from guilt to a kind of indignation, such as 'I was just about to do it, when you interfered!'

The basic idea of accidie was boredom, dejection or even disgust with fulfilling one's religious duty. It appears for the first time in the works of Evagrius (346−49) as 'the noonday demon' which distracts a hermit from the duties of the ascetic life. From its earliest identification it had a double-sidedness: on the one hand, negligence (a behavioural matter), on the other a kind of misery (a matter of feelings). By embedding the negligence in a moral order (one's duty to

God), an emotion (*acedia*) was born, according to just the formula for linking feelings and behavioural manifestations with moral matters through a causal interpretation that we have used, in reverse to analyse contemporary emotions. The range of feelings is quite wide, including sorrow, bitterness, misery and '*taedium cordis*', weariness of heart.

The association of laziness with misery, out of which accidie was born, meant that a certain ambiguity affected the prescriptions for extirpating it. In so far as it involved a failure to carry on with a tiresome, uncomfortable or boring task, the cultivation of fortitude formed part of its remedy. But dutiful behaviour without joy (*gaudium*) was an inadequate response. *Acedia* was only truly overcome when delight in the exercise of one's proper activities returned.

A detailed history of the appearance, flourishing and disappearance, of the emotional state of *acedia* can be found in Wenzel's excellent work, *The sin of sloth: accedie in medieval thought and literature*. Not only is there a shift from emotional state to typical behaviour as the referent of the term, but also a long, analytical struggle to relate *acedia* to *tristitia*. In catalogues of the sins and their progeny the relation undergoes several reworkings. In some, *acedia* is a species of *tristitia*. But in later works (e.g. Aquinas), *acedia* is the root of spiritual vice, and *tristitia* experienced as among its typical manifestations. For this study, the essential issue is the dependence of the very existence of the emotional state on a moral order (duty to God fulfilled in spiritual exercises). Idleness and procrastination are still amongst our failings but our emotions are differently engaged, defined against the background of a different moral order, roughly the ethics of a material production (*see* for example, the emotional state called 'oblomovism', described by Gontacheriff and taken up by T. S. Eliot. I owe the comparison to a conversation with Don Campbell). Perhaps only the scholar who falls into a kind of depression as he or she fails to push on with a project comes close to experiencing the once common emotion of accidie.

*Melancholy: an obsolete mood**

I think it would be correct to say that melancholy, which was of such interest to medieval moral psychology and which played such a large role in seventeenth century personality and clinical psychology, is no longer experienced by anyone. Though we understand what it is to be melancholy, we never confess to this feeling. Bored, depressed, nostalgic — yes. Melancholy — no (though White does include it in a

---

*I am grateful to J. B. Bamborough, Principal of Linacre College, for much help and guidance for this brief study of the history of the concept of melancholy.

written list of moods). A sane but gloomy person would be astounded if his medical adviser diagnosed his troubles as a case of melancholy. Yet Marsilio Ficino made a career out of treating it, and Robert Burton wrote a very large and famous book anatomizing it. Melancholy is obselete. Yet its role in medieval and renaissance psychology was supreme. Some authorities hold that belief in the psychology of melancholy coloured and transformed the admissable forms of personality expression of an entire nation — the English.

Melancholy began its long history as an illness, a bodily malfunction affecting the mind. Ficino's distinction of obnoxious melancholy (*atra bilis*) from congenial melancholy (*candida bilis*) retains the association with an illness brought about by a biochemical imbalance in the body (in those days expressed as an excess of black bile). According to Logan, *The voices of melancholy*, the concept of melancholy developed through the Middle Ages in two contexts: medical practice, in which the theory remained fairly stable, and moral psychology where it was analysed among the passions.

Medieval and late: diagnostic account
Klibansky et al., *Saturn and melancholy* emphasized the extent to which medieval characterology, based on the physiological theory of the four humours, was an echo and re-echo of certain texts, particularly that of Vindician. Excess of one humour caused illness which was cured by increasing its contrary. The seasons of the year and times of the day severally amplify the associated humour. Autumn and night were the times of melancholy. In the course of this period, 1100 to 1300, the melancholic and its three sibling 'complexions' shifted from the status of illnesses to that of temperaments, though without wholly losing their pathological connotations.

Medieval and late: moral account
Hugues de Fouillori is extensively quoted by Klibansky et al. in *Saturn and melancholy*. The text falls into two parts: a short summary of the physiology of black bile, and a detailed account of the associated emotions or passions in the context of moral theology. Thus: '. . . by black bile we may . . . mean grief, which we should feel for our evil actions. But we may also speak of a different sort of grief, when the spirit is tormented by the longing to be united with the Lord.' Later in the same passage the dual nature of the melancholic person is emphasized: 'Bowed by cares, sometimes wakefully directed to heavenly aims.' Popular psychology of the late Middle Ages, according to Klibansky et al. evidently elided and transcended both the medical pathological and the moral psychological theories to create a

genuinely psychological treatment of temperament. Klibansky et al. quote mnemonic verses, which for the melancholic include:

> Invides et tristes, cupidus, dextraeque, tenacis,
> non expers fraudis, timidus, luteique, coloris.
> Envious and sad, eager and skilful, tenacious,
> having no part in cheating, fearful and of a foul and
>   yellowish complexion.

> Auctumnus, terra, melancholia, senectus
> (frigida et sicca appetit et non petit rubea et clara).
> Autumnal, earthy, melancholy, senile
> (cold and dry in his tastes, and he does not aim at being ruddy
>   [cheerful] and bright).

By the late Middle Ages the complex of favourable and unfavourable features of the melancholic temperament were well established and as Klibansky points out, the unfavourable features were emphasized throughout popular and technical literature alike. They cite a marvellous description of the melancholy temperament from the Teuscher Kalender (Augsburg, 1495) in which the melancholic is cold and dry like autumn, the earth and old age. He is timid, lazy, slow of movement, hostile, sad, forgetful, indolent, clumsy, has 'but rare and weak desires' 'owing to his sadness'. At the same time it was widely held that only amongst men of this temperament could true genius be found. Later we have the entertaining spectacle of those who sought to be geniuses, cultivating the melancholy cast of mind, staring out from high towers on autumn nights. Women's melancholy seems to have had no such redeeming features.

By the sixteenth century melancholy had become the main focus of interest of psychology. I shall first summarize a good standard treatment (Timothy Bright, *A treatise of melancholie*) and then turn to one of the great psychological texts of all time, Burton's *Anatomy of melancholy*.

Bright takes pains to distinguish true melancholy from 'that heavy hand of God upon the afflicted conscience, tormented with remorse of sin and feare of his judgement. . .' (p. iii verso). Melancholy has a physiological origin in 'an increase and excess of the melancholicke humour'. In a thoroughly modern manner, Bright identifies melancholy with a particular interpretation of a physiological state: '. . . when any conceit troubleth you that hath no sufficient ground of reason, but riseth only upon the frame of your brain . . . that is right melancholicke' (p. 133). The interpretation is typified by '. . . envious they are, because of their own false conceived want whereby their estate, seeming in their own false conceived fantasy much worse than it is . . . maketh them to desire what they see others to enjoy. . .' (p. 133).

Quite unlike modern depression, melancholy can sustain, indeed can even be the condition of, powerful intellectual endeavours: '. . . melancholie breedeth a jelousie of doubt in that they [the melancholic] take in deliberation, and causeth them to be more exact and curious in pondering the very moments of things — the vehemence of their affection, once raised . . . carrieth them . . . into the depths of what they take pleasure to intermeddle in' (p. 130). Melancholics are both 'diligent and painful, wary and circumspect' and 'doubtful and suspicious', the latter engendering the former.

Burton: melancholy and disaster
With Burton melancholy is neither an occasional disease nor is it a specific temperament, one amongst four. It is a complex affliction to which all are prone, consequential on the general conditions of human life. Burton's work, *The anatomy of melancholy* has provoked two radically opposite judgements in modern authors. According to Klibansky et al. 'the assumption of the generality of melancholy and the uniqueness of each particular case' . . . 'is an entirely literary assumption . . .' (*Saturn and melancholy*, p. 147). Bergen Evans, in *The psychiatry of Robert Burton*, interprets the general/particular distinction as a subtle and empirically well-grounded part of the empirical psychology of the conditions. Melancholy, says Burton is a 'settled humour'. . . '*morbis, sonticus* or *chronicus.*' But the extent of the disorder and the problems of its treatment can only be grasped by a 'sheer, indefatigable listing of innumerable symptoms' (*The psychiatry of Robert Burton*, p. 47). Evans must surely be right.

In two respects Burton's treatment goes beyond that of Marsilio Ficino. It is a 'symbolizing disease', appearing in distinctive forms but it is a condition in need of diagnosis since 'the soul is carried hoodwinkt and the understanding captive'. However, 'there is in all melancholy *similitudo dissimilis*, like men's faces, a disagreeing likeness still' (pt 1, s. 3, mem. 1, subs. 2). In essence, Burton's theory seems to be that there are 'quite natural inward causes . . .' of unfounded 'fears and sorrows' which become the dangerous state of melancholy by virtue of wrong interpretations, as for example by being 'bewitched or forsaken of God' (pt. 1, s. 3, mem. 3). By showing 'to melancholy men . . . the causes whence they [the symptoms] proceed' they can 'endure them with more patience' (pt. 1, s. 3, mem. 3), a remark reminiscent of the analysis of Schachter in *Emotion, obesity and crime*.

Secondly, Burton sees melancholy not as a temperament, among others, but as a condition arising out of quite normal physiological.

states, by some excess. Melancholy, 'in disposition . . . goes and comes upon every small occasion of sorrow etc. . . . .'. 'And from these melancholy dispositions no man living is free . . .' (pt. 1, s. 1, mem. 1, subs. 4). Melancholy to Burton is: 'a chronic or continuate disease, a settled humour . . . not errant but fixed . . . and as it were long increasing, so now being (pleasant or painful) given to an habit, it will hardly be removed' (pt. 1, s. 1, mem. 1, subs. 4).

Despite the enormous variety of ways, dangerous degrees of melancholy are manifested, including unwillingness to speak for fear of uttering obscenities, urges to suicide, hyperchondria etc. 'suspicion and jealousy are general symptoms' (pt. 1, s. 3, mem. 1, subs. 2), leading to a particular kind of attentiveness to all around them, and to morbid fancies of persecution'. And again, 'Inconstant are they in all their actions' . . . 'restless' yet 'if once they be resolved, obstinate . . . .'. And again, 'what they desire they do most furiously seek . . . '; 'prone to love', but 'love one dearly till they see another, and then dote on her'.

But why melancholy? As I understand it, it is the connection with the gloom and despondency that overcomes him or her whose abnormalities and inconstancies lead them into isolation and a kind of miserable idleness near to accidie.

Milton: melancholy as opportunity

The author of Aristotle's *Problems* (xxx, 1) quoted in Logan, *Voices of melancholy* remarks, 'Those, however, in whom the black bile's excessive heat is relaxed towards a mean, are melancholy, but they are more rational and less eccentric and in many respects superior to others in culture or in the arts or in statesmanship.' The suggestion that either as temperament or as mood melancholy subserves and promotes intellectual activity is a common theme throughout its history. Burton is very largely concerned with the pathology of melancholy and the cure of its myriad manifestations. The dual nature of melancholy was an important part of seventeenth century psychology. As Babb puts it in *The Elizabethan malady*, it was on the one hand 'a degrading mental abnormality associated with fear and sorrow', a malady sibling to our contemporary 'depression'; and on the other 'a condition which endows one with intellectual acumen and profundity'. In the twin poems 'L'Allegro' and 'Il Penseroso', Milton displays both images. I offer these lines as an elegant summary of the psychology of melancholy. From 'L'Allegro' we have:

> Hence loathed Melancholy
>   of *Cerberus* and blackest midnight born
> In Stygian caves forlorn
>   'Mongst horrid shapes, and shrieks, and sights unholy

> Find out some uncouth cell,
>> Where brooding darkness spreads his jealous wings,
> And the night-Raven sings;
>> There under Ebon shades, and low-brow'd Rocks,
> As ragged as thy locks,
>> In dark *Cimmerian* desert ever dwell.

In these ingenious lines most of the pathology of melancholy is touched upon. In 'Il Penseroso' Milton gives exactly equal attention to 'constructive melancholy':

> But hail thou Godess, sage and holy,
> Hail divinest melancholy.

> Thee bright hair'd Vesta long of yore
> To solitary *Saturn* bore:

> Come pensive Nun, devout and pure,
> Sober, stedfast, and demure.

The cherub Contemplation and 'mute silence' are among the followers of Melancholy; the connection of melancholy with the scientific approach to nature dominates the last few lines:

> Find out the peaceful hermitage,
> The Hairy Gown and Mossy Cell,
> Where I may sit and rightly spell,
> Of every Star that Heaven doth shew,
> And every Herb that sips the dew;
> Till old experience do attain
> To something like Prophetic strain.
> These pleasures *Melancholy* give,
> And I with thee will choose to live.

What does this story show? — A theory being used to bring into order and compose into a sort of unity a variety of feelings, beliefs and environmental factors engendering both a distinctive mood and a temperament (and personality) of which that mood is characteristic. The original physiological theory upon which the four-temperament analysis of human personality was based, soon became enormously elaborated with astrological ideas; all of this vast apparatus of belief provided a powerful cognitive structure by which to organize one's experience. In the course of the long history of melancholy, the accounts of it take on a prescriptive force over and above their original role in the medical symptomology. By the time of Milton and Burton, melancholy is something one might aspire to and at the same time something of which one might desperately wish to be relieved.

To show that this mood or unique congerie of propensities to emotion is obsolete, a comparison can be made with the symptomologies of contemporary psychiatry. (The fact that they must be looked for there, shows the sad decline in respect for the autumnal emotions.) The best that the American *Diagnostic and statistical manual of mental disorders* III (1980) can come up with is 'depression', which runs as follows:

> Dysphoric mood or loss of interest or pleasure in all or almost all usual activities or pastimes. The dysphoric mood is characterized by symptoms such as the following: depressed, sad, blue, hopeless, down in the dumps, irritable. The mood disturbance must be prominent and relatively persistent, but not necessarily the most dominant symptom, and does not include momentary shifts from one dysphoric mood to another dysphoric mood e.g. anxiety to depression to anger, such as are seen in states of acute psychotic turmoil . . . . . with Melancholia. Loss of pleasure in all or almost all activities, lack of reactivity to usual pleasurable stimuli (doesn't feel much better, even temporarily, when something good happens) and at least three of the following:
> a. distinct quality of depressed mood; b. the depression is regularly worse in the morning; c. early morning awakening; d. marked psychomotor retardation or agitation; e. significant weight loss; f. excessive or inappropriate guilt. (pp. 213−15)

In a typical contemporary account, M. Ostow, 'The psychology of depression and its management' we find: 'Depression is an affect which appears in response to the loss of a love object or in anticipation of some act which would result in the loss of a love object. The characteristic psychic and physical components of the depressive syndrome can be understood as devised to compel protective acts on the part of those who love the patient.' The social−psychological centrepiece of Burton's *Anatomy of melancholy* is a massive and detailed discussion of 'Love-melancholy' which as to its central tenets is, to all intents and purposes, the same theory, even to the role of the linked tendencies to suicide and aggression. Furthermore, the contrast between 'normal' depression and the pathological variety, is drawn much as Burton drew it.

However, the melancholy of the renaissance is double-sided, being both pathological and destructive *and* the foundation of achievement. As John Huarte said '. . . there is none so cold and dry as that of a melancholic, and whatever notable men for learning have lived in the world (says Aristotle) they were all melancholicke.' Or to put it neatly in the Latin of Marsilio Ficino: Atra bilis: id est melancholie duplex est: scilicet naturalis et adusta (*De Triplici Vita* i j. cx.v.)

Melancholy was not only a mood but a temperament. It is as obsolete a personality theory now as its siblings the choleric, phlegmatic and sanguine personalities. It plays no role in contemporary personality psychology. In its stead, new theoretical concepts have appeared and by entering the conceptual apparatus of lay folk have taken their turn as devices by which experience is ordered. A great many people now think of themselves and others as extroverts or introverts. The close parallel between the 'scientific' description extroversion/introversion (and its criteria) and that in use in lay psychology has been established by Semin et al. in 'A comparison of the commonsense and "scientific" conceptions of extroversion – introversion'. They rightly conclude that 'the function of implicit personality theories in everyday life may not necessarily be a predictive one, but a prescriptive one' (p. 84).

6   BASIC EMOTIONS

The four-component theory can find no place for basic emotions. I am fully in agreement with the spirit of Hochschild's ('Emotion work, feeling rules and social structure') 'sociological' theory, in particular with its contention that there are 'feeling rules'. In the four-component scheme a classification will emerge by the interplay between two levels of identifying criteria. I have slipped a classification of the emotions by colour into this chapter: anger is red, envy is green, sadness is blue, pride is purple, misanthropy is yellow. This is based on a fairly straightforward synaesthesia with the phenomenal quality of the emotion. But the cluster of feelings and bodily postures, gestures and so on that are the somatic side of 'one' emotion are culturally selected via presumed causal categories, which have to find a legitimation in a moral order. Why is dread an emotion but not indigestion, exhaustion and pain? Each has a distinctive quality as a feeling and characteristic behavioural manifestations. Plainly these passions do not fall, for us, within a moral order. My unhesitating selection of the right colour for an emotion is not just synaesthetic, but also draws on the cultural associations of those colours, such as the imperial connotations of the purple.

The classification of emotions by colour is not meant to be taken too seriously. It merely illustrates the impossibility of defending an acultural scheme. Certainly no classification of emotions by reference to the biological systems whose workings bring on the passions, so to speak, could be used. It is amusing to notice the blatant ethnocentricity of some schemes which are put forward as candidates for the universal basic taxonomy. For instance, Plutnik's ('A general psychoevolutionary theory of emotion') supposed 'psychoevolutionary synthesis' is readily spotted as an expression of culturally specific moral and political stereotypes.

In psychological research the first question to be asked about some alleged individual cognitive process, such as intuition or some supposed individual condition such as emotion, is this: what contribution does the display of some 'outward' sign of this process or attribute make to the worth of the personality or character that others would attribute to the actor? Under what dramatic convention is it called for? I believe that in some cases a complete explanation for the presence of a display, say in the form or content of talk from which our fellow beings form their opinions of us, can be found by looking at the history of our social conventions, and attributing to the individual actor no more complex a cognitive state than an undifferentiated desire to please. We are relieved of the need to formulate hypotheses about individual cognitive attributes or processes of which our speech and action are displayed as a public manifestation. A conversation may have cognitive properties only because there is a socially maintained cluster of rules which require discourse for people of this sort to take on a certain form. A contradiction may be rejected because there is a social convention to that effect, and we see it in the startled faces of those around us when we bring it out. There may be no logical train of thought which its display exposes as inadequate.

Developmental theory in the light of this conclusion would be thoroughly Vygotskian. Learning is just the privatization of features of public – collective episodes of mutual engagement, and many individual cognitive processes are much what Plato and Vygotsky thought they were, *sotto voce* speech. The fact that talk displays cognitive properties is a collective not an individual fact.

My aim is to show that the basis of many key areas of human functioning is the use by the folk, collectively and derivatively individually, of locally validated theories, in terms of which they create their own modes of experience, thought and so on, including the way they use those very theories. Reflexivity and self-reference will emerge at the very heart of things only if certain theoretical concepts are available to the folk. Psychologically speaking, to be a human being is to be the kind of creature who uses theories to order and so create the forms of experience. To be conscious is not to have a special kind of perception, denied to chimpanzees, but to utilize a theory of a kind that chimpanzees have not and, perhaps thanks to their neural organization, can never learn. The study of psychology is not the study of a natural phenomenon. It is to do the analytical work of disentangling the theories which, as embedded in our thought-ways, constitute the same.

RESEARCH MENU 5

(1) The four-factor theory admits of the possibility of more variations than have been discussed in the text. Once the institution of emotions has been created, it seems conceivable that there could be emotions without feelings: a bodily posture, the cause of it and a moral element could be present together, for instance shushing someone with an out-thrust hand. A modest start could be made by collecting and taxonomizing matters of this sort, and to look for differences and similarities with neighbourly emotions.

(2) There is an enormous repertoire of emotional terms in English, partially overlapping the vocabularies of other languages. The comprehensive symposium edited by M. B. Arnold, *Feelings and emotions*, lists the following: affection, anger, anguish, anxiety, awe, benevolence, boredom, contempt, depression, disgust, disillusionment, distress, dread, elation, enjoyment, enthusiasm, envy, exuberance, fear, grief, guilt, hate, illwill, indignation, irritation, jealousy, joy, longing, love, lust, panic, pathos, pity, pride, rage, regret, remorse, reverence, sadness, shame, sorrow, surprise, tenderness, terror, vanity, wonder, wrath. Far and away the greatest attention is paid to three, anger, fear and rage. Most of the emotions in the list, and many others, have attracted little research attention. The 'four factor' theory could be applied with profit to 'pride', 'ruefulness', 'amazement' and 'pity' as a start, and to many others. The problem of 'embarrassment' has been raised by Sabini and Silver in *Moralities of everyday life*. A great deal of comparative work could be done on the more exotic emotions, using the 'four factor' theory, for instance on 'amaeru'; see Morsbach, H. 'Amaeru'.

(3) In the text I lumped together a number of specific rational properties under 'rationality'. Much research remains to be done on the social construction of species such as 'consistency', 'following from', the social stigmata associated with different kinds of fallacies in different circles and so on. I am unable to find any study of the relation between what counts as conclusive rational demonstration in the public conversation of a subculture and the preferred cognitive forms of individual members.

BIBLIOGRAPHICAL NOTES 5

There is an extensive philosophical literature on intentions and intentionality. It separates out into two strands, the study of the concept of 'intention' as a component of the explanation of action, and the critical working out of the idea that 'intentionality' is the mark of the mental. The former is part of the theoretical psychology of social being and does not concern me in this study; see R. HARRÉ, *Social being* (Oxford: Basil Blackwell, 1979, ch. 12). The latter is summed up in R. E. AQUILA, *Intentionality: a study of mental acts* (University Park: Pennsylvania State University Press, 1977). The 'intentionalist' idea has been used very widely, see G. E. M. ANSCOMBE, 'The intentionality of sensation' (in *Analytical philosophy*, ed. R. J. Butler, Oxford: Basil Blackwell, 1965).

The critical discussion of the sentential – referential form of the intentional criterion begins with W. V. QUINE, *Word and object* (Cambridge: Mass.: MIT Press, 1960) and is still in progress. For the role of conventions see D. LEWIS, *Convention* (Cambridge (Mass.): Harvard University Press, 1969).

Rationality as a social product of discourse figures mostly in the sociology of science, see particularly B. LATOUR and S. WOOLGAR, *Laboratory life* (Los Angeles: Sage, 1979) and K. KNORR-CETINA, *The manufacture of knowledge* (Oxford: Pergamon, 1981). The interplay between the sociological account of scientific rationality and general philosophy of science is described by W. NEWTON-SMITH, *The rationality of science* (London: Routledge and Kegan Paul, 1981). The point about Shakespeare's 'tutorial heroines' I owe to a personal communication from Jonathan Miller. See also F. YATES, *A study of Love's labour's lost* (Cambridge: Cambridge University Press, 1936). How the structure of the conversation can be independent of the rules guiding the speakers is shown by W. B. PEARCE and V. CRONEN, *Communication, action and meaning* (New York: Praeger, 1980).

For general theories of the involvement of social factors in emotions, in particular judgements with respect to standards, see J. AVERILL, 'A constructivist theory of emotion' (in *Emotions: theory, research and experience*, ed. R. Plutnik and H. Kellermann, New York: Academic Press, 1980). The point goes back to Aristotle's treatment of anger revived by A. J. P. KENNY, *Action emotion and will* (London: Routledge and Kegan Paul, 1963). The 'three-factor network' theory of emotion is expounded by H. LEVENTHAL, 'Towards a comprehensive theory of emotion' (in *Advances in experimental social psychology*, vol.13, ed. L. Berkowitz, New York: Academic Press, 1980).

The role of moral orders in the genesis of emotions is very fully worked out by J. SABINI and M. SILVER in their excellent *Moralities of everyday life* (Oxford: Oxford University Press, 1982). Most of the loneliness literature is rather weak, with the exception of the work of L. WOOD which is forthcoming in *The encyclopedic dictionary of psychology* (ed. R. Harré and R. Lamb, Oxford: Basil Blackwell, 1983). The notion of 'display rules' is used by the ethologically minded to mediate between the genetically based 'given' repertoire of emotional expressions and the actual culturally distinctive displays that can be observed. So far as I know, it stems from the work of P. EKMAN and W. V. FRIESEN, *Unmasking the face* (Englewood Cliffs (NJ): Prentice Hall, 1975). The strongest case for ethological universals has been made by I. EIBL-EIBESFELDT, *Love and hate* (New York: Holt, Rinehart and Winston, 1972). The evidence for fine-grained physiological distinctions between emotions is offered by D. T. GRAHAM, J. A. STERN and G. WINOKUR, 'The concept of a different specific set of physiological changes in each emotion' (*Psychiatric Research Reports*, 12, 1960, 8 – 15). The classic studies around which all this revolves are reported in summary in S. SCHACHTER, *Emotion, obesity and crime* (New York: Academic Press, 1971). For an influential early physiological – ethological theory see C. BELL, *Essays on the anatomy of expression in painting* (London: Longman, Hurst, Rees and Orme, 1806, Essays IV and V). M. B. ARNOLD (ed.), *Feelings and emotions* (New York and London: Academic Press, 1970) is a useful compendium.

140   Social foundations of personal psychology

The case for an even more extensive search for social aspects of supposedly psychological and individual attributes can be found in J. COULTER, *The social construction of mind* (London: Macmillan, 1979). See also S. B. ORTNER and H. WHITEHEAD, *Sexual meanings: the cultural construction of gender and sexuality* (Cambridge: Cambridge University Press, 1982).

The history of accidie is beautifully described by S. WENZEL, *The sin of sloth: acedia in medieval thought and literature* (Chapel Hill: University of North Carolina Press, 1960). There is an extensive literature on melancholy, including B. EVANS, *The psychiatry of Robert Burton* (New York: Columbia University Press, 1946) and B. C. LOGAN, *The voices of melancholy* (London: Routledge and Kegan Paul, 1973). The classic study is R. KLIBANSKY, E. PANOVSKY and F. SAXL, *Saturn and melancholy* (London: Nelson, 1964).

The classic study of the origin of romantic love is D. DE ROUGEMONT, *Passion and society* (London: Faber and Faber, 1956). For a thorough study of another obsolete emotion see S. T. TUCKER, *Enthusiasm: a study of semantic change* (Cambridge: Cambridge University Press, 1972). For a detailed discussion of a moral order without the emotion of guilt see B. COLLETT, *The Benedictine monks of the Congregation of Santa Giustina, Padua, c. 1480−c.1568* (Oxford: doctoral dissertation, 1983).

Additional works cited in text are L. BABB, *The Elizabethan malady* (Ann Arbor: University Michigan Press, 1951); T. BRIGHT, *A treatise of melancholy* (London: Vautrolier, 1586); F. BRENTANO, *Psychology from an empirical standpoint* (London: Routledge and Kegan Paul, 1973); R. BURTON, *Anatomy of melancholy* (1621, ed. H. Jackson, London: Dent, 1932); A. R. HOCHSCHILD, Emotion work, feeling rules and social structure' (*American Journal of Sociology*, 85, 1979, 551−75); J. HUARTE, *The examination of men's wits* (trans. of R. Carew, *Examen de ingenios*, from the Italian trans. of the original Spanish by M. C. Camili, London: Islip for Watkins, 1594); W. JAMES, *The principles of psychology* (New York: Henry Holt, 1890, ch.xxv); H. MORSBACH, 'Amaeru' (in *Life sentences*, ed. R. Harré, London: Wiley, 1976); M. OSTOW, 'The psychology of depression and its management' (in *Sourcebook of abnormal psychology*, ed. L. Y. Rabin and J. E. Carr, Boston: Houghton-Miflin, 1967); R. PLUTNIK, 'A general psychoevolutionary theory of emotion' (in R. Plutnik and H. Kellerman, *Emotion theory, research and experiment*, New York: Academic Press, 1980); G. R. SEMIN, E. ROSCH and J. CHARSEIN, 'A comparison of the commonsense and "scientific" conceptions of extroversion−introversion' (*European Journal of Social Psychology*, 11, 1981, 77−86); A. R. WHITE, *The philosophy of mind* (New York: Random House, 1967).

PART II

Modes of Individuality

CHAPTER 6

PERSONAL BEING AS FORMAL UNITY: CONSCIOUSNESS

Theme: Consciousness and self-consciousness are analysed as ways of knowing, the former having prepropositional and propositional forms the latter only propositional. Neither are naturally occurring states, but are structures of belief deriving from certain (implicit) grammatical models.

Contents

1 STUDY OF CONSCIOUSNESS AS STUDY OF GRAMMAR

The primary organization of experience as centred on persons should be ubiquitous in all mankind by virtue of the physical necessities that corporeal embodiment in a world of things imposes on point of view. Extrapersonal experiences and intentions can be universally expressed by first person assertions of knowledge, by virtue of the syntactic necessities that action within a moral order imposes on the grammar of personhood as the locus of responsibility. If this is true then cultural relativity can appear only in the secondary structure of individuals when a transcendental self is introduced (or some other organizing principle) via a theory to organize one's knowledge about oneself and, by reflection, the objects of that knowledge, one's states, beliefs, feelings and so on themselves.

We now have reason to treat the sense of self as a local contingency, as a compilation of two basic synthetic unities, unitary features of psychic organization: point of view and point of action. Each has a double focus. The point of application of power is in the primary structure, where the person is located, while the point of origin of the power is at the culturally idiosyncratic source or apex of the secondary structure.

In this chapter I am concerned to develop an account of the organization of experience with respect to point of view, and its relation to the structure of cognition and emotion, as that is located in the secondary structure, the form of intrapersonal experience. Both point of view and point of action in the primary structure or public world of persons are reflected, I believe, within the secondary structure (and, I reiterate, only in our familiar cultures can we take the 'point' or pencil organization for granted as the object of analytical interest) and both require a sense of continuity in time. I will deal with the pedestrian issue of the founding of that sense in setting out the outlines of the analytical philosophy of personal identity. But the role of temporal continuity in the understanding of the structure of consciousness has played a very important role in phenomenology; see, for example, Husserl's delphic pronouncements on the 'I-pole' and 'temporality' in *Cartesian meditations*. Does the sense of continuity in time underlie personal unity or is it a consequence of a synthesis of experiences to become a unity? The thrust of my argument strongly favours the latter. However, the issue shifts from philosophical analysis to empirical research (*see* research menu 6). Whatever may be the priority amongst the elements of personal unity, the sense of continuity offers an experiential trajectory, so to speak, through which a person has at least the wherewithal for presenting himself to himself and others in an organized account of his own history, incorporating perspectives unique to the unified unities of point of view and point of action in both the primary and secondary structures.

To study point of view as a structuring element in the organization of intrapersonal experience, a study of consciousness is necessary, which will take us through conceptual analysis to the formulation of a prospective research programme. To study point of action, a conceptual analysis of agency is required, again with the hope of leading to a programme of research into the issue of what used to be called 'conation'.

It is my aim in these investigations to distil from the complex conceptual networks which we create in lay psychology to describe and control our personal thoughts, feelings, plans and actions, some structures sufficiently simple and robust, but not wholly inadequate to the subject matter, around which psychological research into personal consciousness could develop. Such research would not occupy itself with the physiological enabling conditions for a being to be conscious, nor would it be brought low by the aura of indiscipline and mystic revelatory confabulation that infects the treatment of consciousness in alternative psychology.

Is there an a priori element in the structure of consciousness, that is, in the way our extrapersonal and intrapersonal experience is ordered? We organize our experience around a supposed self, the core of a person, to which the world of intrapersonal objects of which we are aware and the actions we can perform are ultimately referred, *by virtue of the practice of self-ascription*. I feel indigestion in my midriff, on those rare occasions when more than usually gross self-indulgence brings it on, so geographically, so to speak, indigestion does not require a soul. Yet, in declaring it I do not predicate it of my stomach but of myself. In his Transcendental dialectic Kant tries to show that this deep organization is an artefact, but that it has a necessary (and hence by implication, universal) form. Again in this case anthropological and historical evidence suggests the contingency of the structure of the artefact we call 'conscious experience'. Even if Jaynes' claim (*The origin of consciousness in the breakdown of the bicameral mind*) to have identified the moment at which mankind invented self-consciousness as the experiential aspect of novel practices of self-ascription of responsibility for and sources of intentions to perform actions as sometime between the composition of the *Iliad* and the *Odyssey* is fantasy, the fact that his claim is clearly intelligible (and might conceivably be defensible) demolishes the necessary universality aspect of Kant's claim. To put it crudely, we learn to be conscious, and many amongst our fellow humans may learn to be conscious, to organize experience, in different ways.

The underlying philosophical argument is that when we learn to organize our organically grounded experience as a structured field, and cognitively as a body of beliefs built up of self-predications, we are deploying a concept of 'self' that functions like the deep theoretical concepts of the natural sciences, which serve to organize our experience and knowledge, whether or not they have observable referents in the real world.

This section of the study is not concerned with investigations of the enabling conditions of consciousness, for instance with what level of arousal in what cortical structures awareness appears, but with the description and exploration of structural features of consciousness, in particular of the fact that for each person, that which we are aware of, whether extra- or intrapersonally, is unified and ordered. We shall be trying to discover whether the forms of order are universal features of consciousness (and if any, whether it is by virtue of a semantic relation to what we mean by consciousness), and by what means people come to have them. Are they the result of physiological processes in human beings? Are they the product of a culturally distinctive system of belief? And so on. The case of human experience is complex, since it seems that there are both physiological conditions necessary for its existence and cultural schemata by which it is structured.

I shall try to show that the organization of our experience as 'centred' on self is derived from the organization of our talk about our experience in a discourse made up of speech acts having the form of self-predications, but with the function of expressing feelings, intentions etc. rather than describing selves. My aim is to show that the complex logical grammar of personal pronouns is reflected in the organization of our version of human consciousness, with its characteristic double level. There is awareness (knowing what [that] we are seeing, feeling or doing) and awareness of that awareness as ours (knowing that *we* are seeing, feeling or doing what it is we know we are seeing, feeling or doing). According to this view, 'consciousness' is the product of a complex interweaving of a perceptual—experiential structure and a conceptual—theoretical structure mediated by local grammatical forms as models of organization. It is not some third thing, function or state over and above these components. To understand consciousness then is just to understand these structures, their origin and function, and how they interweave with one another.

All forms of human consciousness will have 'person-centering' in that we perceive the physical world as an embodied being from a place in physical space and time, and we report to others on the view from where we stand by indexing our reports as the speech acts of this speaker. The public—collective concept of 'person' is all that is required both to create and to understand this form of structuring, which produces the structure, to borrow a phrase from the translator of Husserl's *eigenheit*, of 'a primordial sphere' together with an indexical use of pronouns or their equivalents. In this context the geometrical image is literal. To express what we know we are feeling, seeing etc., we use the performative sense of 'to know' — an avowal of rights to be sure and commitment to sincerity of utterance. But to know that I know what I experience as mine, a further conceptual structure is imposed upon our self-knowledge, by virtue of which we come to be able to report it *as* ours, in the light of our knowledge that it *is* ours. The logical form of such reports is perhaps as follows:

I_1 know that I_2 am aware of a tarantula.

In this chapter I shall develop an account of the conditions of use of this logical form, usually much condensed and abridged in colloquial speech. I shall be arguing that amongst the conditions for use is that the speaker should hold to a theory about him or herself, the central theoretical concept of which is a 'self' — the 'true' perceiver and knower — which allows a referent for the second occurrence of 'I' above ('I_2)', which is the 'self' as a hypothetical entity. To explain this, I return to the argument of the first three chapters in which the case was made for construing the 'self' as a theoretical concept derived from the social, that is the public – collective concept of 'person' in just the same way that theoretical concepts in the natural sciences are derived from existing concepts, which already have or are presumed to have an empirical application.

The first phase of the analysis will be devoted to establishing that consciousness has a relational structure, and that it is not a state, condition or simple property of either persons or things. It will emerge that this relational structure is manifested in the form of a kind of proposition, appropriate to attributing experiences to a person. From the standpoint of the basic analysis of consciousness the distinction between those intentional objects which are extrapersonal entities, for instance distinct things, and those intentional objects which are states of that person, that is intrapersonal entities, will play no role.

2   THE 'CONSCIOUSNESS' VOCABULARY

I begin with an exposition of some of the current uses of 'conscious' and 'consciousness'. Later, in the analytical phase of this study, I will introduce an alternative vocabulary which will prove to be more transparent and coherent, and capable of expressing most of that which can be expressed by the current uses of 'conscious' and 'consciousness'.

At least five distinct uses for 'conscious' stand out, but they do not form a metaphysically coherent system.

(1) In an assertion that a certain relation obtains between a person and an object, as for instance 'I became conscious of his hostility (a

light tapping at the window, a discomfort in my foot . . .)'. In ordinary usage there seem to be no obvious restrictions on the kind of entity (be it concrete material, abstract, subjective etc.) that can stand in a consciousness relation to a person. However, the 'left-hand' term is restricted to persons (including collectives) and some animals. When collectives are subjects of consciousness attributions, I propose to read such expressions as '*We* were conscious of . . .' as 'Each of us was conscious of . . .'.

(2) As a state or condition of a person, as in 'Bond remained conscious throughout the flight'. I take assertions of this sort to be referring to the obtaining of an enabling condition without which a person could not stand in any 'conscious of' relations to anything.

(3) In an assertion of a relation between a person and an abstract entity, as in such an expression as 'When Bond regained full consciousness he realized the hopelessness of his predicament'. I propose to treat this kind of sentence as an alternative way of asserting the obtaining of the person-enabling condition (2) above. The 'total' content of assertions like those of (2) and (3) also includes, I think, the obvious implication that the mind of the person involved was not blank, that in regaining or maintaining the relevant capability he or she was, willynilly, exercising it, and so was aware of something.

(4) In an adjectival qualification of mental contents, as in such expressions as 'Bond made a conscious effort to resist the drug', 'Portia had an unconscious wish to be a man' etc.

(5) In ascriptions of contents to a pseudo-space or mental arena, as in such expressions as 'As James Bond lay there a thought drifted into consciousness'.

Taken literally, these usages do not conform to a coherent metaphysical theory. Whatever the referent of the term 'conscious' and 'consciousness', it cannot be a two-place relation, a personal attribute, an attribute of thoughts and actions and a mental arena. Both (3) and (4) can be disposed of as alternative ways of asserting that a 'conscious of' relation obtained or did not obtain between an intentional object and a person, the subtleties of which need not detain us. The uses of this vocabulary reduce to the making of two kinds of assertions, related by the principle that the person – thing relations referred to in the latter can exist only if the person-state referred to in the former obtains.

In all discussions of personal psychology we must consider whether it makes sense to look for a physiological grounding or even a reductive replacement for a state or condition first identified in some other way. The consciousness relation and its terms could not generally be replaced by physiological descriptions since among the variety of intentional objects are many non-personal entities, such as mountains, sunlight, the plans, thought and feelings of other people and so on. Only a heroic solipsistic reduction of all these things to their effects on the sensibility or maybe the nervous system of each person in the whole population of mankind would justify such a reduction. But the person-enabling conditions for any such relation to hold could, in principle, be redescribed physiologically. For example, being awake is to be in a state which is an enabling condition for some 'conscious of' relations to obtain, and a physiological account of that state in terms of level of physiological arousal seems unproblematic, even as a reductive replacement for the concept in all our talk. The essential role of the prior phenomenological identification of the state of being awake, without which just that level of arousal could not have been picked out, could slip back into the social history and etymology of the new 'awake' concept.

However, there is a place for physiological descriptions to enter into discussion of 'conscious of' relations. I have introduced the notion of 'intentional object' without exploration or justification as a convenient generic term for the 'right-hand' elements of the pencil of 'conscious of' relations that can obtain between a person and a field of things. One must allow for the possibility that what one is aware of, which appears perhaps as a physical object, does not exist in the person-independent physical world. When one is aware of a hallucination, say of a visible thing, e.g. Macbeth's dagger, it could be said that one is aware of some physiological condition — but the physiological condition is presented under the concept of a physical thing (a dagger), not in its usual objective (that is, public) appearance as a misfiring of neurones. As far as our mental life is concerned it is modes of presentation, not material groundings, that count, but that priority could be reversed in some other way of dealing with experience, say, psychiatric medicine. The adoption of a less 'latinate' vocabulary than that built around 'conscious' will help to keep these issues straight. I turn now to such expressions as 'awake', 'aware' and 'attend', in terms of which I shall offer a thoroughgoing analysis of the remaining 'consciousness' vocabulary. The treatment I propose, though worked out independently, is encouragingly similar to that set out by Crook in *The evolution of human consciousness* (p. 313). See also his page 263 for a similar theory of the 'self' as a theoretical concept and its role in the construction of consciousness.

To eliminate all the uses of 'conscious' under (2) that I have identified as relational, two common terms seem to suffice, 'aware' and 'attend'. A. R. White, *Attention,* includes 'realize' in the eliminative analysis, but to introduce that term, takes us to a second stage of the refinement of awareness. When the 'consciousness'-enabling condition obtains, a person usually stands in a 'conscious of . . .' relation to a field of many kinds of intentional objects, and usually many instances of those kinds, to things heard, smelled, touched, seen, felt, imagined, concluded and so on. It is of such a field of things that I shall say a person is presently aware. At any moment some things stand out. To these I shall say a person 'attends', 'is attending', 'notices', 'is watching' etc. There are a number of complexities in this mode of talk brought about by the necessity to use both 'task' and 'achievement' verbs (Ryle, *The concept of mind*), as specific modes of attending. For instance, there is watching (listening) (a task spanning some time) as against noticing (hearing) (an achievement, coming about at an instant).

Following this suggestion, 'Is he still conscious?' becomes 'Is he still capable of being aware of or attending to anything?', and 'He became conscious of an ache' becomes 'He began to be aware of an ache', or, depending on just what happened, 'He noticed an ache'. 'Awareness' and 'attention', so I hope to demonstrate, are more transparent expressions than the corresponding 'consciousness' terms, and so their explication will help to clarify this complex and tangled aspect of personal being.

By replacing the 'consciousness' vocabulary with that built around 'aware' and 'attend' a more subtle conceptual system is now available to deal with self-reports.

(1) *'Aware of. . .' and 'aware that . . .'.* The use of the 'aware that . . .' locution depends upon the actual propositional formulation of the experience reported, and that in turn depends on the actual deployment of concepts adequate to identify and categorize the experience in question, to make it, so to speak, reportable. In many cases, exemplified by Wittgenstein's famous treatment of pain-talk, the first person utterance is not (or not primarily) a *description* of what one is feeling, but an expression of it (part of pain-behaviour). I argue that the 'aware of . . .' relation expresses a more primitive experiential state than that expressed in 'aware that . . .' locutions. The conditions under which transition to the 'that' form is possible will be introduced in the next section. It is possible to be aware of an unidentified and inadequately categorized 'something', and it is also possible to be aware of something which enters into experience in a practical rather than in a discursive context. A cat can, in this sense, be aware of a mouse while not aware that the object of its interest is a mouse. In animal thought, I believe, we have many cases of intentional states and actions, without intensions, that is, without the possibility of propositional expression.

(2) *'Attend to . . .' and 'notice that . . .'.* For the analysis of 'attention' we must go to Ryle's *Concept of mind* (ch. 6) and to the further

development of these ideas in White's *Attention* (ch. 2 and 4). According to White:

> The significance of 'attending' is that something has been made the centre or object or topic in regard to which we are actively busy or occupied, whether perceptually or intellectually, or even practically . . . Degrees of attention are not to be explained as more or less intense engagement in one specific activity, but rather as concentrating more or fewer of our activities on one object. (p. 7)

This analysis is in keeping with the conception of attention to be found in so called 'Eastern' practices, for instance in yoga psychology.

> 'Attending' is not a specific form of focussed awareness like looking at or listening to . . . It is a generic term for a variety of such focussed activities. The adverbial form as in 'reading attentively' refers to the exclusion of all else from awareness of what one is reading. (p. 7)

White argues that 'mere perception of something is not consciousness of it . . . we are conscious of something . . . only if it catches or holds our attention' (p. 60). He asserts that 'what we are conscious of is there or is so, and we know it to be there or to be so'. That a person can know that something is there or is so is not to be identified with our knowing that we know without distinguishing it is there or is so, nor does it entail that we can formulate what we know propositionally. From attention, we can sometimes pass to realization. This is the step from mere awareness to explicit propositional expression of what we know in experiencing. I take up this transition in the third section of this chapter.

The 'consciousness' vocabulary in German, like the Italian from which the word-family built around 'consciousness' comes (not from Latin directly, as might be assumed) treats conscious experience as a form of knowing. In so far as the vocabularies of English, German and Italian report the same matters, my cognitive treatment of the English synonyms is confirmed. The German term that comes closest to 'conscious' is *'bewusst'*. It is an adjective that can be used as adverb as well (which is true for most German adjectives). There are, unlike English, two antonyms, *'unbewusst'* and *'bewusstlos'* and, as a further difference, there are two related nouns, *'Bewusstheit'* and *'Bewusstsein'*. Equivalents for 'conscience' (*'Gewissen'*) and derived words exist too (cf. Old English 'inwit').

The verb 'to know' has two distinct senses in English: to be acquainted with and to know cognitively. The former corresponds to the

German '*kennen*', the latter to '*wissen*'. '*Kennen*' may take almost any kind of entity as object (in the accusative). In general it cannot take a clause as object. Clauses can be introduced only in expressions like '*Er kennt die Tatsache, dass . . .*' ('He knows the fact that . . .'); '*die Tatsache*' functions differently in German from 'the fact' in English, since the equivocality of 'to know' allows the English speaker to treat 'the fact' as redundant. '*Wissen*' is followed by a propositional clause or by a pronoun (in the accusative) standing for such a clause. Only some cognitive entities can be direct objects of '*wissen*', for instance, '*Regel*' (rule), '*Weg*' (way), '*Zeichen*' (sign), '*Zahl*' (number) and '*Lösung*' (solution).

In so far as '*bewusst*' retains the philosophical grammar of '*wissen*', it tends to suggest a propositional or 'reportables' view of consciousness, somewhat akin to Dennett's treatment in *Content and consciousness*. Both '*kennen*' and '*wissen*' have etymological relatives in English. There is the 'ken' of Scottish dialects, while '*wissen*' is related to 'wit', as in 'having one's wits about one' or 'doing something unwittingly'. But notice that to do something unwittingly does not imply that it has been done unconsciously, only unknowingly, i.e. not knowing what it was one did, though knowing one was doing something. The usual implication is that it was done unintentionally.

If one took '*bewusst*' as a second participle in analogy to '*gewusst*', one could (re-)construct a verb '*bewissen*' (approximately 'to know about') which does not exist in present German usage though it existed in the Middle Ages. Interestingly enough, even though the word '*bewissen*' seems to have disappeared, it has left traces — not only '*bewusst*' meaning 'conscious' but another that is often overlooked. That trace has kept the original meaning. In this sense '*bewusst*' does not admit of the translation 'conscious'. One may say '*Die bewusste Angelegenheit*' meaning 'the matter in question'.

According to H. Gundlach, to discussions with whom I owe this treatment of the German vocabulary, 'While it is known to etymologists that the Latin root "sci-" in "conscious" has the meaning "to know", the average English speaker is surely not aware of this. However, the relation between "*wissen*" and "*bewusst*" is still part of the sense of the word "conscious" to the average German speaker.'

3 GRAMMAR AND THE STRUCTURE OF CONSCIOUSNESS

Why does one's knowledge (as awareness) of something take a relational form? The relational form cannot derive from an empirical discovery that myself (or yourself) as perceiver is related to this or that intentional object as perceived. The perception just *is* the intentional object, not 'the perception of it'. For any such account to make sense, a third act of perception would be needed in which one perceived the self, the intentional object and that they were related. The characteristic form taken by reports provides both a clue and an explanation. The apparent relational structure of 'consciousness' is just the syntactical structure of reports as individual acts of expression in the primary structure, which are mirrored by the syntactical form of statements avowing experiences, claiming knowledge etc. I need to have mastered the syntax of *indexing* claims and interventions, confessions and so on as mine. But as myself as perceiver could never be an intentional object for me, my capacity to make first person reports, in the form of ascriptions of states or other attributes to myself, cannot require a concept of the first person achieved by ostension or reference.

The outcome of the analysis of 'aware of' and 'attend to' locutions is the general thesis that the psychology of consciousness is a part of the psychology of perception, including the perception of some of the states of the perceiver. In all perception we must acknowledge the intimate involvement of concepts, so that investigating that branch of psychology will include the disentangling of the implicit conceptual systems.

The main thesis to be tested is that prepropositional experience considered in this section is structured in the person — intentional objects form picked out by the relational concepts of reporting vocabulary ('aware of . . .' and 'attend to . . .') by the propositional grammar of the local language. Experience is prestructured in all sorts of practices (e.g. deixis) so that it becomes reportable (i.e. expressible) in propositional form, with subject and predicate, and not just through expressive exclamations, for instance 'Eek! a tarantula!'. Thus the 'aware of . . .' vocabulary is used to report experiences ordered in the form appropriate to 'aware that . . .' locutions, but that form is explicable wholly in terms of indexical force of pronouns and expressive role of experiential predicates.

The problem of the relationship between consciousness as perceiving and consciousness as knowing (that) is just that typified by the relation between 'see . . .' and 'see that . . .'. The objects of the latter are structured by the grammatical possibilities that determine propositional formations. It is for this reason that grammar determines the structure of awareness. The considerations by which the more general Sapir — Whorf thesis of linguistic determination of experience has been refuted have nothing to do with *form*. Colour discrimination has been shown not to depend on the range and inter-relationship of the colour terms in the lexicon of a tribe. To refute the thesis of this work it will have to be shown that the intimate structure of personal being is independent of available grammatical forms (*see* research menu 6).

Strawson, *Individuals,* has argued that the metaphysical basis of human individuality is closely connected to the role of the human body in locating a person's experience in the array of things. As embodied beings we are aware of a great variety of intentional objects which, in various ways, manifest themselves as independent things. The structure of this pencil of relations, from person to things, is centred on a whole person. So the referent of the P term in the $P_{\substack{o_1 \\ o_2}}$ etc. structure is not given in anything other than a thing-like location. 'I' need have no other function than the indexical to serve as the organizing element in this structure. The linguistic function of first person utterances is then comprehended under the principle that they are avowals, claims etc. that is, epistemic performatives, indexed for location in the array of persons. All this carries us no further than the primary structure. Assumptions of consciousness as self-awareness play no role in the understanding of 'mentation' in the primary structure of public−collective discourse. Claims to awareness or to be attentive to this or that nexus in the primary structure are not therefore required to be read as disclosures of the states or occupants of some inner realm, but function like any other public claims to knowledge.

While perception (knowledge of things, states of affairs other than oneself) is person-centred in a world of things in which point of view provides an experiential unity based on the thing-like embodiment of persons, knowledge of one's states is person-centred, in a world of persons, and the person as the common subject of predication is a location in the psychological pseudo-space or array of persons. But not all the intentional objects of personal awareness and attention are thing-based in the primary structure. The existence of thoughts, feelings, memories and the like in a non-spatial *structure* existing in some way other than as disclosures in the public−collective realm, must be accounted for, particularly as that structure, for people of our history, is also a *pencil,* but a pencil whose apex is not experienced. So the properties and origin of the secondary structure must form a part of psychology, and the concept of person, as it functions in the description of the primary structure, will not do as the occupant of the apex of the pencils that realize the secondary structure.

A person in a way yet to be explicated is a competent user of 'I' or the linguistic equivalent. Such a being stands in a one−many relation to a complex variety or field of actual and possible contents, which may have some further characterization. The states of a person realizing these relations are thus intentional, but they cannot exist unless certain enabling conditions are realized. The vocabulary of the expression of knowledge and belief as vouched for by a person in contributions to the public discourse includes expressions like 'aware of. . .' and 'attend to. . .' whose relational structure has syntactical rather than metaphysical significance.

According to Ey 'to be conscious is to live the uniqueness of one's experience while transforming it into the universality of one's knowledge' (*Consciousness*, p. 3). Thus every avowal of feeling, belief and decision will, for a conscious being, have a cognitive 'alternate'. The perceptual verbs I have made fundamental in my analysis of consciousness have their cognitive alternates thus:

> 'aware of. . .' goes with 'aware that. . .' and   (1)
> 'attend to. . .' goes with 'notice that. . .' (and others). (2)

The argument to come against Dennett's promiscuous proposition-alizing depends upon the claim that whether a proposition-forming operator 'goes with' an experience as in (2) is certainly contingent. I can see no reason for thinking it is any the less contingent in (1). We can be aware of something or even attending to it without being able to formulate the content of our experience propositionally, for any number of possible reasons, varying from the complexity of the experience to a lack of appropriate vocabulary. There must be non-propositional knowing to complete our map of perceiving and knowing. However, Dennett wants to introduce a special 'non-conscious' use of 'aware', namely 'aware$_2$ of. . .' to describe the way unattended cues are involved in the control of action. The perceptual apparatus is involved in the control of action when the actor cannot report having experienced the relevant cues, i.e. he or she was not conscious of them. Does it matter how we describe this phenomenon? Whichever way we describe it we must concede that Dennett sets this phenomenon in exhaustive and exclusive contrast to the kind of awareness the content of which a person could, in principle, report (*Content and consciousness*, p. 118).

Dennett's exclusive disjunction between the reportable and the non-conscious emerges as quite implausible when he uses it to give an account of the mental states of animals. The suggestion seems to be that animals are always in the condition we are in when we are unaware of a cue we have taken account of somehow in controlling our actions. This would require the assumption that for all human cases there is an available cognitive alternate for each and every perceptual experience, since that is what is needed to link consciousness, invariably, to an explicit linguistic formulation of the content of the experience, feeling, thought, etc. A cognitive alternate can be formed to express propositional knowledge only if the non-propositional knowledge is categorized with the help of a concept from the stock in hand. To put it briefly: one cannot see that something is the case unless that something has been seen as an instance of some category or other.

To defend the consciousness of animals it is necessary to show that it is implausible to assimilate their mental condition to that of the inattentive driver. Neither can report what they know. The inattentive driver cannot because he was not paying attention to what was passing, and White (*Attention*) is correct to insist that the driver was not conscious of the traffic conditions of which he is taking account somehow. The cat cannot report because he does not have the conceptual apparatus and linguistic skills to formulate statements. But we, as observers, are quite capable of noticing that the driver is attending to the argument he is having with the passenger rather than to the road conditions, while we can see that the cat is wide awake, alert and sharply attentive to his mouse.

There are many occasions in which the distinction between the creature using cues of which it is not aware and using cues of which it is aware but to which it is not attending can quite easily be made, by just the kind of observation which I would make of the driver of a taxi cab in a country where I was ignorant of the language and so could not judge from what he said what he was paying attention to. I need no linguistic entrée to his thoughts to be quite sure of whether he was attending to the traffic or not. Though the cat cannot speak, I can tell whether he too is attending to what he is chasing or merely inattentively taking it into account.

We have two vocabularies in closely related European languages which purport to describe the same range of psychological phenomena. English vocabulary can be reduced to a terminology for modes of perception and their enabling conditions, while German words are embedded in talk of modes of knowing. Knowing and perceiving are in thoroughgoing reciprocity with one another, as witnessed by the co-extension of the English and German vocabularies. The idea that there is some mysterious third 'thing', 'consciousness', which remains to be studied when perceiving and knowing have been investigated, is a mistake. Further, within English, there are two residual uses for consciousness words, that for modes of perceiving (e.g. 'aware of. . .') and that for the enabling conditions for modes of perceiving (e.g. 'awake'). Only the latter is obviously amenable to a physiological reduction.

When the notion of 'self-consciousness' is analysed, it turns out that, unlike consciousness which has both a perceptual and a cognitive manifestation, only a cognitive account will do. To be self-conscious is not to have a special kind of perception nor a special kind of knowledge, but to cast one's knowledge into a special form, the perceptual correlate of which is identical with the perceptual/cognitive content of simple consciousness, but the syntactical structure of which is more complex than that of the immediate cognitive correlates we have been studying in this section. In adopting the more complex form of expression, a new grammatical model or models become available for the organization of experience and thought.

4 SELF-CONSCIOUSNESS

Three different realms of knowledge and/or belief are referred to by this term:

(1) Beliefs about the beliefs which we suppose other people have of us, particularly with respect to how we appear in public — collective activities. What is most commonly meant by saying that someone is self-conscious is that they are painfully aware of bodily appearance, vocal performance and so on. (I deal with this phenomenon in more detail below.)

(2) By self-consciousness we may also mean 'meta-awareness' — what Adam Morton in 'Consciousness', calls 'the state of being aware of one's thoughts, perceptions and emotions', including one's beliefs. On the basis of this kind of awareness, we can form beliefs and make public claims to knowledge. There are perceptual and cognitive alternates for those declarations too. 'I was aware of noticing the bird' has as alternate 'I was aware that I had noticed a bird'; and 'I paid strict attention to the feeling in my muscles' has as a possible alternate 'I was aware that I had a certain feeling in my muscles' and so on. While the first or lasting occurrence of 'I' in the alternate locutions is the indexical of public declarations, what account should be given of the embedded occurrence of I?

(3) The items of which we are aware as our thoughts, feelings, plans, revisions etc. appear to us as organized. Again, to quote from Adam Morton's 'Consciousness' there is 'the system of states of mind which organize and coordinate thoughts and actions'. I propose to argue the nature and origin of this system by my account of the logical grammar of the embedded pronouns in declarations like those in (2) above. Ey calls Morton's 'system' '. . . the configurations of the order that the subject introduces into mental life by commanding a personal model of his world.' I hope to show that these 'personal models' are grammatical models or analogies of use through which the characteristic structures of our personal knowledge is created. For us the

structure is a relational pencil manifested in the expression of personal knowledge as predications of thought, feeling and action upon oneself.

Freud's genius was to provide the wherewithal to create a matching configuration in which to embed unordered insertions into the body of those personal events of which we are aware, by offering a structured corpus of supplementary beliefs, emotions, intentions and appropriate cognitive processes. When one tries the Husserlian exercise of trying to become aware of being aware of something, say the falling snow, little changes perceptually. Nothing new enters the visual field. But the exercise does seem to promote a transition, a change in what I take myself to know. The content of that intuition can be brought out with the cognitive alternate vocabulary, as, for instance, 'aware that I am aware of. . .'. Since 'aware that. . .' introduces propositions, there is the possibility that this item of self-knowledge was obtained by methods other than that by which the knowledge of what I am aware of at the first level is obtained, namely perceptually.

I take it that in the formulation of the iterated proposition the referential content of the original 'relational' proposition becomes itself an object of knowledge. While the referent of 'I saw a tarantula' is the tarantula, the referent of 'I am aware that I saw a tarantula' or more colloquially 'I know that I saw a tarantula' is the relation obtaining between 'I' (in a sense yet to be determined) and the tarantula.

'I', as perceiver, cannot stand in a 'perceived' relation to itself. To know about that which I know and to know it *as mine* must involve a cognitive act or operation other than perception. I propose the hypothesis that this level of knowledge is achieved through the deployment of an interpretative theory to explain the experience at the first, perceptual level. Thus my theory about myself is that I am not only a person among persons but centred on an 'inner core of being', that which 'has' all these experiences, initiates all these actions that at the first level are publicly avowed as mine, that is, located in the 'space' of persons just here. This explains how there can be a cognitive alternate

I know that I am aware of a tarantula

with no perceptual alternate other than 'I can see a tarantula' or 'Eek! A tarantula!'

In summary, a perceptual report can have *two* cognitive alternates, depending on whether the self-theory is implicit or explicit. In the case it is implicit we have the simple alternate, in the case it is explicit the iterative alternate. The 'I' usage is simple indexical in the simple alternate, but has just exactly the duality of indexicality and reference to a hypothetical entity described in the introductory remarks to this chapter.

Some of the force of the iterated form can be brought out by comparing the first person with second and third person cases.

I know that I am aware of an ant in my vest (1)

is, if the above argument is right, the only admissable iterated awareness statement. But

I am aware that (or know that) you are aware of an ant in your vest (2)

is the cognitive alternate of

I am aware of your being aware of an ant in your vest. (3)

While the basis of (3) is probably your squirming about and scratching, it seems to be clear that my squirming about and scratching cannot be the basis for (1). Rather, it would go something like this:

I have just become aware of a sharpish tickle and I have realized that there is an ant in my vest (4)

the second part of (4) being an interpretation (causal) of the first part. Someone as self-controlled as I am could very well be muttering (1) *sotto voce* and so not provide you with the evidence upon which you could say, rather haughtily, (3). (*See* White, *Attention* on the role of realizing in the conceptual system clustered round consciousness and knowing.)

While this makes clearer the proper sense of first person iterated awareness statements, it has methodological consequences for the empirical study of consciousness. No complete study of the phenomenon could be achieved by the use of behavioural criteria alone. This would require a thoroughgoing substitution programme in which first, second and third person pronouns were fully interchangeable. But this, as we have seen, is impossible. I can have criteria for deciding whether it was you or he who was aware of the ant in their vest, but by virtue of being aware of it, I know it. My knowledge does not depend on behavioural or any other kind of criteria.

In the form 'aware that. . .' there is no necessary implication that the awareness is of some intentional object. It is just that one knows something. So in the statement:

I am aware that I am aware of an ant in my vest (5)

the conscious state referred to in the second clause is the ground for the propositional attitude expressed in the first. So the empirical content of (5) is just

There is an ant in my vest. (6)

In the statement (6) above, if my awareness of the ant is nothing but my standing in a certain relation (namely '. . . aware of. . .') to an ant, then what I am aware of is the *ant*. So there is no abstract property 'awareness'. Any such sentence as 'I am aware of my awareness of A' can mean no more than the sentence 'I am aware of A'. In short my awareness of the ant is not an intentional object. It is no more than a kind of artefact pulled out of a grammatically distinctive but content-conserving way of talking about the fact that I know I have an ant in my vest and that I know that by feeling the wretched thing. There remains, however, the question of the logical grammar of the double use of the first person pronouns in the above examples.

So far I have argued that self-consciousness cannot be understood through the idea that I could stand in an 'aware of' or 'attend to' relation to myself as the centre of consciousness or source of action. The simple argument that that which is attending cannot be an object of attention is but a superficial consequence of the deeper-lying fact that the referent of 'I' is a hypothetical entity in so far as 'I' is a theoretical concept. While 'I' in the example below indexes the declaration as mine, the second occurrence of the first person (I_2 below) refers the common subject of the attribution of this and all other mental states or processes.

I_1 was aware that I_2 was paying attention to the game.

In a real conversation this sort of sentence might be used to perform the speech act of rebutting an accusation of lack of concentration.

In general, then, sentences of various forms, including 'I am aware of my attending to the pain in my foot' co-locate various matters at the same person in the array of persons that makes up a social world. If this line of analysis is correct, then the embedding phrase 'I am aware of. . .' and its cognitive alternate 'I am aware that. . .' (available in certain conditions) are propositional operators of the same kind as 'I believe that. . .'.

Expressions like 'I' not only serve as indexicals in person-space but also, I have argued, function like theoretical terms in scientific theories. Their role in personal psychology is to serve as the linguistic bearers of a self-centred way of organizing experience. The distinction I drew in earlier chapters between 'person' and 'self' can now be put to work to explicate the sense of those phenomena which seem to call for a reference to a core of being around which our experience as persons is organized, that is, to a supposed self. This line of thought suggests that 'self-consciousness' in this sense is just the realization a person might come to that his or her experiences are organized in a centred way, that some of their actions are their own responsibility and so on. Again we must note the duality between perceiving and knowing involved in any account of consciousness. To be self-conscious is to come to know how my 'mental life' is organized, but that knowing need not necessarily have been formulated propositionally, that is, it may not yet be true that I know that my experience is centrally organized. I may, for instance, display this knowledge in my sociolinguistic practices, my willingness or unwillingness to accept moral responsibility (*see* research menu 6) and so on.

If the referent of 'I' is a hypothetical entity and the concept of 'self' is a theoretical concept, it follows that 'I' need not be expected to pick out an individual entity disclosed in experience. Modes of organization are not individuals but structures. It also follows that no further components are required for the cyborgs proposed by such authors as Dennett in *Brainstorms* or Farrell in 'Design of a conscious device', to be self-conscious than that each should organize its experience in such a way that it is centred, and that it should have amongst its store the knowledge that it is so organized. It does not need to add an extra box, its 'self', nor any special connections among its modules.

But how is social learning involved in the acquisition of just this kind of theory? Two different but related social practices suggest this way of organizing our experiences. Others treat us as having a *point* of view, roughly as the physical centre of a sphere of things and events literally in space. But those same others also treat us as the centre of an expanding set of ripples of consequences of what we do, in making us members of a moral order, an order of beings who take responsibility for their actions and at least for some of their consequences. But why do we need the theory that we are selves? Why not just continue in the reproduction of the appropriate practices? Only if a person knows or believes that he is the author of his actions does it make sense for him to attend to the quality of his actions and the thoughts, emotions and projects with which they are connected as intentional objects on which he might operate. Thus the relational propositions 'I am aware of this action' and 'I am aware of my doing this action' become essential components in the management of moral orders. It is not surprising then that self-consciousness as a theory forms part of the cognitive equipment with which a person works in the social world. This argument implies that concepts of self as theoretical concepts will vary with the kind of moral orders within which persons are thought to act. But, as I remarked above, indexicality must be universal because unless a language made such uses possible people could not be beings capable of commitment and responsibility, even as members of collectives. There would be no moral orders and so no societies as we know them. But it is clearly a contingent matter whether a moral order includes the ideas of self-discipline, self-attention and self-improvement.

The final step needed to justify this account is to show that even in cases where the pronoun is standing for a logical subject rather than qualifying a state or experience as located at some point in the pseudo-space of person arrays, it is capable of an interpretation that does not need to assume the real existence of a mysterious self. In the exemplary sentence:

$$I_1 \text{ am aware that } I_2 \text{ am aware of a tarantula}$$

the pronouns stand for logical subjects, and the embedded sentence expresses the knowledge I have by virtue of my experience of a tarantula but with the extra ingredient of an indication that I know that it is my experience. A reader might be forgiven for finding sentences such as the one quoted above absurdly contrived. No one I suppose has ever uttered such a sentence. Why then is their analysis of any interest to anyone, above all to those students of the empirical, psychologists?

The sentence in question is clearly grammatically tolerable, put together out of standard components that might just conceivably have been uttered on some occasion. The role of such sentences as examples is to ground the explanation of the limits of the modes of logical grammar by which 'thoughts' of various kinds are constructed. Philosophical analysis of a contrived sentence of this kind enables us to explore the form of a possible thought; a thought in which experiences are not just labelled as mine (the use of a single indexical) but thought as labelled as mine. The capacity to form thoughts of this kind might be one of the things one has in mind in ascribing self-consciousness to a being, even though the thought may never take the form of the clumsy sentence in which it is expressed for study. Are there two subjects, contingently co-present, myself as public person and my 'inner being'? I have argued that the most economical account of the logical structure of the above is that the pronouns I_1 and I_2 are co-indexical, serving to locate the awareness at the same person who is indexed as speaker. But the embedding sentence is not merely the cognitive version of the embedded perceptual sentence, though by using it I am reporting no experience other than my awareness of a tarantula. I am doing explicitly what the embedded sentence, if used independently to make a statement, would do implicitly, that is, locating the experience within the pencil-like structure of my consciousness. I_2 refers to a 'true self' or 'inner being', the logical subject of mental state reports. But just as referring to the gravitational field brings the motion of the moon and a heavy object dropping from the leaning tower of Pisa within the same universal order, even if no existential referent can be secured, so I_2 can order the experience of a person even if its putative referent, the 'inner self' cannot be demonstratively located.

5 ALTERED STATES

The relational theory of consciousness would be undermined if one were forced to admit a literal reading of the phrase 'altered states of consciousness', or to admit the propriety of speaking of the unattended activities of a right-handed person's right cerebral hemisphere as in a 'second mode of consciousness'. I take the latter to be merely a metaphor for 'cognition'. The former implies a more serious threat to the grammatical – cognitive theory of consciousness.

The idea of growth and development of the ability to attend to various objects of which one is aware is implied in the discussions of the last two sections of this chapter. This suggests the possibility of further developments in consciousness beyond those levels that are the normal product of the social practices defining a culture. Recently, there has been a rash of talk about 'altered states of consciousness', particularly in fringe psychology, and along with it the promotion of various techniques by which these 'altered states' could be achieved. This idea has been formulated in a rather muddled way. For this study, the importance of these alleged experiences derives from the implicit theory of consciousness as a state or states. If there are properly 'altered states' then there are states to alter.

Examining the phenomena offered as instances of 'altered states', it becomes clear that they should properly be described by the use of the relational vocabulary. Those 'states' seem to be experiences of novel kinds of intentional objects or novel appearances of ordinary objects. For instance, in an 'altered state' a single vase may come to occupy the whole of one's awareness to the exclusion of all else. 'Altered states' may also involve differing degrees of attention to one's mode of being aware, altering the range of second-order intentional objects (*see* Lee and Ornstein, *A symposium on consciousness*). For a being to be conscious at all, the relational pencil from the self to a field of various objects of awareness, some of which can be attended to, must be maintained. The idea of 'altered states' can be systematized by examining possible points of change in the pencil. The state by virtue of which a person stands in the required relation to a field of intentional objects can change. For example, a person can be asleep or awake, drunk or sober. Considered relative to consciousness, these changes are consequential only as changing the range of possible relata, that is, the range of possible objects of attention. So far as I can see, even the spectacular changes reported by people who have taken psychedelic drugs are always changes in the range of possible objects of attention, and perhaps in intensity of concentration. Novel aspects of things become objects of attention. Though we would say that physiologically the drug affects the person, phenomenologically it is the range of possible objects of awareness that is changed. By 'altered states of consciousness' one must understand 'altered content of perception'.

Drug-taking is not the only technique for altering consciousness that has been suggested. There are all those practices subsumed under the misleading phrase 'consciousness training', including such techniques as 'transcendental meditation'. Again, it seems, changes occur in the range of intentional objects of perception. In transcendental meditation, as I understand it, one concentrates on (attends exclusively to) a single thing. In time one ceases to be aware of anything but that thing. Analytically, all this can be expressed in terms of change in the range of actual objects of attention and awareness. In extreme cases (if they really happen), such as those described by Casteneda in *The teachings of Don Juan*, both kinds of change occur. Casteneda's mentor, Don Juan, not only encouraged him to take drugs, altering the range of possible objects of which he could be aware, but trained him in attention techniques, so altering his capacity to attend to actual objects of awareness within those modified ranges.

Some further distinctions in what could be meant by 'altered states' can be made. If the alteration is considered transitively, in particular as a change in the range of actual and possible objects of awareness, then there is the possibility that a change may occur in how and when a particular entity is located in these ranges. An intentional object may be experienced as belonging to a kind to which it is not ordinarily assigned. Drug-takers' reports of synaesthetic experiences can be analysed this way I believe. They claim to experience colours as if they were sounds and emotional states as if they were attributes of the physical world, fear as a tempest, for instance. In this sort of context 'altered state' has to be understood cognitively. Experiencing fear as a tempest is an act of categorizing, as well as a state of feeling. (*See* also Becker, *Outsiders*, on the relation between belief and experience among drug-takers.) Finally, one should note the distinction between temporary and permanent 'changes in consciousness'. I take this distinction to be an obscure way of referring to the difference between those practices which alter abilities and capacities (say for reflexive attention) which would be permanent, from those which provide novel kinds of intentional objects or high degrees of concentration and attention, exploiting capacities a person already has.

The alleged 'altered states' induced by transcendental meditation provide a third case. Typically, in these experiences the meditator concentrates attention on one of the set of intentional objects of which he is aware and finds that after some time two kinds of changes have taken place. In the first, presupposing still a distinction between perceived and perceiver, the original object of attention comes to occupy the whole field of awareness of the meditator, excluding all other intentional objects. In the second phase, the distinction between perceiver and perceived dissolves, that is, the traditional mode of organization of experience as centred on a 'self', concentric with the person, fades.

In the first phase the changes can be accommodated within the scheme of awareness – attention concepts I have introduced already. The second phase can be understood in terms of the use (and disuse) of culturally specific self-theories in terms of which persons organize their experiences relative to local concepts of 'self'. Adepts of 'altered state' techniques talk of 'dissolving the self' or sometimes of 'decentering experience'. By this they cannot mean breaking up the unity of conscious. It is not a matter of fact that I can be aware of the items of only one 'sphere of consciousness' and that I can remember only those things which I have experienced. These prohibitions touch the deep grammar of the concept 'person', 'aware' and so on. I have argued that an important species of self-consciousness is knowing that certain experiences and states are one's own, a cognitive achievement facilitated by the possession of a theory of oneself as a unified being. The most economical account of 'dissolution of self' experiences is that in the drugged or meditationally induced condition a person temporarily loses their capacity for higher order cognitive activity, including the capacity to deploy the central theoretical concept of their own being. A thought of the form

> Person is aware of intentional object

does not directly involve one's self-theory while

> Person knows that this person is aware of an intentional object

does.

In an 'altered state' the latter cognitive structure may be hard or even impossible to form. The 'dissolution of self' is a temporary cognitive incapacity, not at all to be confused with the selflessness of one who puts the interests or welfare of others before his or her own. Just this confusion is much in evidence in fringe psychology. In neither case is there something special left over, 'consciousness', whose changes we are allegedly recording. (I owe notice of this distinction to an anonymous contributor to a discussion at the University of East Anglia.)

6　SELF-CONSCIOUSNESS AS STAGE FRIGHT

The self of which one is peculiarly aware when one describes oneself as 'self-conscious' is oneself as a person, embodied and public — collectively, that is, socially defined. I shall argue that self-consciousness is a form of knowing or believing.

I take the essence of self-consciousness to be the *belief* that one's physical appearance or one's overt performance and public person is or might be judged to be not as it ought to be in the setting and with the kind of persons one believes oneself to be acting. The normal intentionality of actions in which they are thought as ends or outcomes is suspended and the self-conscious actor focuses on the actions he or she is performing, bringing on that characteristic incapacity in performance we call 'stage fright'. In attending to one's accent, dress and so on, one is acquiring data for assessment according to what one believes to be the standards of others. It is only the existence of the social matrix with its presumed practical, moral and aesthetic standards that provides for the possibility of entertaining the thought that in the 'eyes of others' one might be falling below par. But to assess someone's performance, including one's own, relative to a standard, cannot be a matter of perception, it must be a matter of judgement. The psychology of this condition is made more complicated still by the fact that the very entertaining of the thought that one may not be up to the mark is likely to adversely affect one's performance, and so bring about its own fulfilment. (*See* research menu 6 for suggestions for research into the emotion characteristic of self-consciousness, namely embarrassment.)

Though the empirical referent of the cognitive state is one's public person, the transcendental unified self as actor and ultimate author of one's actions, is also involved, since it is of oneself in that sense that final moral assessment is made. As the author of one's actions one is responsible for them, and so *a fortiori* one is compromised and humiliated by one's public failure just as much, and often more than one is uplifted by one's public successes. Again, this is cognitive. It is to submit oneself to moral judgement, but one that is based on the performance of the public person, who is a member of a collective. The target of moral criticism is, for people who have acquired our kind of 'self'-theory, the 'inner core of personal being', embodied in cognitive structure and grammatical practice.

7　SUMMARY OF THE ARGUMENT

We have now established that the unities of consciousness, by reference to which we assign experiences to ourselves as persons, can be accounted for neither subjectively by reference to experience nor physiologically by reference to some structural property of a cyborg representing our cognitive capacities. Throughout the discussion we have been pressed towards the conclusion that the 'self' is a theoretical *concept* by means of which we organize our experience into the unities presented in the analysis, that is, into a co-temporal field organized as a pencil and a life-continuum organized as a trajectory from the past through the present to the future. Where does such a theory come from? According to Mead in *Mind, self and society* it arises in social interactions with others. But so far as I can follow Mead's argument, his 'self' is not what Ashworth, in *Social interaction and consciousness*, has happily called 'the continued tacit "presence" at the horizon of perception' but that which psychologists call the 'self-concept', a belief about the *kind* of person one is. The 'self' of this chapter is he or she who perceives acts, has beliefs and so on, and can be neither Mead's 'I' nor 'me', and whose organizing presence is required by both of them.

I claim that the 'self' is acquired as a generalization and abstraction of the public person-concept, that is, in use in the public − collective discourse of a community by a slide from one grammatical model to another, initiated by certain social/linguistic practices. As a theoretical concept, 'the self' stands in a peculiar relation to 'the person'. The latter is materially grounded by reference to the human being as a kind of thing, with all kinds of properties. The relation between two such concepts is familiar in the analysis of theory-families in the physical sciences. In the dynamic process by which theorizing structures evolve, the central conceptions can be usefully seen as derived by some sort of analogical reasoning from a source, which among other things involves natural kind rules specifying the metaphysical status of approved entities. A source model then controls the construction of theoretical concepts and so determines the content of an explanatory model. So the concept of the Newtonian particle controls the content of the explanatory concept 'molecule' in kinetic theory, in particular by specifying the natural kind rules to which it must conform. In this way it is possible to construct a meaningful concept before dealing with the question of whether that concept has any real world referent. Such a concept is built up within a discourse, a semantic process impossible in an empiricist theory of meaning. If 'self' is this sort of concept, no wonder Hume could not find the corresponding impression.

In my view the public − collective concept of 'the person' as explicated in the analysis of personal identity, is the source model for the construction of an explanatory concept with which we organize experience, specifying its natural kind as a unity of spatiotemporally continuous point of view and point of action. The criteria for identity of selves are then no other than those for persons — but these can be applied only public – collectively, not subjectively. It is not surprising then that the referent of the concept 'the self' can never be experienced, that is, that the self cannot be discovered empirically, by 'looking into' oneself.

In terms of the defining concepts of the location of psychological phenomena we have a picture roughly as in figure 6.1. Since the pronoun system figures in the discourse of both quadrants 1 and 3, the simplest hypothesis would be to suppose that the medium by which the self-concept is abstracted from the public person-concept is that very system. If it could be shown that a condition for acquiring the use of 'I' were the capacity to use 'you', 'he', 'we', 'Mary', 'John' etc., then the hypothesis would be well founded.

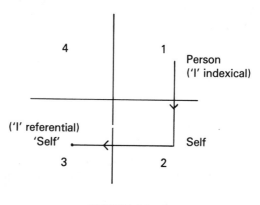

FIGURE 6.1

But the system of pronouns is embedded in various practices such as pointing, acquiring, blaming and praising. The associated research programme of developmental psychology would require a study of the language games involved in the acquisition of the personal pronouns for such various practices as those above, for instance deixis, the acquisition of the practice of pointing *from* oneself *to* a thing. Research into some of the relevant practices has begun but, with the exception of the work of Bruner, not controlled by the idea of 'language game' (*see* research menu 4). Research in the field is made more interesting by virtue of the cultural diversity of language games, and so possibly of systems of self-reference of differing strengths. The work must be related to the theory of moral development, since the language games of praise and blame, assignment of responsibility, repudiation of agency etc. are likely to be involved.

8 CONSCIOUSNESS WITHIN A CYBERNETIC APPROACH

So far, the conditions that have to be satisfied by a being to enable it to stand in a consciousness relation to a set of actual and possible intentional objects have not been very fully worked out. It seems to me that they fall into two main ranges of possibility. There are the cybernetic/physiological conditions that determine the 'soft-ware/ hard-ware' basis for some kind of mental activity, and there are the phenomenological/ontological conditions, determining the cultural, linguistic and social being of conscious entities. For the former we look to cybernetics, for the latter to Kant and his philosophical descendants. The ultimate constraint is that each of these explains, in its way, the singularity and unity of the person as they experience themselves and their thinking and acting. Something of this constraint seems to have been seen by Dennett in the preamble to his cybernetic account in *Brainstorms*.

General adherence to a theory of token identity between mind-states, processes etc. and corresponding brain-states, requires that the scientific framework for treating of consciousness must be the cybernetic rather than the physiological. Only cybernetic concepts could have any chance of generalization from one person to another and from one period of a person's life to another. Mental 'sameness' must be defined in terms of cognitive functions, and they may be performed by rather different physiological 'machinery' in each person, and in the same person at different times.

To understand the import of a scientific theory of an observable process, we need to bring out both its explicit and implicit content. A theory is explanatory if it describes a hypothetical generative mechanism whose behaviour simulates the behaviour of the real world mechanism it represents, and whose structural and other properties are controlled for plausibility by a fairly restricted source model. Swarms of molecules simulate the behaviour of real gases, and are themselves defined by abstraction from what we take to be the real properties of material things. Two explanatory theories are on offer, differing in the source model to which they refer back for plausibility.

The Tart theory

The physical source model is that of electrical resonance and standing waves. Consciousness as an enabling attribute of a person is some form of energy which has the same kind of persistence as does resonance in an electrical circuit. At best, this models an enabling condition; it goes no way at all to represent the physical basis of awareness and attention.

The Farrell/Dennett theory

This theory involves a storage box from which impulses go to an executive box. In Farrell's version the executive box prompts some suitable
kind of action; in Dennett's the propositional theory of consciousness
that he adopts a priori requires the executive box to be the speech-
production mechanism. Farrell's machine is based upon learning sub-
machines, which would work by evaluating inputs through criterial
boxes, the output of which are fed back and stored with the results of
past actions. Two such machines linked end-to-end allow for the
reconstruction of the store and, according to Farrell, for the modelling
of certain features of consciousness.

Dennett's cybernetic model in *Brainstorms* is based upon the idea of
three kinds of access to information by a 'thinking and acting' individual. There is personal access, defined by Dennett as 'consciousness'; there is computational access, needed information, much
of it *in* me but not accessible *to* me; and finally, there is public access.
In explicating the first sort of access, Dennett sets up a strong connection between consciousness of something and its reportability 'at least
to a first approximation, that of which we are conscious is that of which
we can tell' (*Brainstorms*, p. 152). Dennett, like Farrell, attempts a
subpersonal account, setting up a structure of person-components
necessary for certain kinds of functioning that are found in consciousness. In particular, he introduces a short-term relation between a
'memory hold box' and 'a speech production box', called 'M'. To be
aware of something is to have it in M.

To try to fit this model to our analysis we need to say that an object
(be it identifiable as intentional or no) can stand in the consciousness
relation to a being, one of the components of which is such a set of
boxes, if, and only if, the object is held at the pre-speech stage. But this
condition, whatever else one would want to say about it, confines objects of consciousness to representations of real world things, rather
than the things themselves. Secondly, it seems that Dennett requires
that objects in the pre-speech box be 'speakables', but what if the
speaking machine cannot cope with such a thing? Was it not really an
object of consciousness? The only way out would seem to be to define
the 'speakability' of the object as related to some ideal language and not
the actual language of the speaker, but this upsets the original thesis that
identified M as the box adjacent to the person's speaking box, not by
reference to the ideal computational language of the cyborg.

The unity of consciousness as a single field is not represented except
accidentally in the cyborg. There could be two M-boxes, M1 and M2,

each adjacent to the speech box S, and which fed 'speakables' into the box, S, determined by a randomizing device. Being in M1 or M2 would fulfil Dennett's conditions, but since M1 and M2, by hypothesis, do not overlap, there is no necessary unity of consciousness.

The relation of each field of consciousness being necessarily to one and only one person, the transcendental condition on the structure of fields of consciousness as a pencil of relations cannot be represented in either the Farrell or the Dennett cyborg. Whether further structural features could mimic that condition is not clear. As I have argued, that condition is created by the social relations of the conscious beings to a society with certain kinds of practices, which involve, among other things, the acquisition of a theory whose central concept is that of the transcendental ego or knowing/perceiving/acting self. Having learned such a theory, a cyborg would become capable of self-predication, and would have achieved at least a necessary condition for self-consciousness (in the cognitive mode). But this condition does not reflect a structural property of the organization of the modules of the cyborg, but the content of one of the programmes with which it might or might not be endowed.

In Farrell's version of the conscious cyborg in 'On the design of a conscious device', the boxes represent learning and identifying machines. A learning machine, I_1 is devised as in figure 6.2. An 'identifying as' machine, I_2, is created by repeating the machine given in figure 6.2 but allowing for items from store in I_1 to be compared with items from I_2, and only if matched by these to pass through a master evaluator to action (reactivity mode.) I_2 is functionally

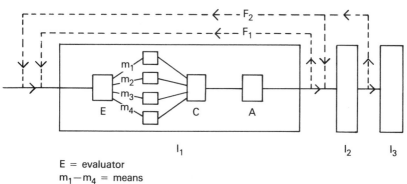

E = evaluator
$m_1 - m_4$ = means
C = classifier
A = action box
F_1, F_2 feed back loops

FIGURE 6.2 (after B. Farrell)

equivalent to a young child of whom we would use 'consciousness' words, 'aware', 'know', 'sees' etc. I_3 is created by adding a third, similar, machine. I_3 represents the state of I_2 as a state of itself, e.g. 'wanting'; we can then add second-order reactivity: 'I want (my coat)'. This system (a) has awareness, but does not have attention; (b) could not fall asleep; (c) does not have *self*-monitoring, i.e. cannot represent I_3 within I_1 or I_2.

However, neither version of this theory admits of a representation of a *unity* of consciousness. The items in M, the memory box, are merely *in* M, not linked necessarily *to* M. Characteristically, consciousness is a pencil of relations centred on me, unified not by any common property of 'my-ness' which each object of awareness so related exhibits, but by virtue of the common centre of the pencil. According to my view, that common 'centre' is a concept, not an object.

Could we pursue the cybernetic strategy a little further, to see if there were some common structural property which would identify all those kinds of things which could be the singular relata of sets of intentional objects? It is not unreasonable to suppose that persons, animals and some kinds of machines have similar information-processing structures. Ought they to be counted as possibly conscious beings? But Dennett's and Farrell's cybernetic analogues could not represent the unity of consciousness by any hook-up of subpersonal components. So the empirical discovery of a common structural feature in all those beings to which we might be inclined to attribute consciousness, as an enabling condition for standing in 'aware of' relations, shows at most that the common structure is a necessary condition for consciousness.

9   WEAKNESSES IN THE PHENOMENOLOGICAL THEORY OF CONSCIOUSNESS

Even if the 'self' is beyond experience in the special sense that as a theoretical entity it is neither perceptible nor imperceptible, perhaps my thoughts are marked or indexed as mine. This idea, I believe, lies behind the phenomenological assault on the problem of understanding consciousness. This is to be contrasted with the theory that I have been expounding, which requires that *I* mark my thoughts, feelings, actions and so on as mine according to culturally distinctive conventions.

The phenomenological approach could be defined by contrast to the ethogenic by returning to Kant's remark about the role of 'cogito', 'I think'. He says of this phrase, 'But it can have no special designation, because it serves only to introduce all pure thought, as belonging to consciousness' (B 400). According to the social construction thesis 'I think' indexes a 'thinking' as that of a particular person, that is, displays its location in the social pseudo-space of the person array, be it private or publicly expressed. There is a field of consciousness at each such location (that is, people do indeed perceive and know things), hence the indexicality function of 'I' is all that is needed to explicate the labelling function of 'I think'. No references to an inner theatre, nor to an inner thinker are involved. But the phenomenological treatment can, 'I think', be seen as an attempt to discern some attribute of intentional objects that, as it were, empirically mark them as mine, as elements of my field of consciousness: something to be discovered rather than something to be imposed.

As far as I can understand Husserl's procedure (in *Cartesian meditations* V, and *Husserliana*, 15) the search for that which identifies an intentional content as mine begins by the 'thematic epoche', that is, by my examining my experience *as if* there were no other persons. This is done by not attending to the ways by which others are presented as persons in my experience. In this way I would reach the *eigenheit* or primordial sphere, that which is properly my own. According to Husserl this move excludes what is given to the consciousness of the other, and 'serves to deny that He and I are the same' (*Cartesian meditations* V, S46). Now all ways in consciousness of referring to the other as a person would be excluded. So what is primitive is my consciousness or at least its contents. We have yet to see whether there is now a residual quality which displays it as mine, that is, as *of* a person. Could it be derived by seeing myself as another?

Other people appear through appresentations. According to Husserl, my experience of others as persons is not by perception, nor by reasoning. It is not a judgement. Just as things appresent their uses (scissors their power to cut), so human bodies appresent themselves as 'lived'. Confirmation of this derives from the harmony of interpretation, as interpretative totality, that comes when we have at least a minimal experience of others as persons. In short, Husserl does not really have a theory of consciousness; the primordial sphere is merely given. Husserl is really presenting his readers with a theory of persons.

Schutz's well-known critique of Husserl's project depends upon realizing that the way my embodiment is given to me experientially is quite different from the way the body of the other is given. So the foundation for appresentation cannot be any analogy between the way I experience myself as embodied and the way I experience you as embodied. By defining the primordial sphere negatively by screening off everything which is indicative of the other, the experience of the other no longer refers to the other. Thus appresentation, at the level of the primordial sphere, fails.

We must now turn to the final reduction by which I try to expunge from experience all marks of the contents of consciousness as mine. In this way we can discover just what these matters were by which the components of the *eigenheit* were labelled as mine. This is the centre-piece of Husserl's Paris lectures, published as the *Cartesian meditations*. Koestenbaum, *Edmund Husserl: the Paris lectures*, offers an elegant summary of this stretch of the argument in his introduction to a translation of the lecture text:

> To understand Husserl we must grant that there is in experience a unique element which can be described, roughly, as the I-pole . . . the existence and nature of which is found in the fact that the careful scrutiny of the given in the experience of objects discloses one pervasive and central truth: every object is given or presented to us as an object-for-a-subject . . . the transcendental Ego . . . is not given as an object, but as the object for which an object manifests itself . . . it is a ubiquitous single centre or pole from which emanate the 'radiations' of consciousness and intentionality. (p.21)

This account requires that experience presents itself as having a basic structure, a vectorial quality. This is Husserl's 'pure intentional look'. This quality remains after the first bracketing or transcendental reduction of experience, which enables us to examine the structure of that experience, which is revealed as vectorial. In the terms in which I have been discussing Husserl's theory, the ultimate mark of experience as mine is to be found in the vectorial quality of experience, which by a further turn is linked to (or maybe identical with) temporality. At first sight, 'temporality' does not seem to be the same vectorial quality of the relation of all experience to the I-pole which was supposed to found the claim for the transcendental ego.

The link comes out like this: (Husserl in Koestenbaum's *Edmund Husserl*, p.26) 'the central ego is not an empty . . . pole, but . . . in virtue of the rules of genesis, it experiences, with each act that radiates from that ego, a lasting determination.' It is 'the enduring subject of persistent convictions.' In this way temporality and the I-pole vector are linked.

There is nothing in this that contradicts the position I have been expounding, but there is one profound difference. Whereas Husserl proposes to find 'I-pole vectors' and 'lasting determinators', like Kant I suggest these features appear in human experience because I, a person, have put them there. In learning to be a self, I learn to organize my experience as a pencil from an I-pole, and as well to synthesize it as the continuous history of one and the same being.

10   EXISTENTIALIST 'CONSCIOUSNESS' THEORY:
J.-P. SARTRE

Sartre's theory of consciousness is embedded in a naïve and vigorous positivism. He begins his major work, *Being and nothingness*, with this remark: 'Modern thought has realized considerable progress by reducing the existent to a series of appearances which manifests it.' A little later he says 'No action indicates anything which is behind itself; it indicates only itself and the total series (presumably of actions like itself).' Thus far, Sartre, Hume and Mach are at one.

His theory of consciousness is based on two concepts that appear to be fundamental to Sartre's account: being-for-itself and being-in-itself. It is in the explication and application of these notions that Sartre differentiates his view of consciousness from the idealism to which, as Berkeley demonstrated, a positivism of appearances is particularly prone. Consciousness is a matter of the former, being-for-itself, and phenomena of the latter. According to Sartre, though they are united in act, that is, we are conscious of all sorts of things, they are realms without communication in theory. What is the solution? To put it in Anglo-Saxon terms, how can one be conscious of something that exists whether or not one is aware of it? I think that the practically impenetrable meaning of the Sartrean treatment in Part II of *Being and nothingness* can be clarified if we subject the central statement (p. 75) to the same translation procedure I used for elucidating the English usage: '. . . we are obliged to admit', he says, 'that the consciousness (of) belief is belief.' I think this is equivalent to our own observation that 'I am aware that I am aware of a tarantula' has as its sole content my perceiving a tarantula, of which the tarantula in question is the only intentional object. My awareness of a tarantula is not an intentional object of some second-order awareness. Rather, the embedding sentence expresses in the cognitive mode what the embedded sentence, if it appeared alone, would express in the perceptual mode, and both express what is expressed by the exclamation 'Eek! A tarantula!'. If we slip into thinking that both 'Is' in the above are referential to 'the self' say, then Sartre objects in the words 'the self does not designate being either as subject or object' . . . 'the self cannot be apprehended as a real existent . . . coincidence with self causes the self to disappear' (p. 76).

The key to understanding Sartre's position is to be found in the remark 'Thirst refers to the consciousness of thirst, which it *is* as to its foundation' (p. 82). To be thirsty is to be conscious of a certain state, namely that of being thirsty. But the prefix 'conscious of . . .' is not dispensable, since it shows how it is that while my canary and I are both thirsty only I can stand in such a relation to that thirst that I *can* come to know that I am. And this, I think, shorn of its bizarre rhetoric, is just the doctrine of common contents I have argued for above.

Sartre comes close to making a distinction between 'self' and 'person' along the same lines as I have advocated, but falls short of an adequate ontology. His positivistic presuppositions prevent him from deploying the notion of 'theoretical concept' as a non-reducible component in a conceptual structure, whether or not it refers to a real entity. Thus his account of shame just fails to gel. He explains shame by the use of the exemplary sentence 'I am ashamed of myself as I appear to the other'. I would like to mark up this sentence as follows: 'I$_1$ am ashamed of *myself* as I$_2$ appear to the other'. Indexed this way we can see that the use of such a sentence would be partly in contexts determined by the public – collective concept of 'person' as I have defined it; that is 'I$_1$' and 'I$_2$' are co-indexicals. To understand the force of '*myself*' in such uses, I think one must treat it as a fusion of two root ideas, that of person in the public – collective sense and that of self in the sense of noumenal author of that person's actions, that is, in the sense of my notion of the self as a theoretical concept and hypothetical entity. I, myself, am the author of my actions, so I, as public person in a moral order, can be ashamed. Sartre seems to see this complexity but does not draw the ontological consequence that J.-P.S. as person is one sort of being, while J.-P.S. as the author of his actions must conceive himself to be another. While only J.-P.S. in the former sense is an actual existent, he needs the concept of J.-P.S. as an inner self to account for how he organizes his experience, including his emotions, such as shame. In the text from which I am quoting, Sartre notices that J.-P.S. as person is given in experience ('for it is as an object that I appear to the other'), but his positivism prevents him from seeing that there is a distinctive theoretical concept at work in these contexts which is not reducible to that experience or concepts descriptive of it. While one wishes to applaud Sartre's aim of eliminating the transcendental ego as a real being, the concept of such a being is ineliminable, since it is only by use of it that we can succeed in generating *our* structured consciousness.

Perhaps 'en-soi' and 'pour-soi' could be explicated as two kinds of reflexivity. In the former there is pure identity between the terms of the identity relation, 'A is A'; while in the latter, there is only a mediated identity, 'A is *A*'; so that though the content of the terms is indeed the same, their modes of presentation are different, in my terms as knowledge and as perception.

RESEARCH MENU 6

(1) Developmental aspects: There are two major research areas opened up by this treatment. What are the grammatical models available in mother – infant symbiosis, involved in the language games of that sort of inter-action? For instance, according to what 'deep' grammatical rules do proper names function in 'motherese' and in early infant talk, and with what practices (such as deixis) are they involved? There has been a noticeable absence of 'language game'-style research in this area. The rapid substitution of 'I' for e.g. 'Mary' as an indexical suggests that 'I' first subserves the same function as the proper name in self-expressive acts. The pronominal difficulties of autistic children point to the correctness of the basic idea that these grammatical models are involved in the structuring of experience and self-knowledge.

The second research area requires a longitudinal study to assess the hypothesis of the acquisition of the duality of function of 'I' etc. by the ad-dition of the second grammatical model in which the 'self' is implicit as a theoretical concept and 'I' takes a referential as well as an indexical force.

It has been suggested by an informant whose name I failed to record that late and difficult language learning, particularly the use of pronouns, and other self-indicating and self-referring expressions, can be correlated with deficiencies in the grasp of the idea of personal responsibility, confirming the extension of the idea of 'self' as theoretical concept to be proposed in chapter 7.

But there are people who acquire a mode of cognitive organization without benefit of the early appearance of linguistic models in their psychological symbiotic 'completions'. These are the deaf mute. The importance of the language game idea, the inter-relatedness of semiotic system and social practice is shown again by these cases, since their modes of cognition, affection and other personal organization will be derived from the practices alone. This introduces a useful dimension of difference by which the general constructivist thesis of personal being could be investigated.

(2) The theory of self-consciousness raises a very different range of problems requiring research. Since the phenomena of self-consciousness are dependent on the tribe holding a certain theory, mediated by the personal pronouns and their associated language games, two directions of research suggest themselves:

(a) What social uses do people make of the various kinds of self-reference allowed for in the theory? Very little research on this issue has been attempted (cf. Mischel, *The self*). I suspect this is largely because outside clinical psychology the fact that psychically oriented speech is directed to the moral order is usually ignored (cf. Fisher, 'Logic and language of defences').

(b) How far do different pronominal systems and their associated ethnographies bear out the central thesis that concepts of the self are relative to the predominant *social* language games, and so vary with the local person-concepts? Cross-cultural work on the 'self' concept has often been vitiated by lack of attention to the actual language games of self-reference which predominate in a culture. The organization of mental activity as thought must be partly associated with the capacity to handle expressions such as 'I know', 'I think', 'I believe' etc. When, and in what language games, is a secure use of these or equivalent expressions established?

BIBLIOGRAPHICAL NOTES 6

Despite the fact that the study of consciousness has not been on the agenda for research of establishment psychology for some half a century, a considerable literature exists, which I divide into five parts:

(1) *Phenomenology*: writings in this genre have typically concerned themselves with 'contents of consciousness', by what marks we distinguish various categories of experiences, e.g. R. H. HOLMES, 'Consciousness revisited' *(Research in Phenomenology*, 8, 1978, 191−201), which gives further analysis of the theories of Sartre and Husserl. There has also been a considerable emphasis on time in personal experience in phenomenological writings, starting with Husserl himself, cf. the sketchy remarks in E. HUSSERL, *Cartesian meditations* (Meditation IV, The Hague: Martinus Nijhoff, 1973).

(2) *Fringe psychology*: three issues have exercised these writers. First, the distinctive kinds of mentation of the right and left hemispheres, cf. R. F. ORNSTEIN, *The psychology of consciousness* (Harmondsworth: Penguin, 1975, ch. 3). Secondly, phenomena called 'altered states' of which the most important author has been C. TART 'Altered states' (in *The metaphors of consciousness*, ed. S. Valle and R. von Eckartsberg, New York: Plenum Press, 1981); though there has also been a rash of romantic literature, typified by C. CASTENEDA, *The teachings of Don Juan: a Yaqui way of knowledge* (New York: Simon and Schuster, 1973). Thirdly, there is a literature on 'consciousness training' closely connected with the material on 'altered states'. From a truly vast literature I select S. VALLE and R. VON ECKARTSBERG (eds), *The metaphors of consciousness* (New York: Plenum Press, 1981), as some of the many facets of that movement. For the relation between altered states and beliefs see H. S. BECKER, *Outsiders: Studies in the sociology of deviance* (New York: Free Press, 1973).

(3) *Analytical philosophy*: the logical grammar of the 'consciousness' vocabulary has been explored by several authors beginning with G. RYLE, *The concept of mind* (London: Hutchinson, 1947). A. R. WHITE, *Attention* (Oxford: Basil Blackwell, 1964), despite its relative age, seems to me to be still an excellent work. Influential too has been D. C. DENNETT, *Content and consciousness* (London: Routledge and Kegan Paul, 1969). The best recent study I have seen is W. PLOTKIN, 'Consciousness' (in *Advances in descriptive psychology*, vol. 1, eds K. E. Davis and T. O. Mitchell, London: Ajai, 1981, p.211). R. L. GREGORY in his recent *Mind in science* (London: Weidenfeld and Nicolson, 1981) takes: ' "consciousness" to be the same as "awareness"

and roughly the same as "sensation" ' (p.451), but he does not address the issue of the central organization of consciousness nor of consciousness as knowledge.

(4) *Neurophysiology*: a very good collection summing up a great deal of recent work is J. M. DAVIDSON and R. J. DAVIDSON, *The psychobiology of consciousness* (New York: Plenum Press, 1980); see particularly the contribution by K. H. Pribam. See also B. COONEY, 'The neural basis of self-consciousness' (*Nature and System*, 1, 1979, 16−31).

(5) *The unity of consciousness*, which must be a central problem for attempts to account for 'centredness' of experience, has been discussed by T. NATSOULAS, 'The unity of consciousness' (*Behaviorism*, 7, 1979, 45−63) and A. WARD, 'Materialism and the unity of consciousness, (*Analysis*, 40, 1980, 144−6), against embodiment as an adequate explanation of experienced unity. This paves the way for my proposal that unity is a cognitive construction on the basis of the holding of a theory. For a more phenomenological account, see R. ELLIS, 'Directionality and fragmentation in the transcendental ego' (*Philosophical Research Archive*, 5, 1979, no.1326), which is an attempt to discuss the problems of an empirical and a transcendental centre of consciousness.

It is worth noting the rarity of social construction theories of consciousness. I have benefited greatly from the excellent study of P. D. ASHWORTH, *Social interaction and consciousness* (Chichester: John Wiley & Sons, 1979), particularly chapters 1−3. For a useful summary account of the variety of meanings of 'conscious' see A. MORTON, 'Consciousness' (in *The encyclopedic dictionary of psychology*, eds R. Harré and R. Lamb, Oxford: Basil Blackwell, 1983).

For the 'standing wave' theory, see C. TART, *States of consciousness* (New York: Dutton, 1975). The two major cybernetic approaches are D. C. DENNETT, *Brainstorms* (Hassocks: Harvester Press, 1978) and B. A. FARRELL, 'On the design of a conscious device' (*Mind*, 79, 1970, 321−46). There are many other proposals, of course, but they seem to me to fall into either a self-reporting theory or a self-ordering theory. Quotations from Sartre are taken from J.-P. SARTRE, *Being and nothingness* (trans. H. E. Barnes, London: Methuen, 1957). I have greatly benefited from reading P. KOESTENBAUM, *Edmund Husserl: The Paris lectures* (The Hague: Martinus Nijhoff, 1964), which has an excellent introduction.

Additional works cited in text are J. CROOK, *The evolution of human consciousness* (Oxford: Oxford University Press, 1980); H. EY, *Consciousness* (trans. J. H. Flodstrom, Bloomington and London: Indiana University Press, 1978); H. FISHER, 'Logic and language in defences', (*Journal for the theory of social behaviour*, 3, 1973, 152−214); I. KANT, *Critique of pure reason* (trans. N. Kemp Smith, London: Macmillan, 1929); T. MISCHEL, *The self: Psychological and philosophical issues* (Oxford: Basil Blackwell, 1977); P. F. STRAWSON, *Individuals* (London: Methuen, 1959).

CHAPTER 7

PERSONAL BEING AS PRACTICAL UNITY: AGENCY

Theme: The self as agent is not a mysterious thing but a belief which endows the believer with certain powers of action in accordance with the interpersonal models available in the society.

Contents

1 THE POWER TO ACT: REDUCTIVE ACCOUNTS

In his fourth letter to Leibniz, Clarke argues against the principle of sufficient reason as a ubiquitous psychological law. Even if the psychological 'forces' are equally balanced between one course of action and another, a man *can* act: in addition to reasons, says Clarke, there is power. If Clarke were right, moral science would need a psychology of action, since the psychology of decision-making would be inadequate to explain how decisions are executed. Since the time of the Utilitarians there has been a tendency to reduce the theory of moral crises to a discussion of the issues involved in understanding the

mechanism of decisions. The fact that we often act in despite of the considerations we consciously entertain has been dealt with by the
introduction of a realm of unconscious cognitions and affections. I am
sure I am not alone in finding myself with an inadequate array of
reasons on occasion, but under a practical or social necessity to act, and
so acting in ways that only a retrospective psychodynamic account can
make intelligible. However, I believe there are also the occasions upon
which, so far as one's grasp of the situation goes, including the
psychodynamic component, the balance of reasons is equal, yet one can
act. Equally compelling philosophically, there are the occasions where
opportunity, intention and knowledge of means are right but one cannot
bring oneself to 'get going'.

If the psychology of action were reducible to a psychology of
decision-making, then cognitive psychology would suffice as a personal psychology of action. The updating of the principle that 'the
reason is the slave of the passions' into the theory of conscious and unconscious motivation, provides a supplement for the conscious cognitions that appear in those clusters of wants and desires of which we
are aware and which are inadequate as explanation. In what follows I
shall try to condense a huge corpus of philosophical discussion to reveal
the essential features of the various main theories. These will provide
a framework for psychological research into agency or rather into what
agency must be taken to be in the light of the philosophical analyses.

To be able to claim in truth that I am the author of my actions, it must
not be the case that some other agent produces them. Yet a strand in the
philosophical discussion of voluntary and/or intentional action leads to
the conclusion that there is just such an agent or agents. Two rather different versions of subpersonal 'powerful particular' theory have been
on offer. In one (I shall call it the 'mental machinery' view) the items
which must be mentioned to give an exhaustive account of the genesis
of action are drawn from commonsense or lay categories of mental entities. The favourite components that are supposed to make up the mental
machinery that produces action are wants (or attitudes) and beliefs. In
the other version, a novel class of hypothetical entities 'volitions' is
proposed, which are to be efficient causes of action.

In both versions it is not people who act, but parts of people or, to put
it more subtly, what we call cases of people acting are really cases of
a subpersonal component causing the action in question. What would,
if expressed candidly, be seen as an alternative account to that in which
people are said to act is offered as (masquerades as) an analysis of
people acting. That this theory, in whatever version, cannot be an
analysis of people acting follows immediately from the fact that the
concept of the unity of the agent does not reappear in the analysans, nor

any acceptable substitute for it. We are dealing with theories of action which are rivals to explanations in terms of personal agency.

Davidson: law of nature account

A typical 'mental machinery' theory can be found in Davidson's 'Actions, reasons and causes'. Davidson's alternative to a personal agency theory of the power to realize one's intentions involves a rather simpler version of the want/belief psychology of lay theorizing. Davidson calls the kinds of reasons he offers as causes 'primary reasons'. A primary reason is a wanting, or having a favourable attitude to, an action conceived under a particular description together with a belief that the action in question is (would be) of that kind. Both components could reasonably be described in the vernacular as 'thoughts'. They are, according to Davidson, when taken together as a primary reason, a cause of action. So reasons for action are causes of action and human agency has vanished, not being needed in the analysans.

Davidson's reduction is aimed at showing that somewhere in the background of action is the nomic regularity we describe as a law of nature. Davidson shifts the locus of power to act from a psychological to a natural necessity. The argument proceeds in three steps.

(1) Admit the propriety of describing the genesis of action in intention/action pairs, which are such that there is some conceptual relation between the intensional content (description) of the former and the intensional content (description) of the latter, as it might be that my action of waving is explained by my declaration of my intention to apologize.

(2) Redescribe the mental state of 'intending to apologize' as its grounding brain-state, but using predicates that ensure that the concept of 'apology' does not appear in the redescription according to the principle that description and redescription are co-referential. Redescribe the action similarly, again preserving referential identity.

(3) The intention is an adequate explanation of the action if there exists a type – type correlation between the referent of the redescription of the intending state and the referent of the redescription of the acting state; this correlation is a (Humean) law of nature.

A striking feature of this analysis is the absence of any mention of the efficacy or power that causes must have. Efficacy is made to vanish by 'splitting it', so to speak, between attitudes and wants, which can 'drive' or 'force' someone, and the nomologicality of natural law.

The fact that a want may be realized in innumerably different ways means that the causal interpretation of the statement that 'this action *B* was done for this reason *A*' cannot depend on some putative law '*A*s always cause *B*s'. There may be no such law. But for there to be a causal relation there must be some description of the events in question, say *C* and *D*, for which a law '*C*s always cause *D*s' is available.

It surely follows from this analysis that reference to persons as agents of their actions is otiose since, if the above says anything, it says that if the want and belief occur then, other things being equal, the action will occur. Davidson notices correctly that knowing the antecedent may often not help in predicting the consequence, since we cannot tell which of the innumerable ways of realizing it will occur just this time. The power to realize intentions in actions is displaced from persons to the nomologicality of natural laws. On the face of it, both weakness of will and strength of will are excluded from the story. Lay explanations of failures to act or notable successes in doing difficult or repugnant actions are usually couched in terms of concepts like 'laziness' or 'force of character'.

There are many objections to Davidson's attempt to reduce human agency to hidden lawfulness. For instance, the argument to show that singular causal statements can be backed by law simply by a redescription of their referents, depends on the dubious principle that event-identity (of a relevant kind) is preserved under the redescription. For instance, it seems implausible to claim that the state of mind 'intending to do *a*' is the same state as 'intending to do *A*', where *A* is a generic term for that which is specified as *a*. The important redescription is to a psychologically 'neutral' entity, the grounding brain-state. But the criteria of identity for the neutral entity are not coherent, since we can be sure only of token identity between mental states, including intendings and their realizing brain-states. We cannot be sure that the same type of intention is always realized, in all people, in the same type of physiological conditions. Referential identity under redescription in relation to a lawful relation between the referents would have to be type-preserving.

When the conceptual connection is broken between intention and action, supposing redescription were to succeed, the lawful relation is supposed to obtain on the basis of a Humean regularity. But if the regularity is truly Humean, that is, if there are no mediating productive processes between the alleged cause and its supposed effect, there is no ground for supposing the relation is lawful. A purely Humean relation has no nomic force and so cannot account for the human power to act.

Davidson is bewitched by a model: actions are events, so they must have causes; compare R. Taylor's criticism of the unexamined adherence to the principle '*Every* event must have *another event* as cause' in his *Action and purpose*. If this criticism were acceptable it would take away only one of the sites of the relocation of personal agency, namely in the operation of natural law. But perhaps the force which impels us to act is the logical necessity of the practical necessity which precedes action. To complete a defence one must also deny that practical syllogism could be an alternative site for the relocation of efficacy.

Aristotle: law of logic account

Suppose the force impelling a person to action were the very same force that compels the mind to draw or to assent to a conclusion which follows logically from explicitly formulated premises. A new way would have been found of eliminating a personal power of action from psychology which cannot be analysed. The practical syllogism is the most ancient and in some ways the most philosophically instructive form of cognitive psychology we have. Syllogistic reasoning could be looked on as a simple form of machine computation using a well-defined algorithm. Provided the premises satisfy the laws of quantity, quality and distribution, conclusions inevitably follow. Logical structure seems to have psychological force. Of course, the concept of inevitability needs some qualification since someone may be too stupid, too distracted or perhaps too drunk to be capable of grasping the logical structure of the argument and so of experiencing its compulsion propositions (and/or their realizations). If it is a description of an action, there is no difficulty in seeing how the logical relation obtains but the original problem reappears: by what force does the sentential conclusion bring the prescribed action into existence?

In neither case can the power to act be ascribed to the sentential structure or reduced to the psychological counterpart of logical necessity. The fact that a distinction is needed between psychological compulsion and logical necessity to accommodate such all-too-human weaknesses as stupidity and laziness, and that the former is not necessitated by the latter by reason of these failings, makes the project of reducing the power to act to a structural property of personal discourse unconvincing.

In her commentary on the practical syllogism in *Intention*, Anscombe makes a point which I shall borrow directly. It is not the logical form of deductive structure that is potent in the acting out of the conclusion of a piece of practical reasoning, but rather the 'want' involved. The 'wanting' is not a premise, rather 'whatever is described in the proposition that is the starting point of the argument must be wanted in order for the reasoning to lead to any action.' Like any 'want' account this leaves open the problem of how to account for strength of mind and weakness of will (interestingly Anscombe's treatment of 'wanting' includes the remark that 'the primitive act of wanting is *trying to get*').

Further, there is good reason to treat the subsequent action as the conclusion of the practical syllogism, and for various reasons the 'reach' of the logical power of appropriate premises does not reach it or its verbal accompaniment, such as 'So I'll do it'.

More telling than these standard objections briefly sketched against both the hidden lawfulness theory and the idea of hypothetical mental causes is the problem of hierarchies of volition. The classic objection has arisen with Ryle, who directs his criticism to those theories of action which, under the spell of the general causal model, bring in a category of hypothetical mental acts, 'volitions', to make good a deficit in our experience, namely that we do not experience mental events *as* the causes of our actions and so supply the potency that wants do not seem to have. Ryle's argument (*The concept of mind*, pp. 63–69) is directed to showing that volitions simply do not exist. They have none of the characteristic features of thoughts, feelings and intentions, or any other mental event, attribute or process identified in lay psychology. So volitions cannot be hypothetical *mental* entities, which we might notice if we looked out for them. Further, if volitions, acts of will, are acts of mind, and presumably voluntary, there must be volitions which bring about those volitions, and so on *ad infinitum*. Ryle, rightly it seems to me, identifies the 'volition' theory as a consequence (and an absurd one) of 'the general supposition that the question "How are mental-conduct concepts applicable to human behaviour?" is a question about the causation of that behaviour.'

Martin Hollis suggests in *Models of man* that giving the reasons for what one does is a complete form of explanation since it is the mark of a person as a rational being. So no further account of acting in accordance with reason is called for. But failure to act must be explained. And this is the place for causes. Attractive though this suggestion is, there seem to be cases when I must force myself to do something irrational, say in response to social pressures. It also seems to be the case that much of the organization of action in accordance with reason is in response to social conventions or imperatives rather than the result of personal cognitive processes. So we cannot eliminate agency in this way either.

I often want something and know how to get it, but remain stuck in the slough of idleness. I have decided to do the difficult thing, and with a great effort I wade in and do it. In the restoration of personal psychology, I want to bring back the study of endeavour, conatus, striving, trying and the like. In the conditions for the use of these concepts I feel the presence of persons as agents rather than as passive passengers on a mental vehicle directed and powered by subpersonal vectors (or information-processing modules) of various kinds.

2 REGRESSES OF POWERS AND TENDENCIES

The problem of internal determinism is complex. As a first step I propose to separate human tendencies to act into those which are grounded
in intentions from those which are otherwise maintained in the human
organism. Among intentions I distinguish those which are sufficiently
well formulated by an actor in propositional form, and which therefore
an actor could declare to his/her fellows, from those of which an actor
may have no clear understanding. I take formulated intentions to
specify a goal and to *express* a favourable attitude to its realization.
Among the resources of a person who is competent in some field of
endeavour is the knowledge of means necessary to the realization of
ends typical of action in that field. I shall take it that it is appropriate to
use agency concepts like 'personal powers' and 'trying' only of formulated intentions. I will return to other kinds of tendencies below. In the
natural sciences agency concepts like 'electrical attraction' are explicated as powers, that is, dispositions, grounded in terms of a regress of
other agency concepts. An electrified body attracts by virtue of its state,
that is, as electrified. But that state is explicated in terms of a structure
of other beings, for instance, electrons, which have their own typical
powers. These powers can be treated as dispositions grounded in the
nature of electrons, analysed as structures of other beings, with their
characteristic dispositions. The same treatment can be given to them
and so on. At the 'lowest' level of such physical regresses are
categories of beings whose nature can be described only as the
ensemble of their remaining unexplicated tendencies or powers. Pure
agency can be defined either as an open regress of powers, that is, of
grounded dispositions, or as a closed regress whose final grounding is
in a kind of being defined by ungrounded dispositions. One source of
difficulty with applying this sort of analysis to the human case is that in
some contexts the open regress seems appropriate (for instance in
explicating what was once called 'the human will'), while in others the
closed regress seems right, for instance in analysing character.

The human sciences are complicated by the fact that we need to make
and maintain a three-fold distinction between dispositions, having to do
with what people will do *ceteris paribus*; tendencies, marking what
people might do *ceteris paribus*; and powers, for describing what
people can do *ceteris paribus*. In the physical sciences we can collapse
these into one another by suitably manipulating the conditions. By im-
posing constraints we can make a physical being display what it can do,
and by tightening constraints we can make it display what it might do.
Even in the quantum mechanical case 'can dos' become 'might dos'

become 'will dos' if we run an experiment often enough to produce statistical ensembles, with a definite, dependable structure. In the human case the transition from 'can do' to 'might do' to 'will do' seems to require human agency or, to put it another way, can be arbitrarily frustrated by bloody-mindedness. I propose to try the regressive analysis in two cases; tendencies based upon formulated intentions, and powers (including abilities, capacities and capabilities).

Having an intention can be treated as the grounding of a tendency to behave in a certain way. The existence of the intention as formulated by that person at that time could be explained by some higher order intention, and the actor having the knowledge that the action first proposed in the lowest order intention realizes the higher order one. So, the lower order intention could be to perform an act which knowledge at the higher level showed was required as a contribution to an act of a higher order intended at that higher level; and so on. The relevant knowledge need not be in the possession of the being currently intending to act. It might belong to his or her collective.

The regress of intentions and knowledge, the 'tendency to act regress', seems to be open in principle. For every intention actually formulated one could imagine another of a higher order. If I formulate an intention to take a certain book from the library, this may be because I know that reading it will improve my musical performance, and I may intend to make an improvement because I intend to offer myself for an audition for a more prestigious orchestra etc., etc. (Wants, intentions and plans tend to offer themselves for attention in describing such regresses, but I shall not pursue that here.)

Intentions come and go. We would not be inclined to tie them other than loosely to someone's nature; perhaps a little more tightly to their character. A regress of powers behaves rather differently. Take a regress of capabilities. A person may be reminded that they are capable of running a business because they are capable of rational decision making, learning how to keep books and so on. Just as the physical regress is closed with beings whose natures are their basic tendencies, so the psychological regress is closed by the idea of a person's nature as the ensemble of his or her powers and capacities which cannot be psychologically grounded, and so cannot be *psychologically* explicated and analysed. In each case 'automaton' man makes his appearance. In the intentions/tendencies regress he may crop up under the heading of 'basic needs', while in the powers regress he appears as a grounding to ungrounded dispositions and abilities.

The argument for internal determinism is sometimes based on an alleged physiological grounding of basic psychological powers. This is the least convincing automaton theory. There is good reason to think that there can be no lawlike reduction of the basis of psychologically identified tendencies to a uniform grounding in physiological states or processes. At best there is only token identity from person to person between a hypothetical psychological state grounding a tendency and its physiological counterpart. The taxonomy of the appropriate physiological sciences is always top down, that is, physiological conditions are identified as psychologically relevant in terms of a psychological conceptual system. We have seen earlier that these two features of physiology preclude any reduction to the material basis of mind through detailed psychophysiological laws that will have transpersonal validity and map psychological functions and processes type by type onto neural activities. So, from the psychological point of view, the final ensemble of tendencies which cannot be analysed is the most basic explanatory level which can throw up transpersonal generalizations. To express these in AI terms is not a reduction programme since, as I have argued in chapter 1, an adequate cognitive psychology *must* be a representation in AI rhetoric of psychological processes. However, the subpersonal psychology of information-processing modules is an automaton theory reducing people to cyborgs. So at this point I have not yet restored *persons* as agents. I have shown only the need for maintaining and developing some sort of conceptual scheme to represent individual activity. So far the tendencies in terms of which the scheme has been developed could be treated as subpersonal but active components of a person. But it is the person who tries, who shifts from the domination of one life plan to another. The final step has yet to be taken. Only if we have reason to believe that some psychological regresses are indefinitely open, has personal agency, in the strong sense I mean, been established.

3   AGENCY ANALYSED

To restore human agency we need: (a) to defend the viability of an activity schema for analysing human action; (b) to identify cases where no means–end hierarchy could provide a complete explanation of someone doing something; and (c) to defend the use of the commonsense theory that human agency is required to provide complete explanations of both action and inaction, based on means–end hierarchies discovered by the techniques of 'action theory'.

I shall develop the concept of agency in two steps. In the first I shall assume the notion of active tendency as an undefined, but intuitively given, root idea and use it to identify two action schemata, one of which represents the exercise of agency. The second step will be to analyse the notion of active tendency as far as possible. I will introduce these concepts in contexts drawn from the physical sciences. This should serve to dispel any idea that physical sciences do not centrally use power and tendency concepts and should make clear there is nothing unscientific about their use. I shall then turn to illustrate their value in psychological discourse. Since physics makes use of tendencies, to draw on such notions for psychology can hardly be criticised as soft-headed.

I shall speak of a particular thing as a patient if, unless it receives an external stimulus, it remains quiescent, unchanging, neither manifesting a new property itself, nor producing a change in anything else. The schema for action of a patient is:

$$\text{Being} + \text{Stimulus} \rightarrow \text{Action}.$$

Patients are such that some stimuli produce an effect only in the patient itself. Liabilities (passive dispositions), realized by a particular category of stimulus, are tendencies for the patient to acquire some state or attribute. A particular being is an agent if it fulfils the schema:

$$\text{Being} - \text{Restraint} \rightarrow \text{Action}.$$

A patient must be stimulated to act; agents need only be released. An agent can act upon itself but also upon other beings.

To complete the account, the concept of 'states of readiness' must be added. In preparing to set off a race the starter creates a state of readiness in the runners with his 'Get set'. The subsequent 'Go' can be thought of as a releaser. A spring must first be wound or compressed before it can be released into action. These distinctions are fully worked out in the physics of energy, with the concepts of 'strain', 'potential energy', 'virtual acceleration' and so on. At some stages of their careers many agents are patients; then, by acquiring tendencies and powers whose realization requires the removal of a restraint, such as a countervailing and inhibiting force, they become agents.

To develop the above schemata one needs to distinguish between those agents whose tendencies to action are self-maintained by virtue of permanent intrinsic properties, and those which derive their tendencies from some surrounding medium or structured ensemble of other beings. In physical sciences the former category is exemplified by acids, which have a tendency to react with bases because they have, among their constituents, and definitive of their intrinsic natures, electrically active hydrogen ions. The latter category is exemplified in the physics of material bodies which acquire their tendency to accelerate by virtue of being located in a gravitational field which is the product of a structured ensemble of other massive bodies.

Inaction may have three different explanations. The being is a patient and has not been stimulated; the being is a potential agent at the patient stage and has not yet acquired a tendency, though it is not blocked; the being is an agent with the appropriate tendency, but it is blocked from acting, from realizing that tendency. In a psychology of the will, inaction is a central phenomenon of interest.

In general, the dispositions or tendencies of agents are to produce effects in beings other than themselves which we might call 'powers', while liabilities involve changes or effects in the being that is the patient. I shall speak of the exercise of a tendency as an influence. On the definitions proposed above, a being considered as a patient necessarily cannot act upon another being, that is, exercise an influence upon or over others. Of course, the patient may become an agent later in its career.

A person is a perfect agent relative to some category of action when both the tendency to act and the release of that tendency are in the power of that person. Reactions in the face of danger are often explicated in terms of this schema. We use the ideas of someone 'screwing themselves up' to act. Henry V's admonitions to his troops before the attack on the walls of Calais is an example of the practical use of that schema. Being persuaded to see themselves as 'tigers' provides the soldiers with the beliefs necessary to create a readiness to attack.

Agency is less than perfect in two cases. Sometimes a certain tendency is outside a person's control. It may be externally engendered, for example, by a reign of terror; it may be the effect of 'internal' automatized processes emerging into quadrant 3, for example as a neurotic compulsion to count and recount the things in one's vicinity. Sometimes a tendency can be controlled by an actor but the conditions for its blockage or release cannot. For instance, a person may be very ready to work but whether this tendency can be realized in action depends on circumstances outside the actor's control. Lukes has developed a version of the imperfect agent schema in his notion of 'power plus or minus opportunity'.

We make use of the former subschema in assigning responsibility in the criminal courts. Psychological hypotheses are debated as to whether or not some tendency, manifested by the defendant in unacceptable conduct, is a permanent disposition, that is, whether the actor has or has not the power to control that tendency even when the conditions for its release obtain. Can a pederast 'control himself' in the presence of young girls in a bathing pool? We often use the latter in assigning moral praise or blame in everyday life in 'He would have liked to help but the opportunity never presented itself' etc. Finally, a being is to be regarded as completely passive if both its tendencies to act and the conditions for their release or blockage are outside its control. For instance, if immunity to disease is biologically based and infection is an environmental hazard, a being is wholly passive in catching a disease. In cultures where disease is drawn into the moral order, such as Christian Science, the pure passivity schema must be denied application to the sick.

To complete the analysis two further steps are required. The autonomy of an agent has to be differentiated from the internal determinism of a pseudo-agent whose action only appears to be self-caused because the causal process which produces it is confined within the envelope (usually the physical envelope) of the being concerned. Further, an account of 'tendency' is still required. As the concept has been used so far, tendencies could be psychological or even physiological forces which carry the person along with them.

Can the idea of open regressive hierarchies of dispositions, tendencies and powers save agency from reduction to a complex form of internal determinism? We can approach the problem by noticing that the regress structure for much of the preparation for human action is not made up of a simple disposition but is a more complex ranking of practical syllogisms in a multi-nested means—end structure. That such structures exist has been well established empirically by the work of von Cranach, Hacker, Tomaszewski etc. (*see* von Cranach and Harré's, *The analysis of action*). Each superior level serves to define a means for achieving a task defined in a formulated intention in an inferior level. The fact that only some of our dispositions appear in the form of fully formulated intentions does not affect my argument. I am not trying to prove that we are fully agents in all our doings, only in some. Thus:

> Intention I (to eat salad) + knowledge (on the cold table)
> + ACTIVATION → action (the doing of what was
> formulated in Intention I).

But a similar structure is required to formulate Intention II. So we get.

> Intention II (to lose weight) + knowledge (salad is not
> fattening) + ACTIVATION → the formulating of Intention I.

The formulation of Intention I is a mental action which realizes Intention II. Further intentions can be added in so far as one has an interest in further explorations of the cognitive processes involved (to look better, to be healthier, to please someone etc.). This looks just like mental determinism, *but* one must do justice to two features of common experience: trying before succeeding, and failing through laziness and procrastination.

A 'mystery' term — ACTIVATION — can be introduced for the moment to acknowledge the reality of effort and idleness. It stands for what was once called 'an act of will'. Is it not just such an act which is required to produce action? All the cognitive preparations for slimming may be complete but I *still* pick up the cottage pie. And when I turn away it is 'I', not some subpersonal module, which masters the tendency, which resists temptation and actually eats the salad. 'Acts of will' are deservedly unpopular as explanatory devices, so what is to be made of the 'mystery' term?

Before I turn to resolving the conundrum, there is an argument that suggests that a personal act of will can be eliminated by supposing that an intention is a powerful particular, and itself has the capacity to engender action. (Madden, 'Human action', has argued for this, and I think Davidson, 'Actions, reasons and causes', believes it.) To extend this idea to cover the cases I have in mind, one would need to add some mysterious force to intentions to distinguish those occasions when I am too feeble to succeed from those when I do master my lower nature. This 'force' would justify the elimination of the reference to 'I' as the active agent. But such a force is otiose. We already have a theory that explains the difference between these cases in terms of further steps in a personal and/or collectively located hierarchy of rational or other considerations, steps which occur on the one occasion, but do not occur on the other. Provided the hierarchy of intentions is open, that is, indefinitely extensible, at no level is there a final non-dispositional grounding to our activity. We choose between principles operative at one level by taking account of those operative at another in the hierarchy, and this explains why on one occasion we choose one course of action and on another, another. It is just such moves, I believe, that we experience when, as it is traditionally expressed, we act 'freely'. The residual power with which I want to identify part of what we mean by human agency does not, I think, need to be defined as the capacity to act without *any* reason at all, as Clarke would have it, but to act according to some reason other than that, according to which in similar circumstances, I am accustomed to act. But we still have to account for our differing capacities to 'hang on to' or to 'opt for' the principles we know to be right. The open hierarchy theory can account for the experience of free action, but not for trying, succeeding and/or failing.

Von Cranach has shown how the constraints in a person's existing hierarchy of reasons for acting can be loosened in another way. Feedback loops can be set up in such a way that intentions of higher order are modified by failure of actions which are attempts to realize intentions of lower order relative to some project. This represents a typical form of self-correction. The capacity to set up these loops requires that people can act independently of and unconstrained by any *existing* hierarchy of intentions and rules of action. It seems to be the case that at whatever level an intention is taken to reside, a further level of intention can in principle be constructed. The regress of possible intentions is open.

In the last two paragraphs I have been talking as if hierarchies of intentions, and the associated corpus of knowledge of the means necessary for their socially permitted realization, are 'internal' properties of individual beings such as persons. While this is sometimes the case, the existence of such hierarchies in individuals is, I believe, possible only because prior hierarchies are features of interpersonal discourse in the conversation among humans out of which our psychologies emerge. Higher levels are represented by the normative utterances of more important, more respected or wiser and more influential persons. One might make a connection with the Freudian theory of the superego, as a version of the theory expounded here, that personal hierarchies take their initial hierarchical form from socially structured discourse.

4   WILL AS SELF-COMMAND

I have argued at length that to understand how we can conceive of ourselves as conscious beings, we need to suppose that we are using a theory to organize our experience, a theory that introduces a unity of self as a theoretical concept rather than as an empirical discovery. In a similar way, I believe, our conception of ourselves as agents should also be understood as the employment of a theory with the active and willing self as its prime theoretical concept. In possession of a *theory* that I am an agent capable of acting against the tide of my inclination, capable of getting myself up and going etc., I have the means for re-adjusting the many means—end hierarchies which are involved in the preparation for action. And I have a way of explaining how my mental life (with others) appears to me the way it does. By being forced to listen to the exhortations of others, I learnt to exhort myself, and by watching others push each other into action, I learn to bestir myself. It is my grasp of the theory that I am a unified being that enables me to understand that I am the recipient both of exhortations and kicks and shoves, and that I can exhort and shove others and, finally, putting all this together, that I can so treat myself.

The most economical version of a person theory would be one in which personal awareness and reflexive activity were centred on the same theoretical entity. In the public world of collective moral orders our one bodily manifestation is the target of all personal attributions by the others, since that is where they think we are and to which they direct their complaints and exhortations because that is from where we act and talk. In the light of all I have argued, we need seek no further for an explanation of the transcendental unity of ourselves as perceivers and agents. It is a model of ourselves created by drawing on our public role as a source.

My final example of a philosophical theory which takes us at least most of the way back to the person-as-agent view is that of Kenny (via Geach and Aquinas) in *Aristotle's theory of will*. He offers an account of 'acts of will' based on the idea of self-exhortation, but without the need to invoke a mysterious mental organ 'the will'. Kenny presents his scheme in a rather complex matrix of moves in philosophical logic, but the scheme itself can be extracted in a rather elegant form. It conforms quite closely to the public—collective to private—individual transition I have been offering as the general account of the mental.

People perform public—collective speech acts of stating, wishing, commanding and the like. Geach suggests (in *Mental acts*, p. 11) that 'any reportable act of judgement is apt for verbal expression'. A private and individual act is modelled on a public—collective performance. In the same spirit Kenny proposes to introduce a generic concept ('to volit') for the kind of mental act for which the models in public—collective performance are expressions of wishes, hopes and intentions, commands, exhortations and the like, that is, action-promoting acts. Thus 'voliting' includes amongst other species 'mentally wishing that p'. If I have understood the theory aright, the public—collective models, which include commanding, make certain mental acts possible as privatized appropriations. Importantly, they include the example that 'to act voluntarily is to command oneself to do'. The content of the volition is just exactly the content of the corresponding public—collective wish, command etc. They are both speech acts of the same species and genus. A number of authorities are cited in support of the 'common contents in different acts, moods' doctrine. A striking feature of this theory, quite apart from the fact that it fits with the 'psychological dimensions' I have proposed in the conservation of the agentive person throughout the development of the theory, '*I*' remains an essential component of the analysis as in '*I* wish that p' and '*I* command *myself* to perform an act which would fall within its descriptive ambience'. In the latter we have once again the duality between indexical uses of personal referring expressions and those I have called 'referential'. It is only relative to the latter that the speaker is an agent.

If, as I have argued, the conscious and agentive self is not an empirical entity existing as referent for the concept of 'self', but is that concept itself as the organizing principle of experience, organized experience should have a distinctive character. I have described it as both synthetic and hierarchical. Sartre, too, offers something like this characterization. In *Being and nothingness*, in the section 'Being and doing: freedom', Sartre, in his inimitable delphic style, says that to be a human being is to be capable of negating everything I have been: 'the permanent possibility of this rupture that is a "nihilating rupture with the world and with himself" is the same as freedom . . . . this permanent possibility of nihilating what I am in the form of "having been", implies for men a particular type of existence.' 'For the "*pour-soi*", to be is to nihilate the "*en-soi*" which it is. . .'. 'It is through this that the for-itself is always something other than what can be said of it.' In short, the possibility of breaking away from any principle of action is what distinguishes the self-as-agent; or, to put the matter organizationally, hierarchies of shifts from principle to principle are the structural mark of mentation organized as a person, that is, as an agent. And of course it is my contention that mentation might have been organized in various other ways.

This takes us back to the active agent schemata of the second and third sections of this chapter. The 'mystery' ingredient I called 'ACTIVATION' can now be identified. It is a complex of beliefs about my own nature with a repertoire of speech acts to go with them. There is no more (and no less) mystery in coming to understand how I can obey myself than in coming to understand how I can obey you. In general, my obedience to your commands is explicable in terms of our relative location in one or more moral orders. (There is the special case of obedience through threat or terror, but this has no analogue in self-exhortation.) Precisely the same must be said of personal agency. There is a moral order in which I stand in various relations to myself, expressed in remarks like 'You owe it to yourself', 'Don't let yourself down' and so on. To understand agency (and its sibling *akrasia*) is to have a grasp of this moral order as it is differently realized in various cultures.

5 PROOFS OF AUTONOMY

Sartrean demonstrations

To be intelligible, an action must be able to be interpreted as an act. Applying the intention—rule schema to understand the genesis of an action is usually based on treating the act as what was intended and the rule component as specifying what is the appropriate action to realize that act in a culture. We have noticed that this takes a hierarchical form in that the intention to perform this or that act may itself be arrived at by the use of a rule, which specifies the act appropriate to the situation or project currently existing, or thought to be existing by the actors. But in such cases there need be no reference to an autonomous agent, since the rule may be thought to have all the compelling force needed to account for the genesis of action. To prove autonomy in the pure sense, the sense Clarke wished to defend against Leibniz, a pure act must be possible, that is, an act not dependent on rule. Sartre's pure acts of commitment to a way of life, to a political position or, in more psychological terms, to a rule system would be the kind of phenomena which would point to the existence of pure agents. But it is doubtful if such acts ever actually occur. How then to defend empirically the reality of a genuine power of decision, and more importantly of action, which I have been suggesting is that power which *must* characterize genuine agents?

By separating practical action from expressive or self-presentational action, the paradox can be resolved. Since the pure agent, that which acts unconditionally, is not an empirically given being, there can be no experience of pure action, that which the pure agent would do. So the proof of human autonomy must be through the demonstration of the existence of characteristic products of autonomous action. The conditions for a demonstration of this kind could be met by performing both the following kinds of action.

An action must be performed which, if considered by practical criteria, is irrational, that is, not according to practical rule or principle. But to show that one is able to act independently of rule of principle, to show oneself as an autonomous agent, is a rational or principled action judged by expressive criteria. Unintelligible as a practical action, it is nevertheless quite intelligible as an expressive action. For instance, the action of shooting the Arab in Camus' *The Stranger* is unintelligible in practical terms, but through it Meursault shows himself to be an autonomous agent, so conforming to an expressive maxim.

An action which is irrational by expressive criteria is now required to complete the proof of one's autonomy by showing that one is capable of acting independently of all expressive maxims. By choosing an action which is rational by practical criteria, one has ensured its intelligibility. So, to complete the demonstration one must find an action which is irrational expressively considered, but principled as a practical performance. For instance, a survivor of an aircrash may save his or her life by eating the flesh of those who were killed in the accident, but by doing so the actor has violated some important maxims for presenting oneself in the best light expressively.

I have set up the Sartrean case in terms of a simple contrast between actions which are rational (that is, accord with rule) and those which are irrational (that is, violate rule). But it might be argued that any reference to rule, whether conforming or violating, is still far short of pure autonomy. An autonomous actor is a-rational, standing aside from the contrast between rationality and irrationality. Meursault's action neither realizes a practical maxim nor violates it. It is an action without respect to maxim. In the terminology of this study it is an action, it was intended, but in doing it the actor performs no act.

The psychological possibility of this case can be established by seeing the intentional structure engendering the action as reflexive. The action is its own act, so to speak. Nothing was intended but the action itself. It points nowhere beyond itself. In this case the act (that which was intended) and the means of realizing it are one and the same. In pulling the trigger what did one intend to do? Nothing but pull the trigger.

Weakness of will

To complete the analysis an examination of various accounts of *akrasia* or moral weakness is needed. In philosophy, the explanation of a concept is often facilitated by studying its opposite. Since agency involves a power to act, the study of weakness of will, of powerlessness to act, may throw some light on the positive concept. There are two accounts of *akrasia*. Cognitive theories of moral weakness involve the hypothesis of a mental apparatus incorporating desires, judgements and so on. The second account involves the actor and his circle, competent in a moral discourse in which there is talk of endeavour, of trying and so on, of personal power which, if inadequate, leaves a would-be actor stuck, incapable it seems of emerging through what is plainly required of him or her.

The 'mechanism' proposed in cognitive theories involves both moral considerations and psychological forces. Episodes of moral weakness have the form: (a) A wants to do x; (b) A thinks x is better than Y by criteria relevant to the larger context of action; (c) A does Y, thus failing to do x. To explain the phenomenon schematized in this episode-plan, x is located in some 'higher' system of beliefs and Y in a 'lower' system of bodily forces and urges, which are often very powerful. Patently a subpersonal explanation, this scheme has no place for human endeavour or lack of it (*see* Taylor, 'Plato, Hare and Davidson on *akrasia*').

Aristotle's theory of *akrasia* is an eliminative scheme, but is wholly cognitive, not requiring any hypotheses of the irresistible psychological forces that typically appear in the alibis of the weak-willed. In the

Nicomachean ethics (book B 1139 a), he sketches a general theory of conduct: 'The origin of conduct, not its final cause — is purpose; and the origin of purpose is desire plus means/end reasoning.' There are various forms and conditions in which this schema can be realized. Evil desires (among them those later to become the basis of the seven deadly sins) provide a groundwork of temptation. The 'temperate' man acts in accord with reason because he does not have evil desires, the 'continent' man acts in accord with reason because he can overcome his evil desires. *Akrasia* is the failing of the 'incontinent' man, within the same cognitive structures. As Kenny puts it in *Aristotle's theory of the will*: 'Even an *akratic*, in fact, does not differ in overreaching goal from a virtuous man; if he did he would not be an *akratic*', but a man with an evil project or no project at all.

How, then, is *akrasia* possible? There are two kinds of *akrasia*. The impetuous man fails to carry out his intentions because he is carried away by the first impulse that comes to mind. The true *akratic* does think things out; he does keep before his mind what he should do, but still fails to do it. Aristotle's theory of this is cognitive (*Nicomachean ethics*, book B, 1145 b 0 − 15). It is not developed in terms of some mental force overpowering the desire for the good. It depends rather on a distinction between knowing something (particularly) and exercising that knowledge. The *akratic* is a cognitive failure, but suffers only a temporary incapacitation since he has the knowledge, though he did not exercise it in identifying an immediate impulse as worthless.

Other scenarios are possible in which the concept of endeavour seems to have a proper place. Another kind of incident in which one would say 'weakness of will' was displayed, takes the following form: (a) *A* knows he/she should (moral/practical imperative) do *x*; (b) *A* fails to do *x*; (c) *A* searches for a *Y*, the doing of which would provide an alibi to self or others for not doing *x*. The failure of will is presented *post hoc* as a choice. Sabini and Silver, *Moralities of everyday life*, describe versions of this scenario. Another incident-form runs as follows: (a) *A* knows he/she should do *x*; (b) *A* tries to do *x* (*x* is within *a*'s power at that time); (c) *A* does not do *x*, nor anything else either, *A* stands rooted to the spot staring past the pile of unwashed dishes out into the yard; *A* sits for some time looking helplessly at a blank sheet of paper etc., etc.

These scenarios involve a concept-cluster around 'trying', 'effort', 'endeavour' and so on as used to attribute a special capacity or power to an actor. This concept-cluster is closely connected with the moral/characterological conceptual cluster which includes 'energetic', 'lazy', 'lively' and 'slowly'.

In an unpublished paper, Gerald Hall proposes a synthesis of the two basic *akrasia* schemes by introducing the idea of 'current perspective', in terms of which an actor deems that the greater but remoter good accruing from doing *Y* (in the 'eliminative' scheme) is too 'effortful', which judgement (and perspective) Hall suggests depends on the current distribution of 'mental energy' within the differences in our capacity to carry through tasks depending simply on how hungry or how tired we are. Attractive though this step is, we have, as yet, no good philosophical account of the commonsense concept of 'mental energy'. I believe research will show it to be part of the discourse apparatus of a moral order(s), having the status of an alibi or, if claimed or ascribed, the basis for an act of self-deprecation.

6   TRAITS AND DISPOSITIONS

Introducing the concept of tendency (and its passive partner, disposition) might suggest the reappearance of the much criticized notion of a trait. Trait concepts were introduced by personality psychologists, particularly Eysenck as explanatory entities. Logically they were clusters of behavioural dispositions, and had a good deal in common with the dispositions Ryle tried valiantly to substitute systematically for mental states and processes. But my invocation of tendencies is to be understood within a quite different theoretical background from that of Eysenck or that of Ryle. For both, dispositional concepts formed a basic explanatory system for psychology.

Philosophers have complained about the practice of locating dispositions and traits at the base of explanatory structures (see particularly Armstrong, *A materialist theory of the mind*). To accept the attribution of a disposition to a being not currently displaying the appropriate behaviour, one would need to know how the disposition was grounded. In the physical sciences, with the exception of the theory of fundamental fields, dispositions (solubility, magnetic permeability etc.) are grounded in the continuing properties (often structural) of the substances to which such dispositions are attributed.

How then are mental and action dispositions grounded? Eysenck proposes a physiological grounding for his traits, such as introversion−extroversion and neuroticism, thereby abandoning the psychological explanation of behaviour at a crucial moment. Ryle does not ground his dispositions in anything. But just as social psychology has come to be based on the idea of a collective cluster of rule systems as the fundamental explanatory level whose further investigation leads into history, so personal psychology must be based on the idea of clusters of belief systems as the ultimate explanations, whose further investigation leads into social processes of personal development. To the question 'Why do people have the tendencies (dispositions, traits) they do?' the personal psychologist must answer 'because they have the belief systems they do'. So in the end the study of personal psychology becomes the study of the differential acquisition and use of belief systems in the affairs of everyday life.

Lately, dramatic support for the general methodological thesis has come from the unexpected quarter of the reworked current form of 'behaviour modification therapy'. Initially it was conceived in simple Rylean dispositional terms and developed as an application of stunning crudity of Skinner's operant conditioning theory. But we are now in the era of 'cognitive behaviour therapy'. Practical experience has forcefully demonstrated that behaviour changes only in so far as the belief systems upon which it depends change. Cognitive 'behaviour modification' is directed towards efforts to change a client's belief system and, not surprisingly, it works.

The Achilles heel of trait theories, the dependence of trait displays on the situations and persons with which the subject of trait attributions is momentarily acting can be explained simply in terms of the relative complexity of personal belief systems. The more complex they are, the more situationally variable are trait displays likely to be. If dispositions or tendencies are taken as the ultimate explanatory entities this kind of variability is mysterious and should be unexpected.

RESEARCH MENU 7

(1) The study of the way agency is experienced is in its infancy. Most research in psychology, particularly in social psychology, is concerned to identify just those facets of human action when some causal conditions lead to the performance of some sort of action. They cannot register agency, so it is washed out wherever it appears as the central tendency is picked up by the statistical methods used. There must be many occasions in psychological laboratories when someone just did not want to do what was asked, but that cannot make its appearance in the final results. Most of the existing studies are summed up by Westcott in 'Quantitative and qualitative aspects or experienced freedom'. This is a field crying out for further research.

(2) The empirical study of 'absolute' agency can only be thought of in the context of demonstrations of Sartrean autonomy. These do occur, but they have been little studied. Why do people perform them? What effect do they have on subsequent relations between those people? Are there, of all things, conventions for the proper display of autonomy?

(3) The empirical study of agency is possible because many means–end hierarchies are or can be made to be under personal scrutiny. The role of the local self-theory, belief in which allows the organization and differential use

of the available and constructible means and hierarchies, can also be studied empirically.

BIBLIOGRAPHICAL NOTES 7

Clarke's famous assertion of the ultimate power to choose is given in his Fourth Reply to Leibniz, sections 1 and 2, 1717, see H. G. ALEXANDER (ed.) *The Leibniz—Clarke Correspondence* (Manchester: Manchester University Press, 1956). The ingenious effort by D. DAVIDSON to enlist natural nomologicality in the causation of action is in 'Actions, reasons and causes' (in *The philosophy of action*, ed. A. R. White, London: Oxford University Press, 1968, ch. 5). For a detailed history of the use of tendencies as explanatory entities in the physical sciences, including an account of the works of R. Greene and J. Priestley, see R. HARRÉ, 'Knowledge' (in *The ferment of knowledge*, eds G. S. Rousseau and R. Porter, Cambridge: Cambridge University Press, 1981, ch. 1). See M. VON CRANACH and R. HARRÉ (eds), *The analysis of action* (Cambridge: Cambridge University Press, 1982) for the efforts of Hacker, Tomaszewski and others to use belief systems in the explanation of action.

Restoration of the legitimacy of the application of the concept of agency through the 'could have done otherwise' move is nicely set out by M. A. SIMON, *Understanding human action* (Albany: SUNY Press, 1982), but we shall meet the issue again in bibliographical notes 8.

A good deal of what I have to say is very close to C. TAYLOR's important proposals in his 'What is human agency?' (in *The self: psychological and philosophical issues*, ed. T. Mischel, Oxford: Basil Blackwell, 1979, ch. 4). Taylor uses Frankfurter's notion of second-order desires but the key step in Taylor's treatment is to situate the decisive actions of the self within a moral order. Thus the self is the moral identity of the actor. But still missing from Taylor's theory is an account of human endeavour. The need to maintain identity by maintaining second-order evaluations does not explain away *akrasia*, in the sense of sloth, only in the sense of choosing an alternative course of action, at the best. See also E. H. MADDEN, 'Human action: reasons or causes: to justify or to explain?' (*Journal for the Theory of Social Behaviour*, 5, 1975, 3—16). For a detailed defence of the psychological reality of residual conation (in contrast to the Sartrean type of moral defence) see B. O'SHAUGHNESSY, *The will: A dual aspect theory* (Cambridge: Cambridge University Press, 1982, vol. 2, particularly ch. 11). See also J. THORP, *Free will* (London: Routledge and Kegan Paul, 1980, ch. 5 and 7).

The existence of irreducible *akrasia* is a key presupposition of my argument. According to Aristotle, the 'incontinent' man, that is, the man who seems to do what he knows full well is wrong or the lesser good, does not pay attention to all the premises in principle available to him. See G. MORTIMORE (ed., *Weakness of will* (London: Macmillan, 1971, ch. 3 and 4). Interestingly, R. M. HARE, *Freedom and reason* (Oxford: Clarendon Press, 1963) introduces 'psychological impossibility' amongst the conditions under which a person does not carry out the actions which the universalization of his principles requires him to demand of himself. I interpret this 'impossibility' in two ways. In one, it lies within a moral order orthogonal, so to speak, from that which engenders the self-injunction, a moral order of will. In the other, it springs from a kind of ignorance, from the absence of a belief in the theory that one *can* do whatever it is that one is calling upon oneself to do. In the former one fails to grasp that one must do something, while in the second that one can. See also C. C. W. TAYLOR, 'Plato, Hare and Davidson on *akrasia*' (*Mind*, 89, 1980, 499–518).

The view that I am presenting in this chapter is akin to Fritz Heider's idea of personal power, which is conceived as 'effort' plus 'ability'; see the summary by B. HARRIS and J. HARVEY, 'Attribution theory from phenomenal causality to intuitive social scientist and beyond (in *The psychology of ordinary explanations of social behaviour*, ed. C. Antaki, London: Academic Press, 1981). I propose that we treat not only ability but also effort as a matter of systems of belief. The latter will be close to Taylor's idea of identity within a moral order.

The literature on the explanation of action is simply enormous. Most does not concern itself with the unfashionable topic of willing. I begin with Aristotle's treatment of weakness of will in *Nicomachean ethics* 1145 b 0–15 and 1139 a 1–33. See R. D. MILO, *Aristotle on practical knowledge and weakness of will*, part II (The Hague: Mouton, 1966). For 'agent determinism' see R. M. CHISHOLM, 'Freedom and action' (in *Freedom and determinism*, ed. K. Lehner, New York: Random House, 1966, p. 11). A useful collection of important papers is M. BRAND ed., *The nature of human action* (Glenview, Ill.: Scott Foreman, 1970). For arguments for the ineliminability of agency, see the venerable but satisfying work of R. TAYLOR, *Action and purpose* (Englewood Cliffs (NJ): Prentice Hall, 1966). I have made great use of A. KENNY, *Aristotle's theory of the will* (New Haven: Yale University Press, 1979). See also P. T. GEACH, 'Ascriptivism' (in *The nature of human action*, ed. M. Brand, Glenview (Ill.): Scott Foreman, 1970), and for his very important thesis concerning judgement see P. T. GEACH, *Mental acts* (London: Routledge and Kegan Paul, 1957, s. 17–22).

For a valuable discussion of the practical syllogism see G. E. M. ANSCOMBE, *Intention* (Ithaca (New York): Cornell University Press, 1957). There is a considerable literature on this subject but still a most useful and brief commentary is D. P. GAUTHIER, *Practical reason* (Oxford: Clarendon Press, 1963, s. 3.1).

Additional works cited in text are D. ARMSTRONG, *A materialist theory of the mind* (London: Routledge and Kegan Paul, 1968); M. HOLLIS, *Models of man* (Cambridge: Cambridge University Press, 1977); S. LUKES, *Power: A radical view* (London: Macmillan, 1974); G. RYLE, *The concept of mind* (London: Hutchinson, 1947); J.-P. SARTRE, *Being and nothingness* (trans. H. E. Barnes, London: Methuen, 1957); J. SABINI and M. SILVER, *Moralities of everyday life* (Oxford: Oxford University Press, 1982); M. R. WESTCOTT, 'Quantitative and qualitative aspects of experienced freedom' (*Journal of Mind and Behaviour*, 3, 1982, 99–126).

CHAPTER 8

PERSONAL BEING AS EMPIRICAL UNITY: AUTOBIOGRAPHY

Theme: Personal identity as a public fact must be distinguished from an individual's sense of singularity. I argue that the former is based upon bodily criteria modified by psychological and social considerations. The sense of personal singularity is construed as a belief based upon a locally valid person theory.

Contents

1 PUBLIC AND PRIVATE MODES OF PERSONAL IDENTITY

In this chapter I set about distinguishing the fact of personal being from our sense of it, now as an application of the private — individual/public — collective dichotomy of person and self. The basic distinction that will be deployed is that between the fact of personal identity (what it is that makes a human being this or that particular person within a public — collective context) and the sense of personal identity (how people experience their unique selfhood). Clearly, there is no necessary coordination between these aspects of personal identity. The former could be well established in a species: for example, members might have no difficulty in recognizing each other as different and distinct and treating each other differentially without any member of that species having a sense of their own personal identity. One might imagine this to be the case among chimpanzees.

We know that they treat each other as individuals, but we are by no means so sure each chimpanzee experiences their lives as developing *auto*biographies, centred on a unified consciousness. What is required for someone to have a sense of personal identity?

(1) Clearly, one necessary condition is that the individual should be self-conscious, that is, be aware of their experiences as constituting a personal unity. A miner, hewing at the coal-face, can attend not only to the things which he is doing, the plans which he is entertaining, but know that they are his, by virtue of his capacity to identify himself as a unique person among others. In the sections below I shall be bringing out what is involved in experiencing one's experience and so one's personal life as a unity.

(2) If experiencing matters as one's own were only an ephemeral or momentary phenomenon, then this would not yield the full sense of personal uniqueness. There has also to be some kind of experiential continuity. In some way or other, an individual woman, for example, must treat most of her actions as developments of and connected with her past personal experience and as attributes of one being, herself. In short, a person's present actions must be located in an autobiography, representing the past and anticipating the future.

In order to keep these complex matters under control, it will be necessary to introduce some basic philosophical distinctions among the kinds of identity with which we might be concerned. These reflect two major senses of sameness. These senses of identity are well established in traditional philosophy.

(1) In one sense of 'same', two individuals are the same when they have closely similar properties, that is, are qualitatively identical. They remain, however, numerically different and distinct, and there are two of them.

(2) Sometimes by sameness we mean numerical identity. 'This is the same person' implies that there is only one individual even though some of its properties at different times are different. The notion of numerical identity raises some interesting philosophical problems about what attributes or properties of an individual must remain the same for it to count as one and only one individual of a given kind. Clearly, some kinds of change, for instance changes in body weight, can be tolerated within a continuous numerical personal identity, whereas others such as extreme changes in personality may incline us, though not force us, to talk of one individual or person changing into another. Some of the more difficult conceptual problems in the area of personal identity arise at exactly this point.

A simple way of setting up the distinction between qualitative and numerical identity can be worked out by relating it to spatiotemporal considerations. If individuals exist at the same time and have all their properties in common except their spatial location, then they are numerically distinct. Sometimes an observer notices, at different times, apparently very similar individuals at the same place. Provided the differences between the apparently distinct individuals do not breach the criteria for identifying an individual of that kind and temporal continuity can be assumed, then we can say that there is one and only one individual persisting in that place. Consider a third possible case, in which there are apparently two individuals, some of whose properties are the same and some different, and the properties that are the same are appropriate for the identity of an individual of that category. But we find these seemingly distinctive individuals at different places at different times. Only if a spatiotemporally continuous path from one place at one time to the other place at the other time can be assumed, are we justified in claiming that we have truly one and only one distinct individual. So by reference to the spatiotemporal system and the grid it lays over the world, we are able to set up criteria which can be used to make coherent judgements of identity.

In the human case, considerations of spatiotemporal location and continuous translation point to the body as the source of the fact of identity. But the sense of identity seems to involve subjective and psychological matters like memory, consciousness and so on. However, bodily identity and continuity play a role in both the fact and the sense of identity; and the following considerations make this clear.

The distinctiveness of one's body serves as the basis of the identification of one's self by others as the same person. One can be re-identified from time to time and in different places through one's distinctive physical qualities and a corporeal bdoy is surely spatiotemporally continuous. Once an individual has been identified, say from an old sepia regimental photograph, as having been present at a particular time and place, say Allahabad 1927, then further questions of identity are usually settled by reference to spatiotemporal continuity from that place and moment to the place and moment at which the allegedly identical individual appears to us now, for example, in the dock at the Old Bailey.

It seems clear that the basis of one's personal sense of identity has also to be, at least in part, referred to bodily considerations. Several philosophers have recently argued for the importance of two associated continuities in human experience (e.g. Strawson, *Individuals*, and Hampshire, *Thought and action*). There is the continuity of one's location in space and time relative to one's point of view. One sees the world from a particular place, relative to which particular aspects and perspectives are disclosed to the perceiver. A moment's reflection on one's autobiography suggests that this way of triangulating one's existence forms a large part of one's sense of a permanent self. Spatiotemporal location is also required to understand where and when one can act. For normal human beings one's point of action in the spatiotemporal system, defined by one's relations with other material bodies, is closely related to one's point of view. Even with the help of causal processes by means of which one can bring about changes at other places and times from those at which one initiated an action, one is nevertheless required to find the sensitive triggers that initiate causal processes near where one is standing oneself. These general considerations will allow us to proceed to more detail in considering the two aspects of personal identity we have identified, the fact of identity and the sense of identity.

2   FACT OF IDENTITY

The problems that are raised by the fact of human identity turn on the way in which the two main kinds of criteria, which seem to be at work in deciding whether an individual with whom we are presented is or is not the same person, are related to one another. Consider the case of the Tichbourne claimant, the man who turned up from Australia to establish his right to a disputed estate. Which criterion has priority in deciding whether he is the same person who left England many years before? There is his bodily continuity and the criteria for deciding that; and there is his continuity of 'psyche', manifested in the public and private displays of what one might reasonably call mental aspects of his being, for example, his personality, avowed knowledge and demonstrated skills. His public right to claim a private sense of identity turns on his ability to remember events in his past life of a rich enough texture to sustain a hypothesis of continuity. The major problem of the balance between bodily and mental criteria arises through the difficulty of deciding, in particular cases, which should have priority (see Williams, *Problems of the self*).

By inventing hard cases, philosophers have tested the force of these criteria to try to disentangle their relationships since they are not always clearly distinguished in practice. The first question to be addressed is whether bodily continuity is a necessary condition for personal identity. That is, if one were able to establish similarity of personality and good agreement as to what an individual purported to remember, would this require us to say that two apparently bodily distinct individuals were really (and perhaps necessarily) one and the same person? By considering fantastic examples, philosophers are able to put pressure on these distinctions to see under what conditions they break down. These examples serve as tests to disclose unconsidered aspects of the use of distinctions taken for granted in ordinary unproblematic contexts. Two kinds of examples are usually offered:

Case 1: The case of the emperor and the peasant exemplifies a typical philosopher's test example. The two people have distinctive bodies: on the one hand, plump and well nourished, and, on the other, gnarled and worn by toil. Each has distinctive memories and radically different personalities. They fall asleep in some contrived situation. When they awake, the man who remembers himself to be a peasant soon discovers he is experiencing the world from the bodily envelope of the emperor and vice versa. Now these individuals are clearly located differently in space at the same time. What are we to say about them? Are they or are they not radically changed? Is the emperor in the peasant's body and vice versa, or has the emperor had a radical change of personality and beliefs about himself?

Suppose the personalities of these two individuals remained associated with their bodies as before, i.e. the emperor's body behaved imperiously and spoke with an authoritative tone of voice, and the peasant's body showed in his cracked tones a suitable deference to authority. However, we are to assume that their memories of their previous lives are radically different. The imperious person remembers being a peasant, and the bucolic individual remembers being an emperor. We now might be inclined to say, not that they had exchanged bodies, but that the peasant now remembers the emperor's past life, and the emperor remembers that of the peasant. We could express this by saying 'He [the peasant, by bodily criteria] thinks he is the emperor'. On this basis, the three possible criterial attributes — bodily identity, identity of personality and sameness of memories are ordered as follows:

$$\left.\begin{array}{l}\text{Body}\\\text{Personality}\end{array}\right\} > \text{Memory}$$

Case 2: There are people who claim to be the reincarnations of famous historical persons. We might suppose that all continuous spatiotemporal links have been broken or are unknown and that we are required to decide whether two individuals, whose existence is widely separated in space and time, are the same, that is, numerically identical. Here our grounds can only be personal memory avowals. We might examine the case for numerical identity presented by a Mr John Smith who exhibits the Napoleonic personality and can tell us in a way that satisfies even the most knowledgeable historian of his memories of the campaigns of the great emperor. Philosophical argument has been used to demonstrate that these mentalistic criteria, without a proof of bodily continuity, are not enough. The argument runs as follows: if Mr John Smith could satisfy these requirements there is, it seems, nothing logically impossible about Mr Bill Brown satisfying them as well. Now what do we have — two Napoleons? Or would we be more inclined to say 'Two individuals purporting to be Napoleon'? It seems clear that there is nothing in our conceptual system which obliges us to say the former. The priority among the three main personal qualities has been further clarified as follows:

$$\text{Body} > \left\{ \begin{array}{l} \text{Personality} \\ \text{Memory} \end{array} \right.$$

The upshot of all this is a clear indication that bodily continuity plays a primary role when the cases become difficult. But is it a sufficient condition for personal identity?

To examine the possibility that numerical identity of the body is a sufficient condition for the personal identity of a human being, we shall again examine some hard cases on the borders of real possibility. The case of Miss Beauchamp, given in Prince, *The dissociation of personality*, provides us with a real example. She exhibited radically distinct patterns of behaviour with seemingly very different personalities, abrasive and argumentative, soft and agreeable, and so on. To make the matter more interesting, there was good evidence that she was not able to remember the activities and thoughts she had had when she was behaving in some but not all of these distinctive ways. One might begin to feel that both the personality and the memory criteria point towards different persons even though there could be no doubt about the numerical identity of Miss Beauchamp's body. The question for the philosopher to examine, before any therapeutic work by psychologists, is whether under these circumstances we would be conceptually obliged to treat Miss Beauchamp as a collection of different persons. Should the differences in behaviour and memory be used to individuate several personalities of the one person or *be allocated to* several persons, conceived as distinctive beings? In the former case, we would have an extension of our ordinary working conception. We could say that the same person has very distinctive personalities, and we would save bodily identity as a sufficient condition for unity of personhood. We could say, though Miss Beauchamp is the same person, her range of personalities is more fully differentiated than those of ordinary folk. One reason for adopting this alternative is the well-established fact that even ordinary folk have very distinctive ways of presenting themselves to different people under different circumstances and, indeed, there is some evidence (Helling, 'Autobiography as self-presentation') that memory is distributed differentially with respect to each personality presented, though not in the radically discontinuous way that it was with Miss Beauchamp.

It now seems we are in a position to summarize the criteria by means of which we decide questions of identity for other people. The hard cases demonstrate that the conceptual system which we operate does give priority to continuity of bodily identity and the criteria of physical appearance based upon it. Though we are prepared to distinguish very different kinds of behaviour, and even different clusters of memories as kinds of unities, nevertheless the comfortable thing seems to be to assign these to entities (such as personalities, roles etc.) which are subordinate to or dependent upon persons rather than competitors with them. So, each individual could be thought to have a more or less radically distinguished set of personalities which would be presented differentially for different occasions.

In all of this I have been following the lead of Wittgenstein, looking for the rules for deploying person-concepts which are *criterial* (cf. Canfield, *Wittgenstein, language and world*). Such rules express the 'deep grammar' in accordance with which we use the public−collective concept of 'person' and with which 'persons', as a category, are created.

3 SENSE OF IDENTITY

To explore the sense we have of our own identity in any disciplined fashion one must avoid vague discussions of what it feels like to be 'myself'. We can follow an alternative route by exploring the idea of a criterion of personal identity: a criterion I might be imagined to employ to decide about myself. What can be made of the questions 'Who am I?' and statements like 'I'm not myself today'? Does the former represent a genuine puzzle, and is the latter an expression of a discovery about personal identity? To answer this one must ask what conditions have to be met for there to be a criterion, for an entity to be judged to be this or that kind of thing (*see* Shoemaker, *Self-knowledge and self-identity*). Clearly, one important condition must be that we admit the possibility of the criterion not being met and candidates being rejected. In attempting to answer the question 'Who am I?', could I make the discovery that I am not, after all, myself? Could I, for example, find out I was someone else? It is intuitively obvious, I think, that these considerations are nonsensical. They are nonsensical because, to query one's own personal, as contrasted with one's social identity undermines one of the very presuppositions that are required for first person utterances to make sense, namely that they are the utterances of an individual person. In short, to have just this sense of any individuality, to treat myself as a possible subject of predication as I treat others, is a necessary part of what it is to be a person. When I ask, 'Who am I?', the most I could mean would be 'Which of various possible social identities, publicly identified, is legitimately or properly mine?'. Amnesia is not a loss of the sense of identity, but rather involves the inaccessibility of various items of knowledge about my public and social being, my past history. The fact that some of the loss concerns private – individual matters shows that the ability to *maintain* a continuous autobiography is secondary. The joint unities, point of view and point of action, make autobiographies possible. The statement 'I am not myself today' can only mean that I do not feel the same as I did yesterday, which presupposes a conserved sense of identity. Since, then, I cannot doubt that I am the author, as it were, of my own speech, the very idea of a criterion for my sense of my own identity is empty.

Philosophers have made this point in various ways. Butler, 'Of personal identity', for example, argued that memory cannot be the basis of a sense of identity since the very notion of memory presupposes that identity. For instance, it is empty to ask whether these memories I am remembering are mine. I can ask only whether what I take to be a memory is an accurate recollection of what happened to me or of what I did. To ponder on whether my recollections are another's memories is at most to ask whether I could perhaps be recollecting someone else's experience. Whatsoever they were, they must, as recollections, be my experiences since I am now experiencing them. At best I can be amazed that my imaginings are like your rememberings, so alike as to be qualitatively identical with your recollections in so far as we can make comparisons. But even in that case, my discovery that you and I have identical, i.e. very similar, recollections of a great many events is no ground whatever for the hypothesis that I am you.

What, then, are the origins of this strong sense of identity? I propose to show that the best hypothesis is that, though the sense of identity is conceptually and logically distinct from the fact of personal identity, nevertheless the former, in the course of human development, derives from the latter. Adequate empirical studies of this matter have yet to be made, but there are pieces of work which can be treated as the first step in a programme of research into the psychological foundations of personal being. The very first step in devising such a programme must be the classification of the relevant features of the notion of identity, brought out by philosophical analysis, features that could serve as the basis of hypotheses to be explored by developmental psychologists.

Bruner's work on 'peek-a-boo' games in 'Early rule structure' would make a good beginning.

The arguments of philosophers such as Hampshire, *Thought and action*, concerning the role of bodily identity in personhood lead, as I have pointed out, to the idea that a person experiences the world from a particular here and now, that is, has a point of view, which is co-ordinated in the spatiotemporal system with their point of action. This doctrine derives from the necessary conditions for the referential uses of words. If I am to be able to refer to something, to point to it, in the world, I must know from where I am pointing as well as to what. That is, I must anchor my frame of reference to the corporeal here and now. Ordinarily, this is done through the indexical presuppositions of the uses of the word 'I', presuppositions which embody the very idea that I am here and speaking now. One might wish to argue that having acquired a language and in so doing grasped the indexicality of referential expressions, a human being is in possession of the concept of numerical identity in space and time, since experience soon provides that person with the idea of a trajectory through a spatiotemporal system which is the locus of their coordinated points of view and points of action.

However, in order to achieve this happy coincidence, the actor must be in possession of the system of personal pronouns and know-how to use them. The indexicality of 'I' depends, it might be argued, upon the grasp of the simple referential function of 'you'. Since 'myself' is not a thing I could discover, it seems I cannot first experience myself and then attach the personal pronoun 'I' to that experience. I must be learning the pronoun system as a whole through the ways in which and the means by which I am treated as a person by others. So that, by being treated as 'you', or as a member of 'we', I am now in a position to add 'I' to my vocabulary, to show where, in the array of persons, speaking, thinking, feeling, promising and so on, is happening. In order to be addressed as 'you', I must be being perceived as a definite embodied person, that is, as a distinct human but material individual by others. This unity of pronoun system might be one of the things that is meant by the social construction of the self. But it depends upon the recognizable bodily identity that I have even as an infant. I have identified these as the indexical uses of 'I'.

I am also treated by other people as having a distinct point of view and being the locus of exercises of agency. So that these very conditions of bodily identity, identified by Hampshire, *Thought and action*, as necessary conditions for having the idea of myself as a person, are also, it seems, to be taken as presumptions that are embedded in all kinds of social practices. For example, the idea that a person has a distinct point of action is embedded in such practices as moral praise and blame. That kind of talk makes sense only upon the presupposition that one has a point of action through which one's intentions and so on can be realized.

So the acquisition of the idea of personal identity for oneself, through which one develops a sense of identity, is at least in part a consequence of social practices which derive from the fact of identity as it is conceived in a culture. Our first preliminary conclusion, then, must be that a human being learns that he or she is a person from others and in discovering a sphere of action the source of which is treated by others as the very person they identify as having spatiotemporal identity. Thus, a human being does not learn that he or she is a person by the empirical disclosure of an experiential fact. Personal identity is symbolic of social practices not of empirical experiences. It has the status of a theory.

However, there is a great deal more to the sense of personal identity than the realization that one has a point of view and can act upon the world at certain places. We must now turn to what I shall call transcendental conditions. These require certain features of personhood as necessary conditions for the possibility of certain kinds of human activities. Philosophers have insisted, and rightly, since the days of David Hume, that in an important sense the self is not experienced. As Hume pointed out, 'I never can catch *myself* at any time without a perception, and never can observe anything but the perception (*A treatise of human nature*, book 1, pt 4, s. 4).

4 SUMMARY OF THE ARGUMENT

The first step towards identifying transcendental features of selfhood involved in the sense of identity was to notice that the considerations advanced above and the analysis based upon them depend upon the assumption of the existence of two kinds of unities.

There is a unity of the realm of consciousness in that, for instance, the experiences I have as a being, spatiotemporally and socially located, and acting where I am, are coordinated in one realm of experience. Consciousness is not divided, and hence does not have to be combined. But this is not to say that that of which I am conscious is not ordered. Clearly, there is an indefinite potential hierarchy of 'knowings' which is given by the possibility of reflexive consciousness. Thus, I can become aware of an orange, pay attention to it, and perhaps, if suitably prompted, can know that I am attending to it, and so on. One of the commonplace techniques of dealing with pain is to attend not so much to the pain but to the relation in which I, as experiencer, stand to that pain.

This leads to a second kind of unity. The hierarchy of experience is paralleled for human beings by a hierarchy of action. I can act upon the things in the world, for instance tennis balls, and I can act upon my actions upon the things in the world, for instance I can improve my forehand style. It would not be unreasonable to say that the hierarchies of awareness and of action involve a regress of the very same self; that the centre of consciousness and the source of action are one self. I act according to a rule; I adopt the rule according to some principle; I accept a principle according to some theory, and so on. It would not be unreasonable to argue that it is the very same 'I' who is aware of the peeling of an orange, who knows that he is aware of peeling an orange, and so on.

It is now clear, I hope, where the need for a transcendental hypothesis comes from. These coordinated unified hierarchies are unified via the self which is presupposed in them. Each time that an individual is able to make a start up the hierarchy of action and hopes, naïvely, to experience the self which makes that step and which is, as it were, the origin of the sphere of experience, that self must remove itself from the realm of experience. The sense I have of myself, then, must include the very complex idea of something not experienced but presupposed as a necessary condition for the form that experience takes; in particular, its unified and hierarchical form. The fine structure of this kind of hierarchy has been perceptively explored by Langford in 'Persons as necessarily social'. From the point of view of the philosophy of science, 'the self' is a theoretical concept, and the sense of self derives from the way we experience our experiences as unified, but is not reducible to it. From the point of view of the philosophy of psychology, that unification is an achievement, made possible by the possession of the chief unifying concept, 'myself'. The 'how' and 'what' of all this will occupy us in the chapters to come.

These matters need to be further elaborated: the idea of an array of persons as the moral order that forms the background of all thought and action; the uses of personal pronouns as a key to the understanding of the structuring of experience; the identification of a mother – infant interaction pattern from which personal being emerges.

5 AUTOBIOGRAPHY AS SELF-KNOWLEDGE

Presented in the course of development with a sense of self, a human being can undertake the organization of memories and beliefs into a narrative of which he or she is the central character. However, autobiography is not just a chronicle of episodes, whether private or public. It has also to do with a growing grasp of capabilities and potentials. As such it involves the exploitation of the conditions for both consciousness and agency. For expository purposes, the structure of the argument of this work can be reflected in three aspects of autobiography.

Consciousness, I have argued, is not some unique state, but is the possession of certain grammatical models for the presentation to oneself and others of what one knows by inter- and intrapersonal perception. These models provide the structures by which I can know that which *I* am currently feeling, thinking, suffering, doing and so on, that is, they provide the wherewithal for an organization of knowledge as mine.

Agency, likewise, is an endowment from theory, permitting the formulation of hypotheses about what I was, am or could be capable. Through this my history is enriched by reference to possibilities of thought and action and so finds a continuous link with the moral orders through which I have lived my life.

To create autobiography out of this some of my beliefs about myself must stand as memories, of what I have at other times thought, done, felt and enjoyed. But as we have seen there is nothing in the phenomenal quality of experiences which authenticates them as true recollections. The category of belief-as-recollection is socially constructed and hierarchically organized. Autobiography involves the social conditions of the confirmation of recollections. The systematic exploitation of this feature of autobiographical work is the foundation of De Waele's 'assisted construction' method in 'Autobiography as a scientific method', for the development of a self-history (*see* research menu 8).

6 SPECULATION: THE BREAKDOWN OF TRANSCENDENTAL UNITIES

I have argued that what makes a being a person is the possession and use of a certain theory, in terms of which that being constructs and orders its beliefs, plans, feelings and actions. I have suggested that the acquisition of the person-engendering theory occurs, and indeed must occur, in the course of changing responsibilities within relationships of psychological symbiosis.

One of the learning progressions which contributes most to the capacity to grasp oneself as a being who perceives the world from a certain point of view is the acquisition of the capacity to use the personal pronouns. With this goes a practical understanding of indexicality, the technique of displaying where in an array of persons something personal is happening. At the same time a nascent person is receiving praise, blame, exhortation, prohibition and so on for what he or she is doing or trying to do. Through these language games a being is acquiring the idea that it can be an actor, with a point of action, that is, has leverage within the world, and with the idea comes the capacity.

The theory I have used to illustrate the social constructivist thesis identifies consciousness and agency, point of view and point of action as one and as mine through the theoretical concept of 'self'. I follow Kant in calling this a transcendental unity, not given in experience, but rather the means by which experience is ordered. There may be cultures where the unity of experience and the unity of action are not unified in a higher order singular conception.

What might be expected to happen to people built up in our way if the unity between point of view and point of action begins to break down? Remember this is not the idea of there being an awareness of some phenomenological disaster, but rather the lapsing of a theoretical standpoint, like ceasing to believe in the unity of electricities.

Failure of memory might make it impossible to order one's experience around the idea of a continuous trajectory of point of view, while one may continue to deploy moment by moment the idea that one acts more or less where one is currently located and in accordance with what one is momentarily intending. This possibility could be realized in some forms of senility. Only against the background of a general belief in the unity of unities does senility appear as a deficit, as opposed to just another form of life.

Another theoretical possibility is that the sense of agency, of being in control of one's actions, may dissolve while one retains a continuous sense of self as a being experiencing the world and one's own states from a continuously developing trajectory of space – time locations and relationships with other people. Certain kinds of schizophrenia seem to have this general character. This is not intended as any kind of rough sketch of a theory of schizophrenia, rather a speculation as to one of the cognitive deficits that might enter into the condition. Then there are cases where, though point of view and point of action are both maintained, they are not unified, but if both dissolve the person has ceased to be.

RESEARCH MENU 8

All the necessary techniques for research into the autobiographies of individual human beings are already available in the work of J.-P. de Waele (*see* De Waele and Harré 'Autobiography as a scientific method'). Whenever this method has been put to work, the results have been very encouraging; see, for example, work of Debi Stec on the autobiographies of the obese currently under way at SUNY, Binghamton. Of course, an autobiographical study takes time and trouble.

BIBLIOGRAPHICAL NOTES 8

From the huge body of literature on personal identity I select the following: S. HAMPSHIRE, *Thought and action* (London: Chatto and Windus, 1959), B. A. O. WILLIAMS, *Problems of the self* (Cambridge: Cambridge University Press, 1973), M. PRINCE, *The dissociation of personality* (London: Kegan Paul, Truscott and Shrubner, 1905), I. HELLING, 'Autobiography as self-presentation' (in *Life sentences*, ed. R. Harré, London: John Wiley and Sons, 1976), S. SHOEMAKER, *Self-knowledge and self-identity* (Ithaca: New York: Cornell University Press, 1963), an excellent work. Much of our modern way of looking at the problems of identity of persons comes from J. BUTLER, 'Of personal identity' (in *The works of Bishop Butler*, ed. J. H. Bernard, London:, 1900).

For the hierarchical nature of the sense of identity see G. LANGFORD, 'Persons as necessarily social' (*Journal for the Theory of Social Behaviour*), 8, 1978, 263–83).

Additional works cited in the text are J. BRUNER, 'Early rule structure: the case of peek-a-boo' (in *Life sentences*, ed. R. Harré, Chichester: John Wiley and Sons, 1976); J. CANFIELD, *Wittgenstein, language and world* (Amherst: University of Massachusetts Press, 1981); J.-P. DE WAELE and R. HARRÉ, 'Autobiography as a scientific method' (in *Emerging strategies in social scientific research*, ed. G. P. Ginsburg, Chichester: John Wiley and Sons, 1979, ch. 8); D. HUME, *A treatise of human nature* (1739, ed. D. G. C. Macnabb, London: Fontana, Collins, 1962).

PART III

Personal Development

CHAPTER 9

MORAL PHILOSOPHY AND
MORAL PSYCHOLOGY

Theme: Moral philosophers and developmental psychologists have concentrated on cognitive aspects of action, particularly on how people decide between possible courses of action. The moral quality of emotions and the moral issues involved in striving or endeavour have been neglected by both. This can be brought out by a study of moralities of honour. A critical account of moral developmental psychology shows how the study of strength of mind and weakness of will can be brought back into the centre of personal psychology.

Contents
1 Limitations of contemporary moral theory
2 Moral development psychology as political rhetoric
  Reservations concerning cognitive development as staging
  Kohlberg's theory of moral development
3 Moralities without decisions
  Moralities of honour
  Moralities of conation
4 An alternative theory of moral development
  Moral orders
  Psychological symbiosis

1 LIMITATIONS OF CONTEMPORARY MORAL THEORY

Philosophical consideration of morality has traditionally concerned itself with a search for and critical assessment of the grounds of moral judgement. Are moral judgements based upon the reasons for an action, for instance its likely consequents, or are they assessments of the quality of an action taken in itself? If the latter, are they descriptions of some special and undefined moral quality which actions may sometimes have, or do they express one's emotional reactions to the action, as contemplated or as realized? If moral judgements of the rightness or wrongness, justice or injustice of actions and policies are based upon reasons, what is the justification for taking those as the reasons that count, and to what ultimate principles would a chain of such justifications lead? Can there be a justification for the ultimate moral principles upon which a morality rests? Such enquiries presume an ability to recognize moral judgements from among all others. But what makes a judgement a moral judgement? Hare, for instance, has argued in *Freedom and reason* that moral judgements are recommendations or prescriptions of courses of action under the condition that the prescription should apply to everyone. Others, for instance Urmson 'On grading', have thought that moral judgements expressed the result of an evaluation of actions or courses of actions against socially specified criteria of worth. A long-running controversy concerned whether the criteria of worth could be grounded in the facts about a society, the nature of man and other natural matters.

If moral judgements are the heart of morality, moral issues will arise over what people do and not over what happens to them, yet much everyday moral condemnation and praise is devoted to people's emotional reactions. It is wrong to feel satisfaction in another's discomfort, to take pleasure in another's pain; and it is right to pity the unfortunate and to sympathize with the bereaved. Furthermore, moral philosophers typically abstract the judgements from the judges, and study the forms of reasoning they require. But what of the moral assessment of persons, as gentlemen, cads, bounders, tarts, bitches, layabouts, gossips, swots, mugs and the rest? If this question is addressed it is usually dealt with in terms of typical actions.

In so far as morality is the province of decisions among alternatives, the weighing up of reasons and the assessment of actions against criteria of worth, the psychology of morality is a branch of cognitive psychology. An aim of this book is to show that many cognitive processes which are treated both by psychologists and by philosophers as if they were individually located and privately performed are modelled on interpersonal discussions under collective conventions, and frequently take their aboriginal form. In this chapter, I hope to show how partial is the cognitive view, both in developmental psychology and in the analysis of the morality of everyday life. In the former case, the classic works of Piaget (*The language and thought of the child; Judgement and reasoning of the child*) and Kohlberg, 'Moral stages and moralization', are flawed through ethnocentrisms. In the latter, the philosophers, with some exceptions, have ignored what I shall call 'moralities of honour' in which the psychology of conation, striving and the exercise of power, replaces the study of cognition as the main empirical focus.

Philosophers are not much given to discussing sin, yet as Sabini and Silver, *Moralities of everyday life*, suggest, the study of sin throws a good deal of light on everyday moral issues. One could begin with the seven deadly sins (pride, gluttony, anger, lust, envy, sloth and avarice), but modern morality shifts its ground a little. Among the modern sins is self-absorption (reaching a criminal degree in psychopathy); among those of the recent past, dishonouring the uniform and the cloth with 'conduct unbecoming . . .'; and in ancient and modern times alike, sloth, with its siblings laziness and procrastination. Among the modern virtues are 'not being at everyone's beck and call', 'not being sticky or priggish', 'not rushing into things', though being biddable, priggish, awkward and impetuous are merely venial.

It is clearly wrong to take pleasure in the pain, misfortune or humiliation of another. Only in German is there a word for this emotion, *Schadenfreude*, but it is a recognizable feeling for most Europeans and universally condemned. It goes along with such moral failings as the satisfaction one feels in retelling bad news. By virtue of a concentration on the problem 'What shall I do?', much contemporary moral philosophy has left uncharted the morality of emotion. To the moralities of choosing and the moralities of acting, we must add the moralities of feeling. In traditional and everyday moralities feeling 'bad' emotions is as much to be deplored as doing 'wrong' things. Yet emotions are passions, and the feeling of them cannot be treated as a form of intended action (though there are those who seek occasions when an emotion of a certain sort is likely to be prompted).

It is worth glancing again at the seven deadly sins. From the psychological point of view they are a diverse catalogue — sloth and gluttony are concerned with 'doing' (too little in the one case and too much in the other), but lust, anger, envy and pride are emotions. Although we condemn rape, aggression, belittling and strutting, the typical action consequences of the 'bad' emotions, my intuition favours the idea that the sinfulness of the emotions is independent of the evil or absurdity of their manifestations.

A moral classification of the emotions should recognize sympathy, love, pity and many others as good, and those who feel them as praiseworthy. Perhaps the moral condemnation of lust, pride and so on could be shown to be derivative from the wickedness of the actions, the subject of these emotions is thus primed to perform, which are judged according to traditional criteria such as whether one would assess them equally for everyone, their utility, whether they involved the infliction of pain and so on. While this may be true of some emotions, perhaps of lust and greed, love and sympathy, it cannot serve to explain the moral quality of all. Neither envy nor *Schadenfreude* issue in typical actions. It is just wrong to feel them. And the same is true for pity, since to feel pity for the unfortunate just *is* good. But these are 'passions'. How can we be responsible for them?

2   MORAL DEVELOPMENT PSYCHOLOGY AS POLITICAL RHETORIC

Reservations concerning cognitive development as staging

The dominant school of moral development psychology, the followers of Kohlberg, presume that the central psychological feature of morality is moral reasoning, and that there is a development in individual competence in coping with moral issues of everyday life. There are reasons to challenge both presumptions. The emphasis on moral reasoning links Kohlberg's theories with those of Piaget, for he above all has promoted the principle of cognitive development through an invariant sequence of stages. Doubts about the psychological reality of Piagetian stages brush off onto the presumptive underpinning of Kohlberg's proposals for staged development in the psychology of morality. I shall begin the examination of the psychology of morality with a brief résumé of the reservations one must have over the Piagetian staging.

It is assumed that differences in the performances of children of different ages are to be explained by the existence of a sequence of stages, marking steps in cognitive development, so that the stage last in time is the highest in cognitive sophistication. Each stage is defined by the nature of cognition yielding processes typical of it; the basic schema is as follows:

> Egocentric cognition
> Concrete operations
> Formal operations

Transition between stages is not brought about by automatic increments due to maturation but is the result of activities which are themselves sequential. New situations force new cognitive performances on children which are first 'assimilated', that is, a skill, technique or idea is merely added to the repertoire, and then 'accommodated' by a reconstructing of the intellectual economy to include it as a proper component. It is mostly by social imperatives that novelties are acquired.

Instead of three stages of ordered cognitive development, the social constructivist claims that there are three kinds of social orders, distinguished by their conversational imperatives, to which a child (or an adult) can belong, not necessarily in the order of succession presumed by Piaget. One's suspicions are aroused by noticing the significant coincidence between the notably logicist philosophy of science of Pierre Duhem, in *The aim and structure of physical theory*, and Piaget's highest stage, formal operations. Métraux ('Evolutionary epistemology') has pointed out the extent to which the order of stages which Piaget presents as empirical fact are reflections of the neo-Comptean philosophy in which Piaget himself grew up.

The idea of cognitive development as a series of transitions between stages, brought about through the mechanism of assimilation (acquired cognitive skill) and accommodation (adjusting one's existing knowledge and capacities to include it), depends wholly on the assumption of an invariance in the sequence of transitions by which kinds of cognitive operations become an ordered series, that is, a development. The alleged order of stages, as offered by Piaget, is a reflection of an ethnocentric view of the relative *worth* of different forms of higher mental functioning. Two features of Piaget's rhetoric should be noticed. He consistently makes use of biological metaphors, leading one to a certain reading of concepts like 'development', a reading which makes the successive stages of cognitive development seem natural. But, he also insists, transitions from stage to stage will not occur without the appropriate experience, and so 'development' is not quite 'maturation'. Comptean metaphysics appears again in comparison between the alleged historical development of science, popularized in the interests of Cartesian logicism by Pierre Duhem, and individual development. So modes of reasoning are ordered relative to a version of cultural history. Since the present is supposed to be a culmination of the past, that is, this version of the cultural history of science is treated as exemplifying progress, a strict and inevitable ordering of stages emerged from the rhetoric, that is without argumentative justification (see Riegel and Rosenwald, *Structure and transformation*). But is cognitive sophistication as defined by the actual development of science really to be found in abstract formalization? Much recent discussion in the philosophy of science has been critical of 'logicism', the idea that ideals of scientific thought can be expressed in abstract formal terms.

Scientific thinking seems to depend, and necessarily depend, on concrete manipulations of intensional content (see Boyd on 'Metaphor and theory change'). So it is at least arguable that Piaget's assumption that we go on to abstract formal operations may be a peculiarity of French culture, a final fling for Cartesianism. The ethnocentricity of the belief that abstract formal thought is 'deep' comes out very nicely in the Duham—Campbell controversy in which Duhem, arguing for a purely formal reading of scientific theories identified 'deep and narrow' thinking with the style of French science. Campbell, defending the 'shallow but broad' forms of English thought in *Physics: The elements*, showed that truly formal theories are arbitrary, there being an indefinite number capable of accounting for (deductively related to) any proposed empirical basis, say the results of some series of observations and/or experiments.

However, it might be objected, has not Piaget shown, by experiment, that the stages exist? Grave doubts have in fact been cast on his interpretations of his findings. For instance, both Bryant, *Perception and understanding in the young child*, and Carey – Block seem to have shown that the famous conservation tasks can be interpreted as what can be called 'pseudo-staging effects'. Piaget's test tasks, for instance the conservation of volume task, called for the joint use of two or more cognitive skills. A child solves the problem by giving priority to one cognitive skill over another, depending on the interpretation the child gives to the question it is asked. If social and linguistic assumptions favour one cognitive skill, it will be displayed effectively masking the fact that in suitable circumstances the competing cognitive skill could be displayed. Of even more significance, the differential rights of different social categories, say child and adult as categorized in modern times, to display particular cognitive skills can also lead to the masking of one capacity by the manifestation of another. It is easy to read the later unmasking, through the growing confidence to handle complex tasks *or* the acquisition of the right to give a certain kind of performance, as the appearance *de novo* of 'the next stage'.

An alternative, but admittedly speculative account of cognitive maturation, preserving Piaget's empirical discoveries as to what middle-class Swiss children can and cannot do, is possible. Suppose one were to begin with Aires' thesis in *Centuries of childhood* that the idea of childhood as a cognitively and morally rudimentary stage of human life is a cultural innovation and a fairly recent one at that. There is a certain amount of evidence that suggests that what children can do is at least partly a reflection of what they are expected to do. For instance, traditional Jewish educational practice treated all children of four years and over as adult in capacity, lacking only the breadth of knowledge and the opportunity for practice to distinguish them from adults. Link this with Roger Brown's suggestion in that full adult linguistic capacity is achieved by about the age of five years, with the grasp of the grammar of tag questions of the 'isn't it?', 'wouldn't you?' sort, and we have the germ of a theory. I can express this theory in terms of four theses.

(1) The full repertoire of cognitive skills is a consequence of a complete grasp of the principles of talk. This must necessarily be so, given

the Vygotsky-style arguments about the nature of thinking in earlier chapters. By the age of five years (we retain the concept of infancy for the period of apprenticeship from birth to five years), logical reasoning at the level of practical syllogism is established, together with the complementary techniques of generalization, for instance the capacity to take another's point of view as equivalent and reciprocal to one's own through the use of the distinction between person and self, and of instantiating, for instance realizing that one's conduct falls under a rule. (Piaget's 'demonstration' that syllogism is not available until very much later seems to be clearly an artefact of his method.)

(2) In subsequent years there are changes, increments and decrements, in the amount and the kind of material available on which to exercise these skills. During what we call 'childhood and adolescence' a corpus of knowledge is built up. I believe that this point can be established through the fact that the autonomous childhood social world has all the conceptual and social machinery of the adult world, but differs greatly in content.

(3) There is a cognitive capacity that does change. This is the ability to deal with more complex tasks and to handle greater masses of material. This comes out clearly in Linaza's comparative study of the game of marbles in 'The acquisition of the rules of games in children'. The simpler the game, the sooner the rules become objects of manipulation and negotiation, contrary to the age-grades identified by Piaget.

(4) Since a body of knowledge is a social construction and since skills, be they cognitive or manual, are manifested in performances, that is, appear as social displays, one would expect there to be cultural and political constraints on development. The social and political position of adults relative to modern children must surely require certain ritual recognitions of superior status in the right to display superior skills. Nowhere has this been more vividly illustrated than in the efforts by certain dons to prevent the admission of 'under-age' students to Oxford University. On the one hand, the processes of person-making must succeed in manufacturing the right kind of social being for the reproduction of the culture, while on the other, these very processes must expressively display the hierarchic nature of that order. So childhood, once invented, becomes both a cognitive stage (stages) and a social status.

But it might be objected, has it not been shown by empirical studies in the field of moral development that certain young people tend to use methods of moral reasoning that display all the expected Piagetian characteristics of the concrete operation stage? However, the empirical work is heavily flawed. For one thing it uses the peculiar documentary

methods of Kohlberg, discussed in more detail below. More importantly, it involves some deep-seated confusion in interpreting the
activities of the 'subjects'. The alleged evidence for consigning the subjects to a lowly cognitive stage is their persistence in applying moral
principles only to their own group and not to 'everybody'. This is supposed to show a cognitive deficit, a lack of the capacity to generalize.
But the very cognitive principle supposedly absent from the repertoire
of the skills of the 'subjects' is actually *displayed* in their reasoning,
since they refer all moral problems of a certain kind to an appropriate
principle, though they apply the principle only to themselves. Unfortunately, in a way typical of the limited sophistication of the moral development research, the 'subjects' were not given the opportunity to
display generalizing capacity in other contexts where presumably they
might have thought they had cognitive rights, for example in cooking,
say 'always salt potatoes'. Nor were they given the opportunity to
handle implicit *ceteris paribus* conditions, such as those that apply
when cooking for someone with heart disease. As I will emphasize
below, in the moral field it may be more sophisticated to apply moral
principles differentially than universally.

These reflections suggest some rather fundamental reservations. Perhaps the very idea of 'cognitive development' is a cultural artefact. We
might suppose instead that in every culture what someone does is a
reflection of their beliefs as to whether they have the right to do something and/or the confidence to carry out a cognitive operation in the
possible or actual presence of certain others. The relations between
rights, confidence and competence are not dealt with in Piagetian research as far as I know (*see* research menu 9). Even if this tangle were
tidied up the problem posed by the ethnocentricism of the comparison
of history of science to individual human development typical of
Piagetian thought would remain.

The cognitive 'development' is a secondary phenomenon, an appearance, a cultural illusion, a way of representing a redistribution of rights
in the changing social structures of psychologically symbiotic dyads,
triads etc. interconnected with a changing capacity to deal with few or
many matters at once (figure 9.1). The curves represent possible
pseudo-developmental trajectories. We tend to regard A as normal. But
B is also a possible life form, for example that of a middle-class child
during a Khmer Rouge regime. And there are many others. To regard
A as universal is to assimilate the local conventions of a moral order
displayed as theory of development to some supposed trans-situational
programme for a generalized human being. Thought of this way,
deviations from A become abnormalities, not normal growth into
alternative social worlds. But if we are to proceed to develop the conse-

quences of these basic ideas in more detail, the theories of the moral developmentalists must be examined as they purport to have mapped the universal and inevitable progression by which cognitively and morally competent persons arise.

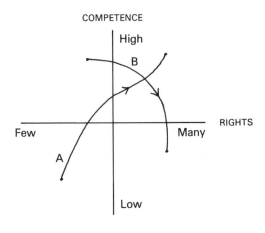

FIGURE 9.1

Kohlberg's theory of moral development

Any theory of how persons are manufactured must include both an account of how the system or systems of rules and beliefs concerning one's responsibility for and accountability to others are acquired and an account of the variety of such systems within which social and personal being is possible. The most important existing approach to understanding moral development is the Piagetian-inspired theory of Kohlberg in 'Moral stages and moralization: the cognitive-developmental approach'. I propose to examine it in some detail since its defects are illustrative of much that is unsatisfactory in contemporary efforts at personal psychology.

Kohlberg's conception of moral development involves two main principles: that central to managing the moral life is a cognitive activity properly to be treated as 'moral reasoning'; and that a person's capacity to carry it out develops in stages, each stage marking a level of cognitive capacity in the manner of Piaget. Individual people can become 'stuck' at a certain level of moral reasoning because of their failure to develop the cognitive capacities necessary for the next stage. This idea is used to explain the supposed prevalence of a certain kind of answer to moral dilemmas posed by psychologists to various kinds of people.

Underlying the account of the stages of the development of capacities for moral reasoning, which most followers of Kohlberg suppose must be applicable to the acquisition of any moral theory, are three Piagetian transitions: (a) from restricted to universal applications; (b) from concrete to abstract representations; (c) from taking principles of thought and action as given to treating some of them as negotiable. These transitions are supposed somehow to be connected. For instance, there is a tendency to take (a) and (b) together as versions of a deeper shift in way of thinking from considering actual objects to possible objects. To treat a moral principle as having universal application, one must take it as applied not only to actual but also to possible people, people one does not know, and this is a step away from considering only concrete cases.

The key questions with which to probe Kohlberg's approach are these:

(1) Can the stages which are specified in the theory as representing steps in a hierarchy from less to more sophisticated modes of reasoning concerning moral issues be shown to be autonomous moral orders?

(2) Can the order in which they are ranked be explained by reference to the ethnocentric moral and political presumptions of Anglo-American middle-class intellectuals?

I believe it can be demonstrated that the 'stages' are not sequential steps in a ladder of cognitive sophistication, but are alternative metaphysical – moral theories, all involving essentially the same cognitive capacities. The Kohlberg scheme is applicable only to moral development in contemporary North American culture, dominated as it is by a naïve conception of distributive justice. It cannot be applied to the understanding of *development* within other moral orders, for some because it already contains them as alleged 'stages' and for others, the important moralities of honour, because their basic concepts have no place in the scheme at any stage. There is no place in the 'ladder' for developing powers of personal resolution. It is perhaps necessary to remind the reader of the main features of Kohlberg's scheme.

According to Kohlberg, there are three methods of moral reasoning: pre-conventional, conventional and post-conventional. In the pre-conventional level of moral cognition, reasons for 'following the rules' are external to the moral principles themselves, perhaps to be found in the fear of punishment for infringement or the anticipation of the pleasures of obedience. In the conventional level, moral principles have authority but there is a *social* differentiation within this level represented, mistakenly as I shall show, as a cognitive distinction. At the lower stage the principles are seen as having authority only within one's own local group, while at the higher stage the authority of moral principles is taken to be universal, at the very least, society-wide. It is at this point that the notion of justice enters the story, borne in on the back of universal applicability. It becomes the dominant consideration in the higher stages. In the post-conventional stage, there emerges the idea that rules may be unjust and that they can be changed, culminating again in a universalistic leap, paralleling the transitions in the second level, when universal principles of justice, such as consistency of application of a rule are drawn on in the moral discussion. At times, Kohlberg seems to believe in the possibility of a final 'level' or 'stage', where even universal principles of justice come under scrutiny.

I believe it could be shown that each level and each stage in a level represents a full-blown moral position (*see* Kitwood, *Disclosures to a stranger*). For my purposes, enough will be achieved if I can show:

(1) That the alleged *advance* within the conventional level, from local to universal applications of moral principle, is not a cognitive step, that is, an advance to a more sophisticated form of *reasoning*, but rather a change from one metaphysical – moral system to another, each of which can be taken to be a dominant form of a distinctive society.

(2) That the alleged step to the idea of negotiability of rules and principles that distinguishes both late conventional and post-conventional reasoning from lower levels is not a function of the cognitive sophistication of the actors, but rather of the logical status of the rules and principles in question. They are not negotiable when taken as constitutive rules, that is, as creating a social order; but they are thought to be negotiable when taken as regulative, that is, used for the controlling of action within an existing order. The distinction between a constitutive and a regulative role for rules is not a difference in cognitive sophistication.

I have already drawn attention to the weakness of the empirical evidence that allegedly supports the idea that the practice of applying a moral principle to one's local group represents a cognitive deficit. No evidence is presented to show that in other contexts people subscribing to that practice do not manage the relation between existential (some) and universal (any, all) quantification perfectly well. This consideration suggests irresistibly that the practice of applying a rule locally is the mark of a certain moral/political position; and there are metaphysical assumptions involved, too. The very idea that there is a contrast between local group applications (say to one's family) and universal societal applications (to anyone) involves a dubious reification of the abstraction 'society'. It could be argued that it is an ideological illusion to believe that there is such an entity as 'society' as a group of essentially similar beings; to build moral reasonings on that premise is naïve.

Behind all this is a deep logical confusion about the nature of social groups. One kind of group exists by virtue of the essential similarity in some important respects of all its members; another by virtue of functional differentiation of members by reference to their locations in a role structure, particularly of a self-maintaining microsystem such as a monastery. The egalitarian moralities whose moral superiority is presupposed in treating moral reasoning as universalistic are slipped in along with the conception of 'society' as a group of the first kind. No place can be found for aristocratic and feudal moralities which involve a conception of society as an order, even as a hierarchical structure, that is, a group of the second kind where universalistic reasoning would be inappropriate. Clearly, to presume that for real human circumstances to reason on a basis of universality of application of a moral rule or moral assessment is an advance is to take for granted that societies which are formed of morally and socially similar individuals are higher forms of human association than those formed of morally and socially differentiated individuals. But this is itself a *moral* position. I will be examining the workings of aristocratic and feudal moralities in detail below, but I hope enough has been said to show the fallacy in Kohlberg's staging of the step to universality. A similar confusion runs through Kohlberg's application of the concept of justice. Justice might be achieved by treating everyone in certain respects alike. It might also be just to treat everyone differently in so far as his or her means, deserts or capacities were different.

In Kohlberg's scheme the alleged transition from reasoning in which rules appear as fixed items (but perhaps axiomatically) to reasoning in the course of which rules are negotiated is an important divide. It reflects the Piagetian discovery that the rules of the game of marbles are first treated as given and only later become objects of manipulation and negotiation, and thus can be seen to be open to reform. The detailed comparative study by Linaza ('Acquisition of the rules of games') of the game of marbles, and the reasoning about it of the youthful players in England and Spain, shows that the difference between the given and the negotiable should not be taken as a mark of stages in the development of modes of reasoning. Linaza found that children did indeed insist that 'You can't change the rules', but he discovered that this principle was held on the grounds that the given rules are constitutive of the game. It did not betoken any kind of cognitive *deficit*. If the rules were to be changed, they would be playing a different game. When Linaza told children that he had seen others playing marbles according to different rules, they replied 'Well, they probably play a different game; each school has its own game'. It is simply a necessary truth that constitutive rules cannot change. Linaza's studies tend to confirm the suggestion broached earlier in this chapter that moral differences do not involve different cognitive powers. Obviously and trivially, greater experience permits the handling of more complex materials. But, as I emphasized in describing psychological symbiosis, more importantly greater age confers certain *rights*. It is not that only older children can conceive of negotiating the rules; only the older ones have the right to create new games. Hence they can (in the moral sense) negotiate new rules. So the issue of whether constitutive rules can be changed depends not on cognitive capacities but on beliefs about rights, that is, upon a specific feature of the moral order of a kind of childhood society.

But why should it seem to Kohlberg that to move to a universalistic mode of reasoning in moral contexts is a development, a transition to a higher stage? Why should the practice of teaching constitutive rules be regarded as a less-developed way of thinking than supposing any rule to be negotiable and hence any constitutive practice manipulatable? By taking these meta-principles for granted, Kohlberg and his followers display their own societal assumptions in the naïve belief in the moral superiority of certain local cultural myths, widespread amongst the citizens of the United States, and perhaps in other bourgeois democratic societies. Kohlberg's meta-principles are Jeffersonian adages as enshrined, for instance, in the preamble to the Constitution of the United States. It is blandly assumed that the Jeffersonian principles represent the cognitively most sophisticated moral order, and at the same time that of the greatest value. One has only to bring out the point to see the flaw that these unexamined assumptions introduce into the heart of Kohlberg's theory. Piaget assumes that his own Cartesian logicism is the highest form of human cognition. In similar vein, Kohlberg builds on the assumption that North American colonial democracy is the most advanced form of human association.

To some extent the difficulties I have raised against what could be called 'classic' moral development theories have been addressed in discussions within the genre. A distinction between the form and the content of moral reasoning is necessary for anything in which differences (staged or otherwise) between kinds of moral cognition are explained by reference to the differences of cognitive competence. So far I have argued that in each stage the same forms of reasoning created by adherence to the rules, the quantifiers 'all' and 'some', de Morgan's laws, practical syllogism etc. are applied to metaphysically and/or morally distinctive content, that moral development as cognitive development is a myth, a disguised way of recommending egalitarian democratic society as the highest form of morality. The only formal differences appear in the degree of complexity of material a person is accustomed to handle. There remains one further, formal distinction in reasoning that might mark a genuine stage-to-stage step in individual development — that between the actual and the possible.

However, by examining the cognitive requirements necessary for each level (or stage) of the Kohlberg scheme, one can see that the capacity to handle this distinction is necessary as much for pre- as for post-conventional reasoning. If somebody is supposed to make moral decisions by reference to anticipated punishments or expected pleasures, they must be able to handle the actual/possible distinction to do so. Again, in the post-conventional level, when someone contemplates a change in a moral principle, the distinction between actual and possible applications is required. Once again the difference between pre- and post-conventional reasoning lies not in the formal distinctions deployed but in that to which they are applied, events in the one case and rules or principles in the other.

Suppose there is no such thing as cognitive moral development. Suppose instead that there are social conventions as to the range of considerations that are properly to be advanced in defensive and anticipatory talk (some of it *sotto voce* in different social milieux. Since any social context will involve some degree of psychological symbiosis with others, the isolated moral reasoner working out his or her own actions in fragments of individual reasoning may be a myth. Yet again, one is made aware of an essentially political and ethnocentric position (democratic individualism) appearing amongst the bases of the theory, as if it were an empirical truth lawful for all mankind. It is empirically true only for those who take for granted the moral superiority of that political position. This suggests taking morally relevant discourse as a text in need of interpretative analysis rather than something for which a literal reading is always available through some supposed shared commonsense understanding. As I have already suggested, it may be determined by the rights of an individual speaker to make certain kinds of contributions. There will perhaps be a display of cognitive procedures (say giving reasons of a utilitarian kind) to establish a persona within the conventions of a particular community. What are the texts from an analysis of which the cognitive moral development theory has sprung? In the tradition of North American experimental psychology, they are both written (that is, documents) and they are administered to and dealt with by isolated individuals. Typically, an isolated individual is presented with a written anecdote describing a moral dilemma of the Judeo-Christian 'What shall I do?' type, and asked to produce another document in commentary upon it. The second document is then analysed to identify the level of cognitive competence displayed in its arguments.

Blasi has demonstrated in 'Bridging moral cognition and moral action', a comprehensive review article, that there is poor correlation between the level of moral reasoning displayed in dealing with the kinds of documents typical of moral development research and that displayed in everyday life, 'level' being defined ethnocentrically, of course. One has only to contemplate the peculiarities of the documentary method to see that this conclusion was almost inevitable. Bureaucratic administrators, Supreme Court judges and the like might proceed by a comparable method in creating the discourse in which moral decisions are presented as rational. These cases are rare. Moral discourse is usually communal talk and is a social, not an individual, production. Furthermore, the simple requirement that texts be written limits the available rhetorics, in particular it automatically elevates the logical−rational rhetoric to the greatest esteem with many further implicit constraints. Finally, the documents enshrine another Anglo-American ethnocentricity, namely that moral psychology is concerned with the study of how people make decisions, of how they answer 'What shall I do?' questions. But for most of mankind, and I suspect for many of us, the central question of moral action is rather 'Given that I should (must) do this, how can I bring myself to do it?'. The investigation of how people answer that question lies in a very different area of secular psychology, that of the study of the exercise of agency.

Kohlberg's moral psychology, as we have seen, is devised so as to lead inexorably to the pre-eminence of considerations of equalitarian justice in moral decision-making (to use Frankena's term in 'Some beliefs about justice'). But in honour moralities the concept of justice is defined in terms of duties and deserts which may be far from equal. The only universal principle is the content-free 'Everyone should get their deserts'. Different categories of persons may have distinct and proper deserts, both in cases of fulfilment and infringement of a code. As Backman in 'Explorations in psycho-ethics' has discovered, jurors still make use of a desert system rather than an equalitarian system of justice. In the classroom, a stupid person is more highly praised for solving a problem than someone brighter. And when the competent get more than the incompetent they are felt to deserve it. On the other hand, more is expected of some people than of others, depending on what is taken to be their natures. Cripples and attractive people are both treated more leniently by juries than are ordinary folk. All this appears in the forms of moral reasoning current in everyday life, the proper province of psychology. Philosophers have a licence to try to persuade us of something more noble, but psychologists have no such right.

Might it not be more sophisticated to make use of those subtle distinctions than to operate with simple universalistic principles? Kohlberg locates the universal *above* the partial. If instead we treat cognitive development as nothing but the capacity to handle greater quantities of material, then the moral developmental aspect of 'taking more things into account' could be just the cognitive step that would permit us to move from naïve egalitarianism to a morality of deserts typical of societies with *differential* structures of honour and duty.

I have suggested that much of the Kohlberg scheme is a reflection of bourgeois liberal individualism still much in evidence in moral and political rhetoric in the United States. Much the same can be said for the prevalent cognitivism of much moral theory (cf. axiological approaches). This comes out vividly in a commonplace linguistic usage, characteristic of contemporary speech, namely the ubiquitous use of the word 'problem'. People are said to have 'drinking problems', 'marital problems' and so on. Problems are complemented by solutions, and there is a cognitive technical relation between them. Couple individualism with cognitivism and oddly, the person drops out of the equation. Drunkenness is no longer a moral dereliction requiring personal effort, but a technical problem to be solved by experts. Only if persons are the residual category of explainers unable to be analysed does the possibility of genuine personal development programmes and projects arise.

Clearly, cognitivism is not a general way of dealing with the forms of moral thought. It is itself a politically loaded moral theory. This point has been overlooked in many discussions of the Kohlberg-type of moral development theory. For instance, Rosen 'Kohlberg and the supposed mutual support of an ethical and psychological theory', proposed a way of filtering out the ethical from the sociological and psychological propositions in the Kohlberg theory. Thus Rosen rightly insists that 'stages represent successive modes of "taking the role of others" ' is an ethical proposition and not a cognitive one, but he thinks that 'stages of moral development represent "cognitive − structural" transformations in concepts of self and society' is not ethical. However, the outcome of the analysis of this chapter is that this too, and others like it, *is* an ethical proposition. Belief in it imposes a psychological structure on the members of society engendered by the teaching of it so that it predetermines which of three possible moral psychologies will dominate the moral order. As we have seen, the very supposition that there are 'cognitive − structural transformations' is to pre-empt the most fundamental moral/political issues of all.

Finally, it cannot be emphasized strongly enough that in neither honour nor conation moralities is there room for individual decisions as to what to do. The code and the sacred text provide one with the description of proper action in all circumstances defined as appropriate for action in that culture. A gentleman and a Samurai do not act outside of those circumstances. How strange to suppose that the moral thinking of gentlemen, Samurai and Caliphs is somewhere in the lower reaches of human capacity.

3 MORALITIES WITHOUT DECISIONS

The difficulties that beset the Kohlberg style of moral psychology go deeper than its associated Piagetian psychological theory. A limitation of moralities to precursors to and realizations of a justice-based egalitarian sort and of moral psychology to the reasoning involved in answering 'What shall I do?' questions is inherent in the very method by which moral development is explored through a documentary method. To define a larger scope for the psychology of morality, I propose to consider a greater variety of moralities than cognitive developmentalists have noticed. One can break free of the dominance of the colonial democratic ideal simply by turning one's attention to real moral issues that confront people in everyday life, say as described by Sabini and Silver in *Moralities of everyday life*, and to the many ways they go about dealing with them as established by Kitwood in *Disclosures to a stranger*.

I propose to discuss the enlarged field of moralities by reference to two polarities. Moralities of deliberation can be distinguished from moralities of honour. In the former, the stress is on the reasons for the action; in the latter, on the moral quality of the actor, which, we will see, in true honour moralities does not depend directly on the morality of what he does. Discussion of moralities of honour finds scarcely any place in contemporary moral theory (*see* Weston, *Morality and purposive action*), but I believe that in some form or another it is the moral system by which most human beings live and have lived. Other psychological processes will come to seem more central than those focused on when the logic of the 'internal' discourse is assumed to be the deliberation taken for granted in current discussions of morality, be they developmental or philosophical.

Aristocratic moralities are amongst the moralities of honour. They range from the corrupt forms of mere snobbery to the subtle distinctions amongst persons involved in feudal moralities where the assumption is that there are given 'places' for everyone, each with appropriate and defined rights and duties. Deviation from the code is a dereliction since there is no sense to be given to choice amongst morally worthy alternatives. To do anything than what is laid down for one as roleholder is to be dishonoured. Both aristocratic and feudal morality work with stable and given codes.

My second polarity is between moralities of deliberation and moralities of action. In the former, the characteristic moral issue to be resolved is 'What should I (you, they) do?'; in the latter 'How can I (you, they) bring myself to do what should be done?'. Modern Anglo-American moral philosophy has tended to stress deliberation at the expense of will, while the existentialists have dealt with a very abstract kind of commitment.

In contemporary moral philosophy the psychological basis of morality is concerned with choice of courses of action. The problem of free will is that of the reality of choice — was the course not chosen a genuine alternative for the agent while he deliberated and passed from deliberation to action? Existentialists have taken Samuel Clarke's brusque resolution of the dilemma of Balaam's ass, starving between two equally attractive bundles of hay, to be the solution to the problem of choice of a code. According to Sartre, choice amongst codes is always possible.

In aristocratic moralities the code is given, not because the actor deceives him or herself into believing that there is no alternative (the Sartrean state of *mauvais foi*) but because the action self-concept (in the psychological sense, that is their beliefs as to their own nature) is bound up with the code, the Samurai with Bushido, the gentleman with 'playing the game' and so on. The psychological basis of honour moralities is not choice but free will in quite another sense, that of endeavour.

In the following sections I shall bring these polarities together in a discussion of morality and honour, conceived as moralities of action, not of deliberation. Contrary to what Cooper implies in 'Two concepts of morality', one does not choose to be a gentleman or a lady. One cannot, and maintain one's identity. If one is in the position to choose between being a gentleman or being a bounder one cannot be a gentleman. The point has been exquisitely expressed by Groucho Marx, who would not contemplate joining any club who would actually have him.

Moralities of honour

Honour moralities exemplify moral orders in which the assessment of persons is the primary focus of moral activity. I distinguish them from 'beautiful people' moralities. In the latter people are seen as worthy by virtue of the degree to which they have individually (and perhaps each in their own way) developed the possibilities inherent in their own natures. Different categories of people may be presumed to have different natures and so different possibilities of development. But in honour moralities worth is determined relative to the typology of proper personhood prevailing in a community from time to time. Pride (tempered with a public display of humility) is widely accepted as a proper sense of personal achievement, while failures are expected to feel ashamed rather than guilty. In the psychology of personal being, self-realization (or 'beautiful people') moralities are the main focus of analysis. In the moral psychology of personal being one's actions count not for themselves but in so far as they reveal and define one's character, besmirch or enhance one's honour and so on. One's standing as a person depends in part on the degree to which one is capable of actually doing what the moral order requires, fulfilling one's commitments etc. So the problem of agency enters into the moral psychology of personal being and, via the world of personal display of character, so do deserts. As Goffman has pointed out in *Stigma*, reputation, that is, the opinion others have of someone, is an essential ingredient of honour, but it is not the nature of honour. One's honour can be besmirched not only by one's own actions but also by the actions of a family member which can dishonour all the family. The same applies to other honour-bound groups, such as the officers of a regiment or the members of a sports team.

A rare and very interesting discussion of moralities of honour is to be found in Michael Weston's *Morality and purposive action*. Weston contrasts the usual role of morality in deciding on means to already existing goals with that morality which 'provides a picture of a certain kind of person to be'. He neatly links honour moralities with the psychology of action (rather than of deliberation) 'Whereas for the mountaineer to blame himself for lack of success is to blame his failure in preparation, it is Jim's failure to act courageously which he sees as blameworthy' (the reference is to Conrad's *Lord Jim*). We might say that to be a hero or a gentleman is not just to live according to the code, but to live up to it. A gentleman cannot say '*I* could have done otherwise'; as a gentleman he can do no other. But his moral virtue accumulates in achieving what the code requires, which is captured nicely in the equivocation of 'has to' in the now banal epic formula 'a man has to do what a man has to do'. Weston notices that in dying for honour 'his death does not assess the relationship (between himself and those who believe in him) . . . but the relationship assesses the death' (p. 37).

In being an officer and a gentleman one accepted not only the tasks and duties defined by one's commitment to the art and science of making war, but also to be bound by a code of honour. To steal from the mess funds was not only to break a law, but also to display oneself as dishonourable. To break off an engagement to marry was not only to break a promise, but to behave like a cad. The study of personal being is concerned in part with what it was to be a gentleman or a cad, a lady or a tramp, over and above performing the actions required by the code. To see how much the distinction between doing and being matters, one should notice that in traditional army morality the punishment for breaking the law by stealing from the mess funds was cashiering and/or imprisonment: but the punishment for violating the code of honour by that very same action could be death. One's brother officers might (and indeed did) present one with a loaded revolver and pointedly leave the room. Carrying the death sentence out on oneself restored not only one's own honour but also that of the regiment, the collective.

As Goffman has pointed out: 'In America and elsewhere at present, however, separate systems of honour seem to be on the decline . . .a human being, like everyone else a person, therefore, who deserves a fair chance and a fair break . . .(*Stigma*, p. 17). Goffman seems to be suggesting that as personal honour declines as a central moral principle, social justice has increasing importance. To be humiliated cuts at the roots of one's personal being; while to be treated unfairly violates one's social being. I shall try to explicate the outlines of a morality of honour in a number of principles and contrasts.

Systems of honour have traditionally involved differentiation of social categories within a social order. There are those persons to whom honour is proper and the pursuit and defence of it a virtue, and those who either do not have it at all or whose honour is, in various ways, dependent on the honour of others. Even in those societies where honour is the prerogative of everyone, such as Spain, forms of honour are highly differentiated. There is the honour of men, and that proper to women (*see* Diaz-Plaja, *The Spaniard and the seven deadly sins*). While an honour morality could, without contradiction, incorporate an egalitarian principle, there is no necessity that it should. In practice, most honour systems involve asymmetrical relations of respect and condescension. In honour moralities justice is related to the kind of person the social order defines one to be. If distributive justice is understood as the principle that 'individuals are to be treated alike in so far as they are, in the relevant respects, alike', the qualification, 'relevant respects', involves some profound differentiations. In Frankena's scheme in 'Some beliefs about justice' the justice of an honour morality is inequalitarian and aristocratic, that related to merit and desert. Honour moralities readily accommodate differential moral demands on different categories of person, for instance 'steadfastness'. Officers should 'set an example for the men'.

There are specific emotions typical of an honour morality. Shame should be felt by those whose loss of honour is through their own self-betrayal. Those who are dishonoured by others should feel humiliated.

Shame is the effect of public displays of self-betrayal. The psychology of concealment of potentially honour-besmirching facts has been exposed to some extent by Goffman in *Stigma*. Dignity (always) and modesty (usually) express a high standing in honour. Both are temperate styles of public demeanour. Dignity is displayed in calmness, while modesty is marked in a certain measure of social reticence. The negative emotions associated with dishonour, shame and humiliation can, as it were, know no excess. But the pride that goes with honour must be temperate. The dangers of excessive pride are clearly set out in such proverbs as 'Pride goes before a fall'. Pride can quickly become 'overweaning'. It can lead the Pharasaical to believe themselves to be 'not as other men are'.

Moral orders involve institutions with which, in a ceremonial and routine way, violations of the moral orders are dealt with. The modern court is the main institution of justice moralities. The system of justice exists not only to punish wrongdoers and to point the way for the virtuous, but to repair the damage done by that wrongdoing. (Psychologically we must, I think, accept all three classic theories of punishment.) In those moral orders built on honour the duel corresponds to the court. In remedying the fault, the duel restores the structure.

There seem to be two types of duels. There are those which mediate between a defect in conduct (an infringement of the code) and the loss of honour. Then there are those which are simply tests of 'character'. A duel consists of three phases: the challenge, the contest and the resolution. In the challenge, the offence is defined by the challenger and the offender is called upon to defend his honour, cast into doubt by his infringement of the code. A duel is not a kind of trial of a misdemeanour. To maintain his honour, the defender must accept the challenge. Failure to do so involves irredeemable loss of honour, whether or not he has committed the fault complained of. Frequently, duels are fought between champions, since typically in an honour morality there are categories of persons, for instance women, who cannot defend their own honour.

A duel is hazardous and its outcome is uncertain. It is quite conceivable that the offender should win and this still purges the offence. In medieval trial by ordeal, God ensured that the guilty were found out and the innocent survived, but in a duel, if the offender (or champion of the offender) survives it does not show that the offence was not committed. It ensures that the offence does not count against character. Don Juan is both seducer and master-duellist. His honour is maintained just so long as he can continue to defend himself successfully against challenges. Whatever the outcome of a duel, its completion restores the moral order. Honour has been satisfied. In some codes, the duellists, if physically capable, shake hands (informal duelling codes, say in a family, may involve 'kiss and make up'). Though duels are hazardous, they are highly formalized and strictly governed by rule. As much as the everyday conduct they regulate, they are themselves regulated, conducted by reference to a well-defined code of both constitutive and regulative rules. If one breaks that code, the code of duelling, one has utterly forfeited the status of a gentleman.

In honour moralities duels can be used as tests of character. The offence is reduced to a formal depreciation of the honour of the other. Among British football fans depreciation is achieved by remarks casting doubt on the sexual definition of the opponent; cowboys impugned the courage of those they wished to challenge, at least in legend.

The challenge must be accepted on pain of loss of honour. Whatever the outcome, both challenger and challenged have maintained their honour. Underlying the possibility of this use for the duel, is a set of shared beliefs linking cowardice, honour and manliness, beliefs identified by Weston (*The morality of purposive action*) in his analysis of the moral order adopted by Jim. It is worth reminding ourselves that whatever may be the official morality of contemporary society, honour moralities are very much part of the fabric of modern life. The moral order obtaining amongst British football fans involves just such a morality.

While the codes appropriate to the honour of men and women may and do differ (*see* research menu 9), the structure of categories for the moral assignment of persons by virtue of their behaviour and attitudes relative to the code seem to me to be similar. The gentleman and the lady exemplify the code, not only in what they do but in what they are seen to be. Their every thought and feeling is appropriate and proper to the code. They are 'true blue right through'. Not only will they be honourable, but they will defend the honour of those morally dependent on them. In non-egalitarian moralities, not everyone is believed capable of his or her own moral defence. Notice how odd it seems to us that a victorian lady thought it right to protect the honour of her servants, a structure of actions that becomes 'patronizing and interfering' when mapped onto our moral system. The cad lives within the code, but knowingly exploits it. The cad is typically one who uses his putative reputation as an overt subscriber to the code to exploit the weakness of others, particularly those that very code recognizes as his moral dependents. Trollope's Crosbie is the very model of caddishness, trading on his reputed status as a gentleman to deceive a young woman (though Trollope depicts Crosbie as torn by his defection, oscillating between remorse and cynical hypocrisy). The cad, once exposed, is seen not to be a transgressor, but an impostor; unfit to be recognized, he is disposed of with the 'cut'. The bounder and the tramp do not purport to be gentlemen or ladies, though they have, so to speak, a natural right to that status, say by birth. They openly repudiate the code. These days, with the decline of honour morality among the middle classes, the distinctions are blurred, but I suspect that among many fragments of British society, particularly the so-called 'working class', honour moralities will be found to be actively maintained, and these distinctions of persons sustained.

In an honour morality one can applaud displays that are aimed wholly at demonstrations of character. Munificence, an elaborate form of generosity, can find an acceptable place. It is as much a sign of superiority of character to destroy one's property in a grand gesture (Doukebhors) as it is to provide gloriously wasteful and lavish entertainments (Maoris).

Goffman's explorations of the workings of honour moralities in 'On face-work' and *Stigma*, though full of details, leave room for many empirical studies to be performed. For instance, in most cultures whose moral orders are built around honour, the most pervasive basis for disclosure of character, and for the insults that impugn one's honour, is sex role. Manliness and femineity provide an almost 'natural' catalogue of virtues upon which a moral order can be constructed, idiosyncratic to a culture. The very interesting study of women's honour in Africa by Shirley Ardener (*Perceiving women*) has no parallel that I know of in European studies (*see* research menu 9).

The distinguishing mark of a moral order based on honour is the presence of the duel as the ultimate ritual for settling moral issues. The fact that in a duel the one who has performed a wrong action, i.e. an action which insults or belittles another, can maintain his place in the moral order by winning is a mark of a pure honour culture. In cultures where some third party adjudicates moral issues and gives a verdict in accordance with law or custom, justice plays a role in the system and some principle of equality has slid in. In a true honour system there is no place for equity and no need for justice.

What sort of moral psychology is needed for understanding how human beings can manage moralities of honour? Moral reasoning of the Kohlberg sort is redundant since decisions between alternatives form no part of living in a moral order based on honour. The cad may well calculate his chances of getting away with it undetected, but this very fact sets him outside the moral order. It is partly by virtue of his resort to calculation that he merits the 'cut'. The Kohlberg ladder describes the moral development of a cad. The code prescribes the proper way a gentleman should act on every occasion, just as the *Qur'an* does for the

Muslims and Bushido for the Samurai. The question 'What shall I do?' cannot trouble a lady or a gentleman, a bounder or a tart. Codes of honour are stern. This gives us the clue. It is weakness of resolve that threatens the adherent of aristocratic moralities. The psychology of honour moralities must be part of the psychology of conation, of strong and weak characters. At the same time, a certain range of emotions is quite characteristic of honour moralities — shame, pride, humiliation, arrogance, hubris, vainglory — so our grasp of this kind of moral order must involve a clear understanding of the structure of these emotions, that is, of their social, cognitive, physiological and behavioural aspects. Moral development in a society dominated by codes of honour will involve not only learning the code, but acquiring the power to act and refrain from acting, to keep up the code whatever the difficulties, and developing the proper repertoire of emotions, pride without arrogance, modesty in victory, resignation in defeat and dignity on all occasions.

Moralities of conation

I have dealt with the need to preserve a residual concept of human agency as power to act in chapter 7. This suggests the possibility of moral orders in which the cognitive work of assessing courses of action is already performed, say through a traditional code or by public — collective discussion, and individuals must needs bring themselves to do that which they must do, regardless of inclination and personal cognitive reservations. The moral psychology of military folk is concerned with this issue. Training, to automatize, is a device for eliminating the need to exercise personal powers in war, as much as to ensure rapidity, effectiveness and uniformity of response. We have also seen how a psychological account of code (honour) moralities requires the psychology of agency as endeavour. There are sophisticated moral systems where the psychology of conation plays the central role. To illustrate these I set out the Muslim doctrine of *Quadar*.

At first sight the Islamic point of view seems to involve an internal contradiction. Some scholars discern a sharp distinction between the lines of thought of the *Qur'an* and the *Sunna* (the non-*Qur'anic* traditions). The *Qur'an* emphasizes the Last Judgement and the responsibility of men for their actions. 'What a man does is his own deed and will go on one side of the balance or the other to his account'. In contrast, the *Sunna* seems to suggest that men cannot do anything unless God wills it, at least in the sense of permitting it. I shall try to show that the psycho-ethics of Islam is a resolution of this apparent contrast.

At the centre of Islamic theological psychology is the idea of belief:

> Being led astray by God is a sort of punishment for unbelief. Verily, those who do not believe in the signs of God, God will not guide and for them is in store a punishment painful. (*Qur'an* 16, 106)

To understand the idea of 'guiding' that is involved in this quotation, we need to grasp the Islamic concept of human action, the centre of their psychology. In Aquinas's system, as indeed in all Western systems, action is thought of as the result of decision and the possibility of decision implies the actual realizability of more than one path. Decision is called for because possibilities of action seem to branch. Agency, then, is exercised in a choice between branches, and the focus of morality is on those choice-points and the reasons and motives for choosing one or the other. The Islamic conception of action is quite different. Action is the result of the exercise of personal power. There is only one path, fixed from eternity, as Abu Dawub says in the *Sunna* (B 16), 'The first thing God created was the pen. He said of it . . . write the destinies of all things till the advent of the hour.' Individual responsibility is located not at junctions in the possibilities of action, because there are none, but according to how far one can move along the predestined path. In terms of this conceptual system, one can understand the notion of being guided, introduced in the *Qur'anic* quotation above. To be guided is to have revealed to one the pre-ordained path; but, of course, an individual may fail to follow it.

A psycho-ethics of personal power leaves the predestination aspect of the *Qur'an* unqualified, whilst being firmly set against an attitude of fatalism. This is called the doctrine of *Quadar*. It is not the idea of the freedom of the will to choose one action or another, but of the power of a man to determine his actions: 'The idea of freedom as such is quite foreign to the Muslim mind' (Watt, *Free will and predestination in early Islam*). The doctrine of human responsibility is formulated in terms of power, not of freedom; of capability to do, not freedom to choose; of the capacity to do what is required, not the freedom to decide for oneself what is desirable or proper. God determines in advance the proper path; man may fail to move along it.

It should be evident that a psycho-ethics and theological psychology based on these principles would lead to a distinctive mode of psychological functioning. Instead of the agony of decision, weighing up this possibility rather than that, the Muslim has only the agony of action. Whereas for us psychological tension lies in choosing amongst possible action and inaction. Our failures are not failures to act; they are failures to act properly. For a Muslim failure is inaction. In so far as Islamic civilization promoted these ideas as the folk theory of the nature of man, according to which people conceived of themselves and their ways of being human, and indeed struggled to realize them, we would expect a very different kind of psychology to be observable among the adherents of the Muhammadan faith.

Muslim moral psychology is the only traditional morality I know of with a well-articulated psychological theory of moral development. It is a conative, not a cognitive, theory. Advances in moral standing come about, not through greater power to reason, but through greater power to act or refrain from acting. Hence all the will-strengthening techniques like the Ramadan fasts and the various other forms of self-denial. They are not to mortify the flesh, a kind of moral sadomasochism; they are to strengthen the will because that is the path of moral development. A Muslim knows what to do since it is prescribed in considerable detail in the *Qur'an*, but has he or she the strength of mind to do it? The psychology of development, in moral orders dominated by the problem of conation, will focus on the development of personal power, perhaps to be understood as the transfer of a psychological locus from one individual, in a psychologically symbiotic dyad, to the other.

4   AN ALTERNATIVE THEORY OF MORAL DEVELOPMENT

Moral orders

A common complaint against Kohlberg's treatment of moral development is that it confuses competence in managing oneself in a moral order with knowledge of moral theories (supposedly characteristic of moral orders). Looked at in the former terms, moral 'development' involves the learning of a widespread bouquet of skills, linguistic (how to account for one's doings) and dramatic (the conventions for the presentation of self as a morally acceptable persona, which involves accounting skills). All this must be coupled with powers to decide and to execute one's decisions; neither to dither nor to procrastinate or, in those moral orders in which the 'laid back' style is valued, to procrastinate with an air of moral superiority. An essential component of this kind of theory of moral development is the notion of *moral order*.

Moral philosophers more or less explicitly assume that the actions upon whose principles of determination they ponder occur in a framework of social relations and in large part maintain them. But the neo-hedonists and cognitivists of the contemporary philosophical schools relate action only to be ghostly simulacra of abstract groups created by assumptions of human similarity in the use of the principle of universalizability. Psychologists of cognitive moral development, more or less in keeping with this tradition, have included the social context of action in a very abstract and schematic fashion, not attending to its structural properties. One searches in vain in the Kohlberg-inspired literature for the idea of a moral *order*.

For the purposes of this discussion a moral order exists among a group of people when there are the following:

(1) Rituals for the public marking of respect and contempt. In a moral order respect and contempt are not just names of the feelings individuals may have for one another. They are symbolically marked categorizations requiring complementary remedies, such as self-deprecation, apology and acts of contrition.

(2) Actions, whatever their practical aim, are treated also as displays of character, in accordance with local typologies of acceptable and context-appropriate personae. For example, in solving other people's problems one can be seen as wise, priggish, nosy etc.

(3) All forms of human interactions are accompanied by actual and potential talk, in the course of which interpretations of and warrants for what is going on can be negotiated. The cognitive dimensions to the moral life may be added before, during or after the performance of an action.

(4) Once the idea of structured and differentiated collectives is introduced, it becomes possible to consider the social organization of a collective, particularly in this context the distribution of rights. As Sabini and Silver point out in chapter 2 of *Moralities of everyday life*, the rights to make moral reproaches are very unevenly distributed and differ front context to context and situation to situation. Even the right to reproach someone for smoking in an area designated for non-smokers is not enjoyed equally by all those whose right to clean air has been violated. Sabini and Silver note that in most everyday cases third parties do not have rights of moral reproach, and if they do indulge in complaints and reprimands they are themselves liable to be morally condemned as meddlers or prigs. Sabini and Silver believe that it is in moral commentary, gossip out of earshot of the offender, that moral norms are promulgated and maintained. The psychology of moral cognition may turn out to be part of the psychology of gossip. In a moral order, then, the three characteristic forms of conduct — rituals, confirmations of respect and contempt and displays of proper character and moral commentary — are permitted only to those who in this or that collective, have the right to perform them.

A coherent and stable society may comprise more than one moral order, provided they are complementary. For example, Carol Gilligan in *In a different voice*, has recently provided a convincing case for treating contemporary American society as comprising two distinct moral orders, one for men and the other for women. The distribution of responsibility between the work place and the family is such that the orders form a stable, complementary pair. The problem of the general conditions in which two or more moral orders are complementary would make an excellent research topic (*see* research menu 9), and how each may require a different psychology of moral development if we are to understand the growth of complementary competences.

Moral orders may be quite modest in size and only occasionally convened. A group of ladies who meet each Thursday afternoon for bridge, a monastic order, the members of the judiciary and a football fan club are all distinctive moral orders. Some attention to the fact that moral judgement occurs in moral orders has appeared in recent moral development literature (*see* Much and Schwaber, 'Moral development'). The studies published in the series *Social Worlds of Childhood* show that there are childhood social worlds in which moral orders are embedded. Like adult social worlds, they are maintained by certain linguistic practices through which social relations between people (such as friendship), between people and things (such as property) and between groups of people (such as team games and social hierarchies) are regulated, and by which social norms or standards for personality, character and physical appearance are promulgated (by, for example, nicknames). I call these autonomous precursor worlds. They have the forms of adult human life, made available by the personal appropriation of certain kinds of mainly linguistic practices from the adult public — collective discourse. Since these worlds are continuously recruited from the advancing cohorts of infants and are relatively immune from influences from 'above' so to speak (games of marbles are learned from other kids, not handed down from parents to offspring), they are immensely stable. According to this theory, transition to adult social worlds involves nothing but changes in the content of the sociolinguistic practices by which every social world is created, practices at which children of six or seven years of age are fully competent. We should structure our understanding of the social psychology of childhood according to the following scheme.

Autonomous non-precursor world

This is characterized by changing structures of psychological symbiosis between infant and mother or mother surrogate; social relations are mediated more by emotions, that is, feelings endowed with social meaning, than directly by conventions. However, I dispute the psychodynamic (Bowlby) view by which the basic emotional structure of infant social relations is treated as non-conventional. Social structures within the psychological symbiosis characteristic of this world are not open to challenge and reorganization.

Autonomous precursor world

This is characterized by the use of verbal and other symbolic means to create and maintain social relations in wholly conventional fashion through rituals. Psychological symbiosis in this world is complicated by the fact that the collective display of psychological attributes, such as rationality, is structurally defined by all the members and that challenges to hegemony take place, sometimes successfully. Personality presentations are controlled institutionally, for example, by nicknames. Further confirmation of this way of understanding children's independent social activity comes from Linaza's study of games ('The acquisition of the rules of games'): 'games continue to pass from one generation of children to another without the adults even noticing it'. The earlier non-precursor world of close adult—child inter-independence is clearly indicated in the way younger children construct 'pretend games' by imitating some of the activities necessary to a real game as they have seen it played by adults or other children. To begin to enter into rule-governed games is to join in a social world in which the *forms* of activity are essentially adult (i.e. it is a precursor world), but the *content* of activities, the projects and rules for their realization, are wholly childish (i.e. it is also an autonomous world).

Transition world

The means for constructing collectives and displaying 'proper' psychological attributes are retained, but the content changes. Contracts, for example, are still verbal but dispose of other forms of property, personalities are still displayed, but controlled by social practices other than nicknaming (*see* Achard, 'Is social stratification possible outside language?').

This theoretical analysis explains the correlations that those such as Sutton-Smith and Roberts in 'Play, games and sports' have demonstrated between children's games and the forms of adult social orders. Traditional unthinking interpretations, imbued with the 'plastic' child fancy, have presumed that children's social worlds reflect and depend on the adult social world. The above theory entails that the correlation is to be explained exactly the other way round — that adult social worlds are transformations by substitution of content, products of the more stable and historically resistant societies children continuously recruit to and maintain for themselves.

Psychological symbiosis

Infant psychological symbiosis provides us with the forms of thought, our basic psychology; the social representations embedded in the collective conversations of our culture provide the rest.

Introducing the notion of psychological symbiosis in Part I, drawn from the work of Richards, Shotter and Newson, I defined the relationship in terms of supplementation of the psychology of one animate being by another. Typically, mother-talk has the effect of presenting an infant to herself and to others as psychologically mature within the local cultural conventions for being a person. I noticed that a case can be made for applying the notion generally, even to the relationships of small groups of adults, but I treated the changes that take place in the mother – infant dyads, by which the locus of psychological work shifts from mother to infant, wholly in terms of changing capacity. The infant can do more, so it does more.

This is insufficient to account for the way symbiotic dyads behave in real life. Some years ago I was studying the way small children assign meanings to times and places in the Skovangsveg Bornhaven in Aarhus, Denmark. By chance, I noticed something odd about the behaviour of parent – infant pairs. At the end of the day a parent, sometimes the mother, sometimes the father, would call to collect their child. In leaving, farewells were exchanged with the Kindergarten director. When the child was collected by its mother, the director bade farewell to the dyad by speaking only to the mother, but when the father appeared, both infant and parent were addressed. This suggested that symbiotic dyads have an internal social structure. One way of describing that structure would be in terms of differential distributions of rights to conduct this or that part of a performance. With the father, a child has separate social rights from when it is in symbiosis with its mother; social rights recognized both by the father and by the Kindergarten director. Do we find a similar distribution of rights for the display of cognitive competence? Bronwyn Davies has shown in *Life in the classroom and playground* that there are differential rights of display for competence in moral reasoning. Since cognitive skill is part of the criteria that determines standing in our social world, it is clear why there are differential rights of display.

If my intuition that psychological symbiosis is a ubiquitous phenomenon is correct, psychological development theory must take on a very different colour from the one to which we have been accustomed. Not only do the capacities of members change, but so too can their rights.

What someone does on an occasion will have to be analysed in a two-dimensional space, one axis representing personal capacity, the other socially recognized rights (figure 9.2).

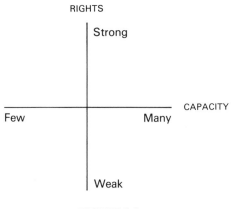

FIGURE 9.2

Empirically observed 'development' must be taken apart to look for several possible growth processes: there may be stable rights, embodied in the discipline of the dyad and changing capacities; there may more often be stable capacities and changing rights; and cases where both are labile. An important case in practice is when children know they have a capacity for something, but also know they do not have the right to use or display it. Bronwyn Davies, 'An analysis of primary school children's accounts of classroom interactions' has described an interesting case where children control an adult by playing on this distinction. They show a teacher that they can use adult moral reasoning, applying a moral principle universally, but when the adult is trapped into engaging them in a debate on this level they leave him mouthing and gesticulating by reminding him that they are only little kids, with whom it is improper to engage in such an argument. This move is made possible just by the ambiguity in the fact that little children do not use adult moral reasoning techniques at least in conversation with adults. Is it because they lack the capacity so to reason, or is it because they are tacitly, or sometimes explicitly, denied the right so to do ('Don't give me any of your lip', for instance)?

The dual nature of psychological symbiosis should preoccupy developmentalists in search of the origins of personal being. Cognitive and moral development research has of necessity to be conducted by creating a public discourse (in Kohlberg's case in the form of written or printed documents), to which an individual taken to be typical of, say, an age group, makes a contribution abstracted from the moral order within which he or she usually engages in dialogue or monologue about moral issues. The research presumes that there is no problem in deducing an attribute of an individual person from an attribute of a public discourse to which he/she contributes. The ambiguity of this technique is something like this: there is a difference between the explanation of the production of a saying for which an individual can or could formulate a practical syllogism and the explanation of the production of a saying when the speaker feels that what others have said provides for and often requires that speech act. The train of reasons are what the others say. In strong symbiotic dyads there might even be promptings ('What do you think?'). In the second case, the train of reasons is public – collective and there is no need for any one person to recognize it as having a logical structure provided that each contribution is seen as right or wrong, proper or improper, according to social convention expressed by the local arbiters of propriety. The very same saying might be said in the one case as in the other but the cognitive capacities involved could be radically different, depending on the social relationships of those present. Socially dependent capacities would only show up by their extinction when an individual is isolated. But equally, if the individual is isolated, what he or she can then do by way of generating practical syllogisms does not show what they can be called upon to do in the course of everyday life, but their moral practice may (and usually does) depend on the latter. All this is a matter requiring research, I believe (*see* research menu 9).

We must also take into account the recent discoveries in developmental psychology which have shown us reciprocal influences between the members of a symbiotic dyad. The behaviour of infants calls forth a certain specific subrange of the possible repertoire of speech acts available to the mother, ensuring the suitability of her supplementations. This sets out the agenda, as it were, for the psychology created by supplementation. In so far as these early forms of infant behaviour are biological, seeking a food source, for example, they are universal and so set boundaries to a supplementation process.

In the linguistic aspects of psychological symbiosis, the infant's initial contribution is necessarily zero. The question can be raised as to whether there are any intentional movements intelligible to the mother before her speech contributions. One could also ask whether there are any structurings of conscious or other mental fields before the acquisitions of the speech forms which are the vehicles of the local self-theory by which a person organizes his or her experience. I believe that the evidence is far from clear. Perhaps all mind organization comes from the learning of theories in language games (*see* Bruner's study of 'peek-a-boo' in 'Early rule structure'); but again this is a matter for empirical research.

The weight of the argument lies against the idea that somehow intentions arise spontaneously, naturally and individually, and that these are encoded in speech or some other semiotic form such as gesture. Rather, an infant first acquires the capacity to issue speech acts: for example, in displays of intentions the possibility for which has been created by its mother by issuing speech acts on the child's behalf. Since the mother is creating the initial intentions and emotions of the infant and acting towards them, her actions *must* be coordinate with the infant's intentions or emotions. A course of action can be biologically inappropriate, but initially it cannot be psychologically inappropriate. The differences between mother−infant interactions must be graphed on to a space defined by two axes: biological appropriateness on one and sophistication of psychology implicit in talk on another (figure 9.3).

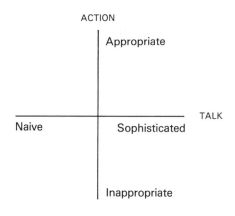

FIGURE 9.3

An infant will have a complex psychology in so far as it is embedded in more than one psychological symbiotic relationship, since father, siblings, aunts etc. provide supplementing speech of differing kinds. Further, in each dyad the infant usually has different rights to provide for a reading of its actions as displaying 'proper' psychological features by its own contributions (*see* research menu 9).

In the light of these discussions, what are we now to make of the work of the greatest of all developmental psychologists, Piaget? The distinction between precursor and non-precursor worlds is both social and cognitive. It involves the distinction between a child as merely the occasion for the speech acts of others, until at about the age of five or six years he or she becomes a location for the display of an evident mastery of social uses of speech, including those we call cognitive. The linguistic vehicles for thought may not be those of scientific/technical civilization, but their effectiveness is as great. For instance, the use of nicknames to promulgate and maintain desirable categories of persons is as effective as any explicit catalogue could be. On this view adult and childhood social worlds differ only as to content.

Piaget's most persistent principle is the setting of concrete operations before abstract operations in his developmental hierarchy. But if no a priori grounds for the priority can be found in the history of science, nor can any social – practical task of the autonomous precursor world or its adult successor be facilitated by moving to abstract cognitive management (including everything from studying science to the management of war, cf. Chomsky's *For reasons of state*) where does the developmental direction towards and clear implications of superiority of abstract forms of reasoning come from? In Métraux's terms, why should Piaget's early acquaintance with Duhemist philosophy of science have continued to provide the underlying priorities of a lifetime of research?

Discussions of Piaget's work have almost always treated it as empirical, and criticisms have been couched in those terms. However, suppose instead, in the spirit of the theory of social representations, we take his work as a normative scheme presented in the rhetoric of science. A social – educational scheme whose products will fulfil the person-specifications of the Gallic, francophone social universe will present a developmental schedule which *must* culminate in the cognitive style appropriate to the normative classifications of that universe. If the culture is aimed, so to speak, at producing people who reason abstractly and formally, then its practices will necessarily appear as a sequence of stages by which one of the many possible modes of human thinking comes to overtake and supersede the others. Piaget's work is a brilliant exposé of a cultural tautology. But so too, in a more pedestrian way, is the work in which *that* judgement appears, namely this one!

RESEARCH MENU 9

Above all we must start a long way from Kohlberg's dilemma of Heinz and the medicine!

(1) Emotions are subjected to moral evaluation. I know of no research on the growth and development of the sense of right and wrong emotions. Is there

a rationalistic ground given for the prohibition of delight in the pain of another? There must be a rich field of family interactions in the course of which tender and soft emotions are demonstrated as preferred and so on.

(2) The distinction between competence at a skill, practical or cognitive, and the right to display it. A vast field of research opens out here to follow the redistribution of rights and skills over time.

(3) Gilligan, *In a different voice*, has shown that a society can function smoothly with two distinctive and interlocking moral orders. How is that possible? How are resolutions along the border achieved and so on? Along with this there could be study of contemporary honour moralities, at present out of vogue in psychology, but still in vogue among the folk. Ardener's often-cited study of courts of honour among the West Africans could be applied 'at home' so to speak, to help us look for indigenous courts of honour amongst ourselves and to discover with what psychological processes and theories they are worked. (See *Perceiving women*.)

(4) The idea that the Piagetian stages may be ethnocentric *evaluations* of equally effective cognitive modes ought to be testable by cross cultural studies. Unfortunately in both Warren, *Studies in cross-cultural psychology* and in Triandis, *Handbook of cross-cultural psychology* the same author, P. R. Dasen, is responsible for reporting on Piagetian cross cultural studies and in both reports he so structures the research that the question of whether concrete or formal operations are most valued by the culture is not addressed. He believes, on the authority of Piaget, that formal operations come last as the most sophisticated (allegedly) so he just studies concrete operations. Much more promising is the excellent study by J. J. Goodnow in Warren, *Studies in cross-cultural psychology*, vol. 2, ch. 5, where she develops the idea of socialization into 'proper intellectual behaviour' and the really prescient idea of 'intellectual manners'. Her work deserves to be strongly followed up.

BIBLIOGRAPHICAL NOTES 9

The close relation between Piaget's developmental hierarchy and Duhem's philosophy of science is well documented by A. MÉTRAUX, 'Evolutionary epistemology' (in *The history of recent psychology*, ed. C. Buxton, New Haven, Connecticut: Yale University Press, 1983, ch. 13). See also K. F. RIEGEL and G. C. ROSENWALD, *Structure and transformation: Development and historical analysis* (New York: Wiley, 1975). The most recent attack on 'logicism' in the philosophy of science is R. BOYD, 'Metaphor and theory change: what is "metaphor" a metaphor for?' (in *Metaphor and thought*, ed. A. Ortony, Cambridge: Cambridge University Press, 1979).

Recent research has shown that the transitions which Piaget read as steps up a hierarchy are actually complex interactions of existing skills, social and environmental constraints and interpretations. See P. BRYANT, *Perception and understanding in the young child* (London: Methuen, 1974), M. DONALDSON, *Children's minds* (London: Croom Helm, 1978) and J. SANTS (ed.), *Developmental psychology and society* (London: Macmillan, 1980). How a child's choice of pattern of reasoning for a task in hand is situated with respect to certain categories of others is well demonstrated by B. DAVIES, *Life in the classroom and playground* (London: Routledge and Kegan Paul, 1982), and for a later age group by T. KITWOOD, *Disclosures to a stranger* (London: Routledge and Kegan Paul, 1980).

The failure to check 'cognitive deficit' hypotheses across the board, so to speak, is evident in much moral development research; see, for example, A. COLBY, 'Evolution of a moral development theory' (in *Moral development*, ed. W. Damon, San Francisco: Jossey Bass, 1978, p. 89). For more complex moral orders than the simple egalitarian–democratic assumed in Kohlberg staging, see C. BACKMAN, 'Explorations in psychoethics: the warranting of judgements' (in *Life sentences*, ed. R. Harré, Chichester: John Wiley and Sons, 1976, ch. 12), and also the unjustly neglected L. B. MURPHY, *Social behaviour and child performance* (New York: Columbia University Press, 1937), which establishes a variety of moral principles in use by young children. For the classic account of moral 'staging' see L. KOHLBERG, 'Moral stages and moralization: the cognitive-developmental approach' (in *Moral development and behaviour*, ed. T. Lickona, New York: Holt, Rinehart and Winston, 1976). The monumental review by A. BLASI, 'Bridging moral cognition and moral action: a critical review of the literature' (*Psychological Bulletin*, 88, 1980, 1–45) leaves little doubt that the Kohlberg 'documentary' method is missing something central to the management of action in moral orders.

For an elegant summary of contemporary moral philosophy, see M. WARNOCK, *Ethics since 1900* (Oxford: Oxford University Press, 1971). Moral philosophy based on universalist principles can be found in R. M. HARE, *Freedom and reason* (Oxford: Clarendon Press, 1963). For evaluation theory see J. O. URMSON, 'On grading' (in *Logic and language II*, ed. A. G. N. Flew, Oxford: Basil Blackwell, 1953).

For the variety of justice moralities, see W. K. FRANKENA, 'Some beliefs about justice' (in *Freedom and morality*, ed. J. Bricke, Lawrence: University of Kansas Press, 1976). 'Rosen's filter' appears in B. ROSEN, 'Kohlberg and the supposed mutual support of an ethical and a psychological theory' (*Journal of the Theory of Social Behaviour*, 10, 1980, 195–210).

A rare examination of the foundations of honour is M. WESTON, *Morality and purposive action* (Oxford: Basil Blackwell, 1975, p. 16). N. COOPER, 'Two concepts of morality' (in *The definition of morality*, ed. G. Wallace and A. D. M. Walker, London: Macmillan, 1970, ch. 5) is a clear exposition of the individualist–reductivist treatment of collective psychological aspects of morality. In the same volume T. W. SPRIGGE, 'Definition of a moral judgement' (in *The definition of morality*, eds G. Wallace and A. D. M. Walker, London: Macmillan, 1970) hints at an honour morality with his remark that those who infringe public opinion 'will be less readily accepted members of any community'. For a massive informal study of an honour morality see F. DIAZ-PLAJA, *The Spaniard and the seven deadly sins* (trans. J. I. Palmer, London: Gollancz, 1968). For Islamic moral psychology see W. M. WATT, *Free will and predestination in early Islam* (London: Luzac, 1948). C.

GILLIGAN, *In a different voice* (Cambridge (Mass.): Harvard University Press, 1982) has shown how there can be distinctive moral psychologies within a common cultural milieu. The evidence for the autonomous precursor world theory of development is massively assembled in Routledge and Kegan Paul's *Social Worlds of Childhood* series; see particularly B. DAVIES, *Life in the classroom and playground* (London: Routledge and Kegan Paul, 1982), A. SLUCKIN, *Growing up in the playground* (London: Routledge and Kegan Paul, 1981) and J. MORGAN, C. O'NEILL and R. HARRÉ, *Nicknames* (London: Routledge and Kegan Paul, 1979).

The argument in this chapter parallels, for the moral order, the general analysis of V. WALKERDINE, 'From context to text: a psychosemiotic approach to abstract thought' (in *Children's thinking through language*, ed. M. Beveridge, London: Arnold, 1982, pp. 129−55). See also G. BUTTERWORTH (ed.), *Infancy and epistemology* (Brighton: Harvester, 1981).

Additional works cited in the text are P. ACHARD, 'Is social stratification outside language?' (address to the *Language and Power* conference, Bolagio, Italy, 1980); P. ARIES, *Centuries of childhood* (trans. R. Baldick, London: Cape, 1962); J. BRUNER and V. SHERWOOD, 'Early rule structure: the case of "peek-a-boo" ' (in *Life sentences*, ed. R. Harré, London: John Wiley and Sons, 1976); N. R. CAMPBELL, *Physics: The elements* (Cambridge: Cambridge University Press, 1920); N. CHOMSKY, *For reasons of state* (Suffolk: Collins, 1973, ch. 5); B. DAVIES, 'An analysis of primary school children's accounts of classroom interactions' (*British Journal of the Sociology of Education*, 1, 1980, 257−78); P. DUHEM, *The aim and structure of physical theory*, (Princeton: Princeton University Press, 1954); E. GOFFMAN, *Stigma* (Harmondsworth: Penguin, 1968); E. GOFFMAN, 'On face-work' (in *Where the action is*, London: Allen Lane, 1969); J. LINAZA, *The acquisition of the rules of games by children* (Oxford: doctoral dissertation, 1982); J. PIAGET, *The language and thought of the child* (London: Routledge and Kegan Paul, 1926); J. PIAGET, *Judgement and reasoning in the child* (London: Routledge and Kegan Paul, 1928); N. C. MUCH and R. H. SCHWABER, *Moral development* (San Francisco: Jossey-Bass, 1978); B. SUTTON-SMITH and J. M. ROBERTS, 'Play, games and sport' (in *Handbook of cross-cultural psychology*, vol. IV, ed. H. E. Triandis and A. Heron, Boston: Allyn and Bacon, 1981); H. C. TRIANDIS (ed.), *Handbook of cross-cultural psychology* (Boston: Allyn and Bacon, 1980); N. WARREN, *Studies in cross-cultural psychology*, vol I (New York and London: Academic Press, 1977).

CHAPTER 10

IDENTITY PROJECTS

Theme: What personal development is possible will depend on the theories actors hold. Certain person-theories will promote self-knowledge and self-mastery, others will inhibit them. The public fact of identity invites social displays of idiosyncracy, while the private sense of singularity is promoted by metaphorical transformations of appropriated forms of thought.

Contents
1 Psychological conditions of self-development
    Self-knowledge
    Self-mastery
2 Moral dimensions of self-development
3 Identity projects: the achievement of uniqueness within a moral order
4 Identity as personal being: the private creation of difference

The dimensions public − private and collective − individual provide a two-dimensional space of four quadrants to represent matters psychological. This conceptual system allows me to formulate four phases of development. The transition from quadrant 1 to 2 I have called 'appropriation'. It has been the focus of the first nine chapters of this work. This phase encompasses processes of development which create minds that are reflections of linguistic forms and social practices. Mind is formed on the basis of grammatical models and locally acceptable episode structures. In a way the first nine chapters draw out in detail the original insight of G. H. Mead, that the self owes its form and perhaps its very existence to the circumambient social order.

In this chapter I turn to a second phase of development. Individuals transform their social appropriations and, so to speak, take over their own development. The transition from quadrant 2 to 3 I call 'transformation'. The creation of distinctive personal being by the transformation of one's social inheritance is by no means inevitable. There are culturally distinctive institutions of self-development. It is to the study of such institutions and the practices they legitimize that I turn in this chapter.

My psychological 'space' admits of two further transitions, two more steps in a developmental cycle. Idiosyncratic transformations can be brought out into the public arena, a process represented as a transition from quadrant 3 to 4. I call this 'publication'. At this point an actor stands on the threshold of radical recategorization, since, depending on the reaction of that public, his personal innovations may earn him assessments running anywhere between 'madman' and 'genius'. It is to this phase that the study of creativity is germane, but that lies outside the scope of this work.

The cycle of development is completed by a transition from quadrant 4 to 1. I call this 'conventionalization'. It comes about when the personal innovation is taken up into the conventions of the social order in which it has been publicized. The study of this transition occupied the fourth part of *Social being*, the first volume of this study. The cycle of human development can be represented in figure 10.1.

It must be emphasized that whether a transition from one phase to another takes place is a complex matter, involving the interweaving of social conventions as to the kinds of personal transformations that are proper with the degree of personal resolution than is brought to the task. In this chapter I try to chart, in outline, the ways that personal transformation could be accomplished. I have nothing to offer on the subject of the conditions under which it will.

By the presentation of self in public one creates one's social being. One's personal being is the product of appropriations and transformations of social resources, including the local theory of selves. Two principles of ethogenic analysis must now be drawn into the discussion: that everything psychological comprises appropriations from and perhaps transformations of something social, and that human experience is always an interpretation of what nature provides. For example, emotions are not feelings, but interpretations of personal states, *within a moral order*. I have laid great stress on the central role of language and other cruder semiotic systems in the mediation of the process by which individual psychology is constructed out of appropriations from the social. In every psychological field one must pay close attention to the dependence of psychological possibility on available sociolinguistic resources together with the constraints on the possible that are imposed by the local moral order, constraints which often go unnoticed by workers in the experimental tradition (see the discussion of the work of Duval and Wicklund in chapter 1). It follows that under certain conditions one's own personal being can become one's own project. Personal development takes place within cultural conventions. In accordance with those conventions the people-makers have been teaching us theories, including the most important of all, that

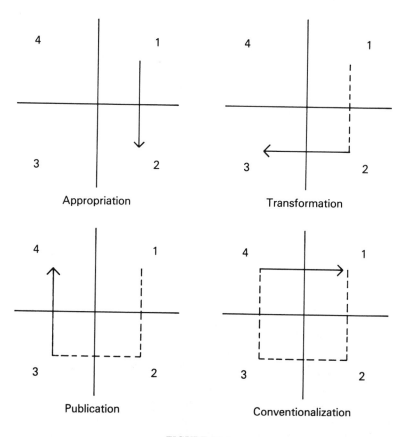

FIGURE 10.1

we are selves, active centres of experience. As psychological symbiosis dissolves, we take over the work of the dominant member of the dyad within which we were created, and that includes the people-making work. For cultures like ours the key question must be what kind of people-making work is facilitated by the kind of self-theory common to the culture. For us, I shall be trying to show, it facilitates reflexive cognition or self-knowledge, and reflexive action or self-mastery, or at least the idea of these activities as projects. Amongst the many projects made possible are identity projects in the sense of work towards the achievement of uniqueness, both as a social being and as a personal being.

1 PSYCHOLOGICAL CONDITIONS FOR SELF-DEVELOPMENT

Self-knowledge

It seems that what self-knowledge is possible to a being must be dependent in at least two ways on what semiotic resources are available to that being. There must be an apparatus of self-referential devices available, and there must be a conceptual system providing the wherewithal for identifications, predications, and so on, itself dependent on the concepts available in the culture and the extent of individual appropriations therefrom. This suggests the possibility of a fairly large-scale research project relating the form taken by institutions of self-knowledge to cultural resources and to the level of acquisition of those resources typical of individuals of certain categories. Capacity for self-knowledge, like all other psychological abilities, must be understood in terms of social relations. It follows that the actual degree of self-knowledge displayed by an individual human being may be a poor index of the extent of that individual's appropriation of the resources of the community since, like every other psychological manifestation, it will usually be displayed as part of a collective process in some symbiotic dyad or triad.

But why talk of 'institutions of self-knowledge'? Is not self-knowledge just that form of cognition which has no institutional basis? I believe that there is evidence that what we take to be a product of an individual's own isolated mental activity, self-perception and self-assessment appears in other cultures as a social process involving others in quite definite social relations to the person at the centre of the cognitive work (see research menu 10). Students of Japanese life, for instance Lyman in *The Asian in the West*, have drawn attention to the way the Japanese use the reactions of others, rather than the results of their own self-scrutiny, as a technique of self-assessment. The 'triangular diary' is a document created by first writing up a personal problem, as if it were the dilemma of a 'friend', and passing it on to another person for comment who returns with advice for the 'friend'. Self-assessment is a public–collective (quadrant 1) rather than a private–individual (quadrant 3) activity. There are obvious connections with psychotherapy and the role of therapist as 'external conscience', and the psychodynamics of this kind of activity amongst the

Japanese would be of great research interest, for instance whether 'transference' occurs (*see* research menu 10). How far is something akin to the 'triangular diary' a routine feature of the psychology of self-assessment in the solipsistic West? It probably figures quite largely outside the world of middle-class academics who have been passing off their curious customs and those of their students as the psychology of all mankind. 'Conscience' and 'gossip' could form foci of research needed to test out these ideas. (See Sabini and Silver, *Moralities of everyday life*, on the role of gossip in the social institutions of moral reproach. Perhaps conscience is the individualized institution of moral reproach, and its form in a given culture a reflection of the public – collective institutions from which it was appropriated. Thus the superego may become a researchable entity.)

Finally, it should be noticed that self-knowledge in this sense must be organized by the very same 'self' theory at work in the structuring of experience as a 'pencil' or whatever geometrical analogue catches the local person-theory. Self-knowledge requires the identification of agentive and knowing selves as acting within hierarchies of reasons. It follows that this kind of self-knowledge is, or at least makes available the possibility of autobiography. But, as Hamlyn has convincingly argued, self-knowledge as history lacks the dimension of moral assessment that is at the heart of self-knowledge proper. I think it can be shown that self-knowledge as history cannot exist independently of self-knowledge as moral assessment.

The self-knowledge as accumulated information about this being here and now, which becomes possible for those who have learned a theory which permits them to organize their experience around a central unity, could be analysed into beliefs about how they are now (self-awareness, that is, consciousness as a form of knowledge of one's own states); how it has been with them (memory, that is, autobiography); and how it could be (personal dispositions). I follow Hamlyn in thinking that items accumulated in each of these categories, based just on personal self-scrutiny, gathered 'solipsistically' so to speak, would not count as self-knowledge proper. One's dispositions, for instance, are realized in one's interactions with others, just as what counts as a memory is certified by a social institution in which certain persons have the right to declare what is authentic and what the reworking of hearsay, and so on. But, as Hamlyn rightly points out, self-knowledge is not just knowledge of how one responds to, interacts with and is assessed by others. Such interactions provide important, perhaps indispensable conditions for self-knowledge but they do not exhaust its content.

Self-knowledge is coming to see oneself in relation to a moral order. As Hamlyn puts it, it is for a man to know 'where his values lie, what he truly wants, and where he stands in relation to those wants'. It is not a knowledge of what he would do in certain circumstances that encapsulates a man's self-knowledge because only in making a decision may we 'become aware of what really matters to us.' Self-knowledge arises through involvement in our actions, as those are engaged with others.

Once again, as I have stressed throughout this work, without attention to the way what we think is embedded in local moral orders, the most fundamental psychological issues will be glossed over. This is just what has happened with the psychologists' notion of 'self-concept'. Our beliefs about ourselves, unless set against a thorough investigation of the normative system within which they are to be realized, miss the core of personal being (cf. in this regard 'A helical theory of personal change' by Ziller).

Self-mastery

The reflexive powers which our self-theories endow us with appear in many cultures wrapped up in institutions of self-mastery. (Psychological work has slid past the issue of the involvement of moral orders; cf. work on the resistance to temptation and more recently studies of the use of *sotto voce* speech in self-control.) We need to put together a more subtle conceptual scheme to study self-mastery empirically.

Hollis has argued in *Models of man* that reasons are enough and necessarily enough to explain rational actions because persons are just those beings who do sometimes act in accordance with or by reference to reasons; irrational actions typically call for causal explanations, that is, explanations not involving the actor as agent. This distinction must run through any treatment of self-mastery.

A cluster of physical metaphors dominates our vocabulary for referring to the causes of behaviour. We have 'forces', 'impulses', 'tensions' and 'drives'. The rest of the conceptual space is taken up by terms with pathological implications such as 'obsession' (that of which one cannot help but think) and 'compulsion' (that which one cannot help but do). In the psychology of everyday life amongst the speakers of English, 'self-control' applies mostly to the mastery of that which is potentially a cause of behaviour as, for instance, impulses and obsessions. In what does that mastery consist?: in the presence of the impulse and in relation to the local moral order to do something other than realizing the impulse ('impulses to generosity', however, are not to be diverted or gainsaid). This will turn out to be a species of a more general capacity which I believe underlies all notions of self-control, which will emerge as we look more closely at rational action.

The work of von Cranach (reported in *The analysis of action*) has demonstrated as clearly as one could wish that amongst middle-class Europeans non-compulsive action is controlled by the construction (in some cases collectively and in others by an individual appropriation) of means—end hierarchies. In constructing a system for action control a person(s) *both* sets an ultimate goal and some of the intermediary achievements necessary to realize it *and* chooses among currently and locally acceptable ways of realizing it and such intermediary goals as have been already specified. We could call the considerations involved in goal setting 'maxims' and those in realizing goals 'rules'. This provides a cognitive structure characteristic of prior preparation for action, current control and retrospective accounting. Both maxims and rules are, in principle, subject to public assessment as to their compatibility with local moral orders. (Notice the furore created by the publication of a guide to successful suicide published by the EXIT society. Moral objections were raised not only to the end but to at least some of the means.)

How will *self*-control appear in a von Cranach structure? It must be in the choice of maxims and rules, since once they are chosen means and ends are fixed. Once again one can turn to the Clarke—Leibniz controversy or, if one prefers, to some existentialist writer. For the question to be addressed is whether every choice of maxim or rule is to be referred to another maxim or rule? Must we admit the residual possibility of unprincipled choice, a direct, immediate and ungrounded act of commitment? I tried to resolve this issue in chapter 7 in Kantian style, in favour of the view that claims to be exercising pure agency are to be judged not as contributions to the empirical theory of choice, but as expressive displays in accordance with a local principle. This is the principle that the greater the degree of reflexive self-control that can be exerted, and the ultimate degree will be that in which action is unconditioned by any rule whatever, the greater the moral worth of the actor. The only question of interest left for research after the studies by Von Cranach and his co-workers is the study of the social conditions under which displays of 'pure choice' are routinely put on. One would search in vain for empirical evidence to support or dispute the verisimilitude of the fictional representations of acts of ultimate commitment offered by the existentialist literature. At best, as I have argued, we have evidence for complementary acts, the one unprincipled in the practical order and rational in the expressive, the other rational in the practical order and unprincipled in the expressive. The complement must be unprincipled rather than irrational, since there is no suggestion that the existential act is the product of apersonal causal forces in the complementary order, but a pure and arbitrary personal act (see, for instance, the interrogation of Roskolnikov in Dostoevsky's *Crime and punishment*).

In the everyday context self-control is treated as a conflict between compulsions, impulses and the self, in that the issue turns on whether someone can or cannot succeed in acting other than as realizing an impulse by reference to a rule or maxim. The presence or absence of cognition will not do to identify the cases where self-control has 'succeeded', since though impulsive actions are carried out without thought, compulsive actions occur despite thought. The commonsense picture runs something like this: in so far as thought is taken and action is undertaken in accordance with principle, maxim or rule, in the presence of the tendency to impulsive or compulsive action, an agent is exercising self-control. But this picture is defective in several ways, the most important in this context is the lack of any sketch of how thinking of the maxim is related to acting in accordance with it. Is this to be understood as acting in accordance with the higher order maxim 'act in accordance with maxims'? And how is that 'acting in accordance with . . .' to be explained? Furthermore, the picture suggests that impulses are completely analogous with maxims and principles. Yet the impulse is offered as a source of the actor's actions which stands over against the actor as the source of action him or herself. Alternatively, and this is the way I propose to move the discussion, the impulse or compulsion becomes part of the cognitive structure to which the self-organizing activities of a person are directed, and hence a fit subject for the exercise of what we loosely call self-control, only if it can be found a place within the existing cognitive system. 'Name the devil' says the folk wisdom of self-mastery. For the agentive process to occur, that is, for a person to work their way around clusters of guiding principles, an obsession has to appear as a guiding principle. (To put right a habitual fragment of incorrect fingering, a musician plays the incorrect fragment deliberately, that is, as an action in accordance with rule. Once this is achieved the correct fingering which had previously eluded the player is easily established.) But for the incorporation to be possible there must be linguistic or other semiotic resources available by which the compulsion or impulse can take propositional form.

The common theme running through both traditional and official psychological conceptions of self-control (once these are stripped of their religious and scientistic rhetoric) is that of somehow embedding the causal in the rational. I follow Kenny in the view that providing oneself with reasons is to create a private discourse in which such speech acts as self-command can be performed. There are two conditions for such a discourse to be possible:

(1) The actor must be in possession of a theory amongst the concepts

of which are devices adequate to set up a dialogue in which he or she, the actor, appears in more than one part.

(2) There must be a public discourse to serve as a model for the private discourse realizing local conventions of debate, command, reprimand etc. Research on 'locus of control' has ignored issues of the relation of implicit distinctions in locus of control to local moral orders. Casual observations suggest that there are marked cultural and national differences in these matters. In the United States, people tend to look to 'external' sources for self-control, to medication, group support, attachment to gurus, marriage guidance, psychiatry, health farms, road signs and so on. In Europe and Japan, folk practices tend to place much greater emphasis on 'internal' or personal control. Ironically in North America, the land of Mead, the philosopher of the 'I' and the 'me', debates over troubles which are expressed in terms of impulses and compulsions, are now often conducted between one person and another (or vicarious other as in 'Alcoholics Anonymous', psychotherapy etc.), while in other societies such debates are conducted between a person and him or herself. (To my knowledge little serious comparative research has been done on this remarkable difference.)

Notoriously the discourses of reason are not enough to hold the devil at bay. There is personal power to be included in the formula, that residual aspect of agency that is reflected in the prayer for grace, and systematically excluded by all forms of subpersonal psychology except the medieval mystery play. So far I have treated personal power as the unanalysed residue of the dispositional analysis of agency. But it too can be incorporated within the ethogenic approach, that is in part the psychological aspect of the personal appropriation of a form of public discourse, the discourse of injunction and command. The general theory in use throughout this study can be related to that of Evreinov, *The theatre in life*, as a kind of mirror image, defining the relation of the study of personal being to that of social being. Whereas for him monodramas were public social events displaying psychological interplay between the subpersonal components of the mind as personal relations, for me the structures of the mind are appropriations from the public – collective discourses of social life. To treat myself as someone to be ordered about, I borrow as a thought-form the structure of a discourse between persons whose roles define super- and subordination between them, a discourse in which one person commands cajoles and implores another. In the public discourse there is *A*, the master, a *B*, the vassal. In the personal thought-form there is me, the moral weakling, and another me, the better self. In folk techniques of self-control much is made of addressing reprimands, exhortations and commands to oneself. (For instance, the techniques proposed by

M. Coué). In accordance with the general theory upon which this work is based, the psychological structure of self-control must be a reflection of the culturally available discourses of command, unless deliberately altered by private–individual activity in quadrant 3 of our psychological space. Again a topic requiring research opens up here as a test of this aspect of the general theory (*see* research menu 10).

I have argued throughout that persons are the product of a certain kind of work done on beings who are merely animate by nature. The work is essentially the teaching of a theory to that being in terms of which it can conceive of itself. The possession of such a theory and the exact form that its self-conception takes is intimately bound up with the language it learns and with the social rights it can conceive of itself as having. Persons can be 'grown' from any kind of being capable of learning such a theory. Some suitable beings may be inanimate, though I have confined my discussion in this work only to the growing of persons on animate beings. Animate or inanimate, to be a person is to have certain cognitive linguistic capacities, to be in possession of certain theories by means of which reflexive discourse can be formulated, and to have certain rights to the public display of those skills and knowledge. It is not to be embodied in any particular way.

It follows that personal development must involve each of the aspects of personal psychology left out of the behaviourist–cognitive ways of conceiving of human beings. The mere fact that each of the traditionally psychologies, in its own way, aims at the universal in human nature necessarily leads to a neglect of the unities which are the basis of human individuality — consciousness, agency and autobiography — since I hope to have demonstrated that the unities are culturally distinctive. 'Reflexivity' is the magic ingredient by which persons are created as self-conscious, self-controlling and autobiographically aware beings. But this is by acquiring a local version of the theoretical concept of 'self'. This suggests thinking of personal development in just those terms, as I have emphasized at each stage in the analysis. Related to the transformation of consciousness to self-consciousness will be the possibility of growing self-knowledge while the skilled recollection of one's past enables one to elaborate a cluster of autobiographies, within the conventions of the local moral order. Each reflexive activity requires that the being be capable of performing the other two.

Though knowledge of one's own history as one's own is a condition for the sense of personal identity (the essence of the 'memory' requirement suitably elaborated into a skein of overlapping sequences of recollections), growth in autobiographical knowledge, say through the use of the method of assistance pioneered by J.-P. de Waele (see chapter 8), is an important part of self-knowledge in the sense brought out by Hamlyn, since that involves what one has done and what one believes one could do against a background of moral evaluation. Development of self-control, as one is freed from psychological symbiosis with others, and as one maintains distance from the roles defined by institutional rule systems (cf. the Eichmann story), is a necessary condition for the achieving of the identity projects that the concept of personal being allows one to formulate. The mastery of reflexive discourse is self-consciousness and so all three unities combine to define a fundamental moral principle for personal development moralities. To see this last step one must take account of the necessary conditions for achieving the three modes of personal being. A person must have acquired a person-theory sufficiently rich to enable sustained self-reference to be possible, and which sustains and *legitimates* the construction of mental structures independent of the public – collective orders, the realm I have called quadrant 3. There are societies in which a personal mental life is immoral, and the person-theory at least officially admits personal reference only within some form of psychological symbiosis. Thus we reach another necessary condition for personhood as we conceive it: it is that psychological growth, which involves the appropriation of powers by the junior member within a symbiotic dyad or triad, will be *permitted* to restructure the dyad so that 'locus of control' will have shifted to favour the junior partner. Unfortunately we cannot just borrow from traditional psychology with the help of a few references to the literature, since, without exception, it has failed to treat 'external locus of control' as socially structured and morally loaded with respect to the individual actor, and altogether missed the point of distribution of rights.

All this has been worked out on the assumption that those who are endowed with capacities and abilities and the right to use then will, when the occasion seems right, use them. But that assumption must be called into question. Wittgenstein has taught us that between knowing a rule and applying it there is a deep psychological chasm, not to be bridged by the addition of yet more rules to the psychological endowment of the actor. There must be some generic power to use the abilities and capacities that are within one's rights. The final step in my argument is to try to show that this is not a psychological problem but a matter of moral orders.

The abilities discussed in the first part of this chapter are important because the moral issues arise only for intentional action, whether that action is directed to others or to oneself. The personal transformations I am concerned with in a theory of personal being conceived as set within a moral order are those which an actor can be thought to have brought about, sometimes with the assistance of someone else, in some sort of psychologically symbiotic relationship. But there are other personal transformations which come about despite the projects of the actor as, we believe, falling in love, religious conversion and the like. In so far as these events are indeed in spite of the projects of an actor, they lie outside the scope of this study.

The argument so far has been directed to setting out the conditions for achieving personal power over and responsibility for one's own personal being. In so far as I have discussed temptation it has been in the context of the mastery of 'forces', the folk psychological account of obsessions and the like. If we give equal attention to moralities of the will as to moralities of decision, the morality of the exercise of personal power must include a discussion of the moral issues that surround weakness of will, *akrasia*, procrastination and sloth. In the morality of *social* being the exercise of personal power plays a quite different role, since it is the psychological foundation of fascism. As I argued in that context, the central moral focus must be on the right to have one's account of oneself listened to and incorporated in the negotiation of social reality. But from the moral necessity to abrogate the social exercise of personal power it does not follow that it should be abandoned for the province of oneself. Radical social actors need not be personal slobs, though there is a recognizable frame of mind in which resistance to hierarchical social control is generalized to an abrogation of self-control. I turn to an account of procrastination and sloth based directly on the treatment of those sins of everyday life by Sabini and Silver in *Moralities of everyday life*.

Some 'puttings-off' are rational, that is, they involve principled assessment of the relative worth of goals. Only irrational 'puttings-off' are procrastinations, and of those only cases where the idle or the self-distracting person knows full well and is attending to what should be being done. There is no issue of decision in the sense of choosing a right course of action for the procrastinator. Sabini and Silver propose four psychological mechanisms each underlying a form or 'strain' of procrastination.

The first case involves the substitution of one goal-directed activity for the one duty calculation or advantage enjoins. This case is irrational or procrastinatory only when the actor continues throughout to subscribe to the superior worth of the original goal. 'Busy-work' of the middle-aged academic sliding from research into administration is something most of my readers will have seen, and surely indulged in from time to time.

'I'll just watch five more minutes of Wimbledon, then I'll start marking those exam scripts!' Very soon a succession of such moments becomes an hour. The second form of procrastination involves, according to

Sabini and Silver, a rational calculation but on an irrational time base.

In the third form there are no rational calculations or decisions to do something else 'before I get started'. One just drifts into a distracting and meaningless activity. One is still, as it were, in the posture of work, but not actually working. Sabini and Silver include in this category the bearing of what they call 'tokens of sincerity', e.g. taking one's books on holiday but not opening them.

Finally, there is 'perseveration' — toiling at a preliminary but easy task and never actually getting on with the job in hand. One can spend years looking up references and build up a remarkable card index and yet never write the learned article, just as one can spend hours running up and down C major without getting on with memorizing A minor.

Much more empirical work needs to be done to develop this promising start. It is obvious that the third category or strain of procrastination is something of a hotch-potch. But reflection suggests a deeper query. Are not all four categories still conceived within the framework of the 'Protestant ethic' so to speak? In each case procrastination is achieved by some kind of alternative *doing*, and in three of the cases the doings are intentional. Even the sophisticated Sabini and Silver slip into a 'North American' theory of procrastination. What of sheer idleness — just doing nothing in the face of the task to be accomplished — the legendary vice of those who live south of the Rio Grande? (For some suggestions for further work in this area *see* research menu 10.)

Sloth and procrastination are sins in the cultures to which most of us belong. So there must be a moral dimension to the enhancement of personal powers. A rough preliminary distinction can be made between 'powers to do' and 'powers to be'. The former are the ordinary or extraordinary capacities people acquire to carry out tasks and projects. I have in mind physical strength, linguistic capabilities, practical and cognitive skills and the like. These powers are defined relative to task performances whose outcome is extrapersonal, though there may be personal consequences, but they are grounded in permanent or semipermanent properties of the person who has them. One may take a course to improve one's Spanish in order to be better understood, and in taking the course one acquires a vocabulary.

But 'powers to be' are reflexive and second order. The object on which they are exercised is oneself, and the tasks which their enhancement enables one to perform are intrapersonal. Muslims regard the fast of Ramadan as a period of training to augment the power to act and refrain from acting we call the will. Self-knowledge and self-control are reflexive powers, 'powers to be'. Without them our power to acquire powers to do can be seriously impaired. Unless you can 'keep yourself at it' you will never acquire an enlarged Spanish vocabulary.

This is such a commonplace of folk psychology that to insist upon it may seem to be to emphasize a mere banality. Yet in that commonplace lies, I believe, a principle of central importance in the moralities of everyday life. It is as follows.

To work to enhance one's powers to do has moral value only derivatively from the moral quality of the extrapersonal tasks those improved abilities bring within one's capability. Mere body-building as an end in itself is thought by most people to be as morally grotesque as the torsos it produces (*see* research menu 10). But in so far as one's reflexive powers grow and are exercised this, in itself, is regarded as moral advancement in the moralities of everyday life. Here we have the psychological foundation of personal development moralities. While the first order abilities of the yogin have moral worth derivatively from the worth of what he can do with them, his second order abilities, his reflexive powers, endow that and other personal development regimes with moral quality. For devotees of the oriental martial arts enhanced powers of self-defence play a very small role in the assessment of what is good in Tai Chu'an, Tai Kwan Do and the like (*see* research menu 10).

We are now in a position to make a little progress towards understanding a well-known problem in moral development psychology. Why have the persistent attempts to secure an advance in the 'level' of moral action by teaching people advanced cognitive skills failed? (*see* Blasi, 'Bridging moral cognition and moral action'). The problem is complicated by the fact that the projects so far undertaken have been based on the supposed universal order by which the forms of moral thinking form an ordered hierarchy. We have found reason in the last chapter to reject the very idea of such an order as a reflection of an unexamined ethnocentric presupposition. But it was also assumed that the psychology of the moral life rests on cognition, and that it involves competence. We have seen that a study of the moralities of everyday life reveals the role that conation plays in real moral orders. 'Does one know the code?' is one sort of issue. 'Does one know oneself?' is another. Much of the moral life is a matter of self-mastery, of the power to do that which convention or reason enjoins. To progress in the development of one's powers of self-mastery the Kohlberg theory makes no contribution whatever.

The final stage of our project will be to marry the results of the discussion of the variety of moral orders with the theses concerning personal development that have emerged from the critical discussion of this and the previous chapter. The structure of personal psychology has turned out to be the final consequence of a generalization of the Vygotskian idea of appropriation. The four quadrants of the space defined by the axes individual – collective and public – private provided speculative dynamics for the development of personal being. That dynamics has been further refined by considering the conditions under which people-makers can transform a merely animate being into a person. The prime condition turned out to be that it should prove possible to teach that being a theory the central core of which is some concept of itself, for our culture that of an active, self conscious being. By means of some culturally distinctive version of that theory, a being organizes its experience, beliefs and so on so that its perceptions are centred on a point of view, its feelings are interpreted as emotions by reference to its dealings in a moral order and its workings in the world can become more independent. The gift of reflexivity creates personal being. The thrust of my arguments, both critical and constructive, has been to highlight reflexivity and the maintenance of personal being as the core of the two moral orders that I believe, contrary to the emphasis given by philosophers to moralities of justice and of consequences, are the realizations of the moral systems within which mankind has usually conducted its affairs. These are the moral orders of honour and of 'will', of personal standing and personal (as opposed to social) power.

At the corresponding point in *Social being*, I proceeded by taking the empirical conditions for a human individual to be a social being, and by trying out various valuational loadings of those conditions, tried to reveal the hidden political dimension of my social psychology. But to be a social being is not in itself a moral status. I follow Steven Lukes in his assumption (in *Individualism*) that personal being is a moral status in itself. Persons, and we may dispute about just what conditions a being has to satisfy to be one, are accorded a morally privileged condition, shown marks of respect and have, of right, certain unearned privileges. They are not to be used as a means to someone's minor gratifications so should not be eaten, raped or forced into degrading work. However, the fact of psychological symbiosis makes the analysis more complex. Some animate beings are persons only when they are in psychological symbiosis with a partner willing and ready to do the person work for them. One's personhood may be displayed, not through one's own efforts, but by the supplementation of one's defective display by the senior partner of the dyad. The conditions for personal being are more stringent than those for being a person. Agency and honour can be ascribed to *me* only when the symbiotic relationship has dissolved to some notable extent. Since the dissolution of psychological symbiosis is a matter of growing competence and redistribution of rights, he or she who strives to achieve personal being must seek both honour and autonomy.

I am not suggesting that consequence moralities, justice and so on have no place in human life, nothing so silly, but that underlying them is a *psychologically* more fundamental moral order — that in which persons are created. Means–end reasoning seems out of place, since apart from the glory of God and the reproduction of society (neither of which figure in the day-to-day worries of modern folk) persons are not created *for* anything. Only within moralities of honour and reflexive power can we give an account of person-making as a moral activity, and perhaps make some headway in the psychology of moral development, a field vacated by reason of the culture-bound limitations of the Piaget–Kohlberg approach.

How can value accrue to persons as bearers of honour and agentive power? The ambiguity of this question will reveal the duality of the issues involved. Can philosophical analysis show honour and agentive power to be fundamental and interconnected values in a world of persons? We might also be asking 'By what social practices are personal beings, in the course of being "grown" by person-makers endowed with these supreme values?'. The latter question *replaces* the cognitivist query to which the Piaget–Kohlberg theory supposedly framed an answer. Posing it is the final step in replacing Franco-American individualism with a thoroughgoing collectivist viewpoint.

Recent discussions of the concept of 'person', as we are accustomed to employ it, have emphasized two attributes that must be at the core of any person-concept. These are the capacity to act intentionally, in contrast to one's behaviour emerging from a nexus of causal chains, and autonomy, in the sense of the capacity to adopt one principle rather than some other in the management of action. Different features of personhood have been emphasized by other authors but I content myself with these as illustrative of how this line of thought goes.

To be rational is to display one's actions as being in accord with some socially valued discourse principle. It may be obvious to one's co-actors that one's actions are rational in this public–collective sense, but sometimes work must be done, particularly talking, by means of which what one did can be provided with a description under which it can be seen as in accord with a shared principle or custom. I have already argued for the view that rationality may rightly be attributed to someone without entailing that the action so praised emerged from the workings of an impeccable personal logic machine. Action and talk are not transparent windows into the soul; they are mentation in their own right. In this light, a connection from rationality to a moral order is easily forged. To display oneself as rational is to make a sustainable claim to worth. Rational actions are those which can be justified within a certain belief system, and relative to that system a rational being is just one who is seen as acting in that kind of justifiable way. But all the actual work of justification may be performed in public – collective discourse. And a person may be seen as rational even when the justifications for his or her actions, when called for, are routinely provided by a partner, and the same may true for the daily life of someone seen as irrational.

Rational action and talk is, in our way of life, a mark of one worthy of respect, a form that honour takes. When the military mode dominated our life-forms, honour was expressed in the more belligerent virtues. It is worth noticing that the academic debate can become a duel of honour. (An interesting example of this was the question-time after S. J. Gould's address to a biological conference at which he proposed the theory of punctuated equilibrium.) If an academic debate is a moral as well as an intellectual contest, it should conform to the social psychological structure of the duel (*see* research menu 10).

Value accrues to human beings just in so far as they are seen to be intentional actors because by that alone they can lay claim to personhood, to a place in a moral order. This is not because they are then seen to be responsible for good actions, but because of the respect due to beings who are capable of planning and acting. This is itself not just because displaying these capabilities is a show of competence, but because the fact of displaying them is illustrative of the right to do so. In so far as capacities for self-knowledge enhance one's capacity to display one's actions as intended, so self-consciousness emerges as a derivative virtue.

In traditional moralities of the will, moral assessment of persons cannot be in terms of what they do. The proper line of action is prescribed collectively or by divine decree or in other ways. To do something other than what is prescribed is not to choose to do that as an alternative good, but to fail to do what is required. Every sin is a form of *akrasia*, procrastination or sloth. The moral assessment of human beings is only by reference to 'strength of character'. We have seen the inadequacy of interpreting the will in cognitive terms as an extra subpersonal module. The will is a personal power. Moral assessment by reference to will is just another assessment in the familiar form of loaded dichotomy. It adds the polarized continuum 'lazy – energetic' to the familiar 'socially useful – socially useless', 'misery-inducing – happiness – inducing', 'contemptuous of the rights of others – respectful of the rights of others' and so on. In various moral orders these have figured as the ground base of moralities of social being. As social beings, human kind are subject to some or all of these other regarding principles. But as personal beings, while their necessary location in collectives is reflected in their submission to moralities of honour, in carving out their own identity they must submit themselves to a morality of will. The ultimate personal power is just that to act. It is no more difficult to judge if someone has it than it is to tell if someone has mononucleosis or is just plain lazy. And this shows that diagnosis of mononucleosis is more a moral assessment that a clinical judgement.

3 IDENTITY PROJECTS: THE ACHIEVEMENT OF UNIQUENESS WITHIN A MORAL ORDER

Identity is manifested in quadrants 1 and 3 of my basic psychological space. There is identity as a social being and identity as a personal being, and in each mode of being a person can strive for uniqueness. In public – collective space it will be achieved by virtue of an idiosyncratic display, and in private – individual space by the creation of a unique discourse. I shall take up each type of identity project in turn, taking first identity as a social being, the public display of difference.

We know very well that there may often be disparities between private beliefs about oneself and the limited public presentations of self from which the beliefs others have about one may derive. More poignantly we all know of cases where there is a disparity between a person's publicly displayed beliefs about themselves and their private aspirations. These disparities suggest the possibility of projects in the realization of which such disparities might be remedied and resolved. I have emphasized the fundamental psychological distinction rooted in a deep philosophical dichotomy between personal identity and social identity, between the individuality one has as a numerically identifiable being and the attributes one shares with the others that make up some relevant reference class.

What, then, might be the rough outline of a theory of social identity projects? The first step would be to identify people in a predicament which would define the range of possibility for efforts of various kinds to modify one's identity displays and so the perception of one's social identity by others. The sociological category of 'the marginal' seems exactly suited to this. I take it that 'marginal people' are those who do not share, but might aspire to share, a certain social identity. Typically, amongst such people would be immigrants, those who are moving from one kind of social world to another, for example, the socially mobile, children on the way to being adults and so on. It is clear that these people are in a position to experience the kind of disparity in terms of which I defined identity projects above. They are able to realize what it would be like to have the attributes of the group to which they are nearest and at the same time to have it borne in upon them in various ways that they do not possess them. This is a very heavily researched area, although most of the work has been individualistic and statistical.

It is clear, then, what a social identity project might consist of. It would involve efforts to acquire the attributes of an existing social identity, and I shall look into what these efforts might be in a moment. One necessary condition must be noticed. In order for there to be the possibility of an identity project of this sort, one has to know what the attributes of the desired social identity might be and, furthermore, one has to be right about them. The social world is full of people who are, or have been, aspiring to social identities which do not exist, either because they have never been or because they have recently ceased to be. Presuming, then, that a person realizes what social attributes he or she must acquire, the next step is to convince others that one has these attributes and that one has them as of right, whatever that right might be. For example, it may be necessary to perform in such a way that others take one's social attributes to have been inherited, and so on. Again, the Tajfel notion of social comparison might properly identify a cognitive condition necessary for the accomplishment of such a project; though such a process, presuming individualistic comparisons between persons, cannot be relevant to projects involving fancied or extinct social identities.

Efforts of this sort can be separated into two different categories.

(1) There are actual role performances by which the attributes that one wishes to have ascribed to oneself are displayed in the appropriate circumstances and with the right degree of verisimilitude. These might consist of such attributes as correct speech, proper manners, impeccable dress, appropriate job, and so on. Veblen, in *A theory of the leisure class*, proposes that this feature of social identity projects is ubiquitous in Western society and has provided a powerful dynamic for the strange gyrations of fashion. In his studies of hypercorrection, Labov, 'The study of language in its social context', has examined the dynamics of identity presentation in speech.

(2) But the Veblen-like process of social emulation (and the reasoning involved could fit Tajfel's 'social comparison' theory), which drives the persons in Western society who occupy as of right identities to which others aspire to more extravagant means of representing their differences, is only one aspect of an identity problem. As I have already pointed out, it is necessary to establish that one has the attributes as of right. In general, rights in the social world are established by the existence of appropriate biographies, i.e. beliefs about a person's previous life held by others. So, part of an identity project involves a construction directly, or by implication, of an appropriate biography or autobiography. (cf. The Australian cousin searching the parish

registers for impeccable British antecedents. Here, if there is social comparison it is with a mythical social identity type.) Indeed, such projects involve quite radical changes in presentational features, such as changing one's name, e.g. by adding 'de' or 'von'. They must also require successful concealment of one's real biography (*see* Goffman, *Stigma*).

So far I have pointed to the outlines of a theory of social identity projects in which an individual strives for social identities real or mythical, but social identity projects might take another form. There might very well be cases where an individual's problem is to retain a given social identity against various destructive influences. So far as I can see by a priori reflection on the matter, the psychological structure of the reasoning involved in managing those projects already suggested would be identical to that required for positive social identity projects. But whereas in the former the actor can presume a shared knowledge of the matters of the identity aspired to, in the latter an actor's problem would be to secure that others (who might conceivably doubt if there is or ought to be such an identity) came to accept that such an identity existed. One would also need to make sure that the moves appropriate to the public display of that identity were widely enough known for one to be able to be seen to have achieved it. It seems theoretically possible that the actual efforts which a real person might undertake would turn out to be the exact complement of the demands of the positive identity project. It may be that a person is seen by others to have certain attributes and is believed to have a certain biography. The problem for that person might be to create in others the impression that these attributes and this biography is not some idiosyncratic failure to achieve the attributes and biography of some worthy social identity, but is already the achievement of a mode of social being which has been forgotten, overlooked or not understood by the others. In short, it will be to make public the existence of a social identity corresponding to the personal attributes which are displayed and known. (cf. Peter Weinreich's study of Muslim youths in British schools in Breakwell, *Threatened identities*) and Lyman on Japanese-Americans of the first post-immigrant generation (*nisei*) in *The Asian in the West*.

These remarks provide a theoretical background for studies such as Weinreich's. They are an attempt to lay out the various aspects of social identity projects, aspects which derive from a conceptual analysis of the notion and commonsense understanding of its application. Like any theory, they stand in need of empirical investigation, justification and test. Further reflection suggests that the way in which the cluster of hypotheses above ought to be tested would be by some form of ethogenic method. A prior social analysis would be checked against the beliefs of the various folk involved, access to which would be obtained through an analysis of their accounts. Further elaboration of accounts could be obtained through the use of the methods of George Kelly (*see* Bannister and Fransella, *A manual for repertory grid technique*). These methods would be appropriate for this part of identity investigations because what we are in search of is the system of beliefs, knowledge etc. which are the necessary conditions for the success of the reasoning required of an actor in the production of the action in which the realization of his or her project consists.

Ordinary action theory of the type developed by von Cranach (*see* von Cranach and Harré, *The analysis of action*) and others should be an adequate basis for empirical studies of the reasoning involved. According to action theory, the activities by which people go about realizing their knowledge and beliefs are conceived of as controlled by reasoning which can be represented by hierarchical means—end structures. An end or goal could be represented in an intention and the means of realizing it in a rule or convention. The means—end structures which make up the intentional aspects of an actor's psychology could be very complex. It would be necessary to use account analysis to investigate the appropriate systems of beliefs and interpretations to provide the decodings necessary to understand the meanings of particular public performances by the actor engaged in a project. Unexamined common-sense could lead one widely astray unless one already shared the criteria for the social identity in question. At most 'social comparison', if it occurs in the real world, could yield either the realization that one is stigmatized and/or knowledge of the public requirements of other social identities (and perhaps some of the private—collective as with those forms of social comparison that have been explored by Goffman in *Stigma*).

Personal identity projects, on the other hand, depend upon an individual being well established in a role position or in some more general social category. By well established, I mean that both the actor and the other persons who constitute his or her social environment are agreed on all hands that this person has the social identity manifested in public performance as of right. We would be dealing here with centrally located people such as certified office-holders, arbiters of social propriety such as the powerful women who determine what is and what is not upwardly mobile speech in Philadelphia in Labov's 'Study of language in its social context', well-defined role-holders such as bank managers, policemen, members of the picket line, males who believe they are men, and so on. The identity problem for such centrally located people is the obverse of that for the marginal, namely, how are they going to be seen to be both worthy exemplars of the social identity they rightly claim and individual persons. There is a second kind of threat to identity which was perhaps not envisaged in Breakwell's original formulation of that interesting notion in her book *Threatened identities*.

The bulk of the traditional 'research' into the pursuit of personal uniqueness is summed up in Snyder and Fromkins' *Uniqueness: the human pursuit of difference*. Their study is an almost perfect example of the particularity and ethnocentricity of what is passed off as 'human', that is, 'true of all mankind', in traditional psychology. Shorn of the barbarous scientistic terminology of 'dimensions' and 'encodings', Snyder and Fromkin suggest that the psychology of the enhancement of personal identity, conceived primarily as a public (behavioural) display, rather than as the development of personal psychological space in the private – individual domain, depends on four bases:

(1) That people regularly and normally, that is routinely, make comparisons between what they take themselves to be like and the way they think other people are. Comparisons may turn on almost anything: physical appearance, intellectual skill, biography etc.

(2) While people are ready to accept that they may be moderately like others, they find it unacceptable that they are very similar or very dissimilar.

(3) Those who believe they are very dissimilar will try to appear more similar; while those who believe they are very similar will try to be somewhat less so.

(4) Behind this, according to Snyder and Fromkin, lies the belief that most people are fairly but not wholly similar to others, and the discomfort of finding oneself 'out of line', one way or the other.

In short, efforts to display uniqueness are just one more facet of conformity and stem from the unpleasantness and implausibility of discovering that unlike most people, one is too similar to others to conform to the norm: '. . . the "pursuit of difference" . . . is not an unquenchable thirst and total desire to be different . . . but it . . . represents a striving to maintain a moderate sense of dissimilarity relative to other people.' It will come as no surprise to learn that this theory has its origins in North America. Unfortunately, Snyder and Fromkin's researches are presented in the all-too-familiar causal rhetoric of the pseudo-scientific 'experimental' tradition, and the empirical work reported is almost all drawn from the use of the highly suspect documentary method of American academic psychology. Nevertheless, just because of its limitations its results are fascinating if interpreted as a display of a local cultural imperative.

The documents with which the experimental participants worked and those they were required to construct were mostly written descriptions of overtly displayed personal attributes, many of them performances of other people (real or imaginary) in similar documentary tasks. The issues of 'sense of self' and of the structure and content (if any) of private – individual cognitive space, that which I have called quadrant 3, are thus not able to be addressed, since only what can be written about in non-metaphorical and easily grasped sentences can be addressed. Not surprisingly the participants came up with the 'bureaucratic norm'. The format allows almost no other form in which a person could present him or herself. Neither their dreams, nor their poems, nor their aspirations were made space for.

The ethnocentricity of the 'bureaucratic norm' is amply illustrated in the content of the Synder – Fromkin 'theory'. To the outsider it so obviously reflects thought patterns characteristic of the unique historical paradox of contemporary North American society, the immensely conforming and rule-bound character of everyday life (the making routine and 'professional' of even the most intimate rites), coupled with the myth of 'individualism', universal subscription to which is part of the very anti-individualist conformity, so glaringly apparent to the outsider. That myth I believe, nowadays represents a part of the ideology necessary to sustain late capitalism. In the psychiatric society the unacceptability of eccentricity is only too obvious and very well recorded (cf. K. Vonnegut, *Breakfast of champions* and Szasz, *The myth of mental illness* and so on).

Ethnocentricity is apparent not only in the results but in the substantive assumptions of the research. The authors clearly believe that 'social comparison' is a ubiquitous activity of human beings. While social comparison is typical of the psychological activities of immigrants, of the marginal and of highly mobile and personally competitive but rule-bound societies like the United States, it has next to no place in traditional and aristocratic societies where one's place in the order is fixed, and the appurtenances, both physical and moral, proper to it are decreed by custom and law. Even the Veblenian pursuit of finery is impossible in the context of sumptuary regulations. Yet it is in just those societies that the cultivation of personal uniqueness flourishes to the point of eccentricity, for instance the intense interest in personal tailoring of the ubiquitous uniforms of the Peoples' Republic of China. I turn now to investigate identity enhancement projects in the absence of an institution of social comparison, and where individuality need not be displayed to be felt.

There are those who are so well integrated in the social order, whose public performances are such perfect manifestations of what is required of them, whose biographies are impeccable to the last degree, that their problem is to resist dissolution into no more than the cypher at the centre of the role. What is threatened in these cases is personal identity. Again, there are two forms of action that are necessary to create personal identity in the midst of a tight-knit social order.

(1) The role performances, the demonstrations of impeccable claims, must somehow to be put on in such a way that they are given what Martin Hollis, *Models of man*, perceptively called 'the stamp' of one's uniqueness. As one king succeeds another, how are we to notice the difference between them? A good beginning can be made with the help of physical peculiarities. Successive presidents look different from one another, have different names, but that is only the beginning. There must be some way, and it is very apparent in the utterances of such persons that a presidency is to be marked by a particular style of doing prescribed presidential actions. Just as when a new committee takes over the management of the local jumble sale, the new role-holders try to introduce some differences which mark this year as theirs.

Though this point has been made now for some considerable time, and I suppose goes back to remarks by Goffman in *Stigma*, very little empirical study, so far as I know, has been devoted to the way in which marks of personal identity are imposed upon standardized role performances. Partly, I suppose, this is because the interest of social psychologists in recent years has been focused on the positive ways in which social identities are generated, i.e. what sort of role performances are required for the marginals to acquire relevant identities, rather than ways in which, given those role performances, they can be modulated in such a way that a distinct person emerges from them. Could this be because many social psychologists are themselves marginal people with dubious biographies?

(2) Complementary to the activities of the holder in attempting to generate a personal identity, there are the interpretative procedures by which the others are able to see him as a distinct person. Such a person has to convince the others that he has the special attributes which his ways of performing lay claim to. (There is an interesting catalogue of uniqueness 'marks' in part III of Snyder and Fromkin's *Uniqueness*, which includes material possessions, unusual names etc. Only in chapter 9, the discussion of 'performances-uniqueness motivated behaviour', does a strongly ethnocentric strain appear; but as an essay in the anthropology of the American middle-class, it is of considerable interest.) And, of course, many of these attributes will be invisible, such as a claim to ancestral or genealogical worth, special kinds of private thoughts and feelings. Indeed, those claims are themselves double-edged since a kind of claim may be initiated by someone who wishes to mark his social identity with a personal stamp and is so suc-

cessful that shortly it generates a new social image. For instance, in the late Victorian era it was perhaps part of the way in which someone engendered a personal identity to display his humble origins as a self-made man, a tycoon risen from the people. Notoriously, that claim very quickly became standardized, and indeed there are apocryphal cases of persons with impeccable middle-class antecedents faking up a working-class background in order to have the right social identity, e.g. some British Labour politicians.

Just as the more interesting cases of social identity projects have not been carefully studied, so I believe little has been done to look at the way in which personal identity projects may be realized. Again, an ethogenic approach seems appropriate since one must be dealing with the interplay between the personal and social distribution of knowledge and belief, accessible through accounts, and the actual performances in terms of which this knowledge is realized. The reasoning by which these performances are controlled should be accessible through the study of means – end hierarchies. Little has yet been done to investigate either aspect of personal identity projects.

One further point needs to be made. I have argued that the appropriate methodology should involve the analysis of accounts in terms of which performances are to be interpreted, using the interpretations of actors and interactors. So, in the above theoretical remarks I have tried to emphasize that these projects, whether of social identity or of personal identity, necessarily require social display because they involve the achievement of collective convictions. I have taken it for granted that the achievement of human beings engaged in these exercises are of those who have a private sense of personal identity and that that is not at issue. In short, this conceptual scheme and the suggested empirical projects which go with it depend upon the assumption that the individuals with which we are concerned are sane. There are cases, of course, where the disparities between aspiration and achievement are so great that what becomes problematic is indeed the private sense of personal identity and this is a matter for the psychiatric psychologist to investigate.

4 IDENTITY AS PERSONAL BEING:
THE PRIVATE CREATION OF DIFFERENCE

The organization of mentation as personal psychology is the product of belief, and the form it takes a realization of the grammatical models used in that talk which takes personal action and knowledge as its subject matter. Saving a dramatic reordering of experience, with a redistribution of one's beliefs about responsibility for one's actions or the origins of one's thoughts, as might occur in madness, much of what is to make one's mentation unique must involve meaning, the transformation of a system of collectively imposed uniformities into an unstable structure of individually modified conventions. But meaning is a notoriously troublesome concept, and no common understanding of it can be presumed. I begin with a brief outline of the interrelated notions of meaning upon which my account of personal transformations of the common stock will be based. Two conditions are necessary for an item to have a meaning:

(1) The item in question is located at a node in a network of relations to other items in the same semantic system. The network or semantic field is made up of two kinds of relations. (a) There are relations of sequential organization; adjectives precede nouns in English; requests precede takings and takings are followed by thanks and so on. (b) There are substitution and exclusion relations between items in any actual structure, say a sentence or an unfolding social episode, and other items in the system, 'cat' can be substituted for 'pussy'; in hearing 'cat' we exclude 'chat'; 'Bye bye' can be substituted for a wave and so on. The totality of such relations forms a multidimensional network within which an item is uniquely located. The network defines the 'value' of an item, which is an intrasystematic aspect of meaning.

(2) The item in question has extrasystematic reference, effects etc. including objects denoted and social acts achieved. The extrasystematic relations of an item are its 'significance'.

These conditions are generalizations of de Saussure's conception of meaning in *Course in general linguistics*. Significance and value interact. For lexical items such as words, the rules of grammar and conventions of synonymy and antinomy that define the location of an item in a multidimensional value field are related to the significance of the item. So the fact that in one of its uses 'horse' is synonymous with 'steed' and a noun is not independent of the extralinguistic reference of the term. Rules for the placement of actions, and for what is to count as socially equivalent alternatives, the social value of an action, are intimately linked with the social significance of action as act, that is, with the extrasystematic significance of the action in the social world in which it has a place. Instead of thinking of value and significance as fields of relations, they could be thought of as sets of rules of use. These sets would include Wittgensteinian 'deep grammatical rules' which as determinants of language games are criterial for the use of key terms, actions and so on.

To link this meaning theory to the concerns of psychologists we must introduce intentions. Intentional actions are directed by the actor to practical and/or social ends. The former are related to action by causal processes, the latter by social convention. It is customary to call conventionally defined social outcomes 'acts'. Acts modify the existing social order in various ways, by setting up new relations and dissolving old ones, by creating expectations in the interactors and so on. Such expectations, particularly when expressed as impersonal norms of behaviour, are sometimes called 'meanings'. For instance, the handshake that seals the deal has meaning in this sense, that is, it creates obligations and expectations in and for the actors.

But many social commentators (e.g. Marx, Durkheim, Habermas and others) have insisted that there is another 'level' of meaning revealed by a technique derived from that by which biblical scholars interpret a text, hermeneutics. There is the way actions as acts portray the basic relationships of the social order.

How is personal meaning possible? How can there be value and significance which are both individual and private? Wittgenstein's famous argument against the possibility of a private language casts doubt on the stability of any semantic system which attempts to maintain meaning by some sort of private act of denotation. But even if that difficulty were overcome what would be the role of a semantic system which *a fortiori* could have no use in the public domain since it had no collective reality? Such meanings could exist perhaps as a shifting texture of fragile structures, loosely approximating the semantic fields of public languages, but their use, if they had one, would have to be confined to quadrant 3 of psychological space. At the most, a private – individual meaning could inform a private fantasy and the dreams of the mad, but not for long. Yet we feel, perhaps, that part of what it is to have a place in a *social* order as a *personal* being is to be able to contribute to the conversation of the primary structure some disclosure of thoughts and feelings that are uniquely ours, particularly in the context of the argument of this work in which the attainment of personal being is to be seen as much as a shift in moral standing as a change in attributes or skills. There are two ways in which a bridgehead to intelligibility could be maintained.

(1) The ramblings of mad persons are sometimes provided with meaning by another person. This is a special case of psychological symbiosis, and there are any number of ways in which this might be done. R. D. Laing once advocated a kind of interpretative analysis by which the speech of schizophrenic people could be trawled for expressive and oblique references to their family life. The study of the vicarious construction of personal meaning will involve, in each case, the differentiation of intended figurative speech by the speaker from the interpreter's prior commitments to a certain conception of the

public–collective structure or process he or she purports to find embedded in the mad person's contributions to the public discourse. However, in this work I am interested in the creation of personal meaning by *intended* figurative speech and other, perhaps non-linguistic, catachreses.

(2) In the sciences the bridgehead to intelligibility is maintained by metaphor. I propose that the intelligibility of our private–individual thoughts and feelings is maintained by ourselves, for ourselves, in just the same way. Personal meaning is individual metaphor. But what is metaphor?

Metaphorical uses are displacements of lexical items into domains of discourse in which they are not customarily used. We must avoid too ready an assumption that literal meaning is a given. By virtue of this displacement a term, in a metaphorical use, 'stands across' a number of applications. This 'holistic' feature of metaphorical use has tempted some linguists to take metaphor as a more primitive feature of language than literal use. By standing across a variety of applications a metaphor draws them into relation with one another, creating the possibility for similarities and differences, not hitherto noticeable, to emerge. In this respect metaphor differs quite fundamentally from simile which depends on the comparison of known ensembles of attributes of its two subjects, and serves merely to single out one or more in a particularly forceful way. Metaphor is like a Kantian schematism, bringing into being, if apt, the new feature which it serves to express, forcing a similarity to emerge. Boyd has perceptively described this process as 'gaining epistemic access' since the appearance of the similarity permits further investigations of the hitherto unfathomable matter under description to be undertaken. (See 'Metaphor and theory change'). Similarity is a relation, so the forcing of it in the tenor, what the metaphor is about, reciprocally forces it in the vehicle, the term which carries the metaphor. This mutual forcing has been called 'inter-animation' by Richards. In the private–individual quadrant metaphorical discourse provides the wherewithal for us to gain epistemic access to ourselves, to the personal realignments and reformations or transformations of the public–collective endowment I called appropriations, and partly brings them into being. What we will find in ourselves will then be a function of the metaphors available in the public–collective domain. And here the study of personal being connects up with that of *représentations sociales* (*see* research menu 10). This is yet another facet of the principle that we strive to become what the best authorities tell us we are.

If metaphors are interanimations, then personal meaning, however fleeting, must modify the available uses of the terms involved. In the display of personal meanings in 'public space', in their publication so to speak in quadrant 4 of psychological space, the essential step in creativity is achieved. In this picture creativity is not something mysterious that occurs in quadrant 3, but is an assessment that the public makes of the display of semantic novelities in its presence. 'That's creative . . .' is a judgement from the public – collective world on the appearance within it of items from the personal stocks of individual persons. Creativity differs from madness, on this view, only in the degree to which it can be absorbed into the collective conventions of the primary discourse to become part of the psychological resources taken for granted by ordinary folk.

Once one is in possession of a transformed semantic system one could put it to work, to become poet, inventor or madman. But that will not depend wholly upon oneself, but also upon the cultural conditions and social structures of the community in which one publishes ones private discourse. At this point the study of personal being merges into literary criticism, psychotherapy and the sociologically oriented philosophy of science.

But such personal mastery as we may achieve is within the small, dimly lit area of those of our actions and beliefs of which we are aware. There is much that is extrinsic to the consciously monitored processes we can routinely take command of for ourselves. In my four-quadrant psychological space quadrant 1 (the public – collective) and quadrant 3 (the private – individual) stand out as locations for the incoming thrust of influences over whose origins and forces we have no control. As I emphasized in *Social being* we live embedded within structures of social relations that ramify beyond the capacity for current techniques of discovery. And from the dark foundations of the private – individual arena there emerge the thrusts of biological imperatives to be clothed in the civilizing garb of acceptable interpretations, of which that discovered by Sigmund Freud is only one. According to this view psychodynamics becomes an alternative scheme *for* structuring mentation, rather than a multi-levelled hierarchical description *of* mentation. It follows that, like every other general psychological theory, it must be assessed, not for verisimilitude, but in relation to some moral order, that is with respect to the kinds of lives belief in it enables people to live.

RESEARCH MENU 10

(1) What are our 'institutions' of self-knowledge?
(2) What happens during psychoanalysis in Japan? Is there transference and how do analyst and patient handle this?

(3) Why has the psychodynamic theory of the human mind found so little favour in China, though they have been familiar with it for many years?

(4) Is there something natural about our capacity to follow rules, and is this the psychological resolution of Wittgenstein's famous problem of why it is that we can follow rules without further rules to guide us?

(5) What are the discourses of self-command? And from what grammatical models do we take them? Are they the same for everyone?

(6) The opening moves in procrastination research by Sabini and Silver are of great interest but clearly far from adequate. This is an open field for non-experimental research.

(7) By what criteria do outsiders and practitioners assess physical self-development practices morally? Compare body-building of the Charles Atlas kind with yoga.

(8) How far do academic debates take the form of traditional duels?

(9) What happens to the moral orders so strongly associated with oriental martial arts when they are introduced into the West? For instance, are they incorporated in some local form of moral assessment?

(10) How far are the 'metaphors we live by' (Labov) the result of the absorption of social representations and so still within the confines of convention?

BIBLIOGRAPHICAL NOTES 10

For the relationship of self to culture see P. HEELAS and A. LOCK, *Indigenous psychologies* (London: Academic Press, 1981, ch. 1 and 2). See also T. VERHAVE and T. VAN HOORN, 'The temporalization of the self' (in *Historical social psychology*, ed. K. J. Gergen and M. Gergen, Hillsdale (NJ): Erlbaum, 1983). The Japanese institution of self-appraisal is described by S. M. LYMAN, *The Asian in the West* (Reno: Western Studies Center, 1970). For D. Hamlyn's theory of self-knowledge, see 'Self-knowledge' (in *The self*, ed. T. Mischel, Oxford: Blackwell, 1977, ch. 6). See also R. C. ZILLER, 'A helical theory of personal change' (in *Personality*, ed. R. Harré, Oxford: Basil Blackwell, 1976, ch. 5). A very interesting step in the direction of the thesis of the present work is to be found in G. ZIVIN (ed.), *The development of self-regulation through speech* (London: Academic Press, 1983).

Hollis's important distinction between the completeness of 'good reason' explanations and the incompleteness of other psychological accounts, if offered in terms of reasons, is to be found in M. HOLLIS, *Models of man* (Cambridge: Cambridge University Press, 1977, ch. 6 and 8).

For A. KENNY's argument for self-control as self-exhortation see *Will, freedom and power* (Oxford: Blackwell, 1975). The origin of the idea of grammatical models as determining the form of mental activities can be found in N. EVREINOV, *The theatre in life* (trans. A. I. Navaroff, London: Harrap, 1927). For a development of it as an explanation of personal concepts, see R. HARRÉ, 'The self in monodrama' (in *The self: Psychological and philosophical issues*, ed. T. Mischel, Oxford: Basil Blackwell, 1977, ch. 12). The discussion of procrastination is taken from J. SABINI and M. SILVER, *Moralities of everyday life* (Oxford: Oxford University Press, 1982, ch. 7). The moral climate of scientific debate is discussed by B. LATOUR and S. WOOLGAR, *Laboratory life* (Los Angeles: Sage, 1979, ch. 5) in the notion of cycles of credit with credibility as the currency. The 'Gould affair' was very fully reported in *Newsweek* at the time (1980). Emulation forms the basis of T. VEBLEN's, *A theory of the leisure class* (New York: Macmillan, 1899), and no doubt forms part of the implicit explanatory matrix for W. Labov's well-known work on linguistic change, summed up by him in W. LABOV, 'The study of language in its social context' (in *Sociolinguistics*, ed J. B. Pridle and J. Holmes, Harmondsworth: Penguin, 1972). For techniques of identity management see E. GOFFMAN, *Stigma* (Harmondsworth: Penguin, 1968).

Repertory grid techniques have been described in several works, but for an introduction see D. BANNISTER and F. FRANSELLA, *A manual for repertory grid technique* (London: Academic Press, 1971). For a discussion of work in defence of social identity see P. WEINREICH, 'Emerging from threatened identities' (in *Threatened identities*, ed. G. Breakwell, Chichester: John Wiley and Sons, 1983). For the political and moral issue of autonomy, see T. SZASZ, *The myth of mental illness* (New York: Hoeber-Harper, 1961) and many further derivatives by the same author. The moral issue of psychological models is to be found in M. HOLLIS, *Models of man* (Cambridge: Cambridge University Press, 1977, ch. 7—9). Also see E. GOFFMAN, *Asylums* (Harmondsworth: Penguin, 1968).

The Saussurean theory of meaning is set out in F. DE SAUSSURE, *Course in general linguistics* (trans. Wade Baskin, London: Peter Owen, 1960). For the relation between 'deep grammar' and 'criteria' see J. CANFIELD, *Wittgenstein, language and world* (Amherst: University of Massachusetts Press, 1981), particularly pp. 190—1.

Hermeneutics as psychological method is superbly summed up by J. SHOTTER, 'Hermeneutics' (in *The encyclopedic dictionary of psychology*, ed R. Harré and R. Lamb, Oxford: Basil Blackwell, 1983). Langean and other 'sympathetic interpretation' views can be found in P. REASON and J. ROWAN (eds), *Human enquiry* (Chichester: John Wiley and Sons, 1981, particularly ch. 25, 28, 31 and 34). The general theory of metaphor can be found extensively discussed in A. ORTONY, *Metaphor and thought* (Cambridge: Cambridge University Press, 1979) and D. MIALL ed., *Metaphor: Problems and perspectives* (Hassocks: Harvester Press, 1982).

The idea of a reflexive study of psychology itself as producing or inhibiting the possibility of personal being is very new; see K. J. GERGEN, *Toward transformation in social knowledge* (New York and Heidelberg: Springer Verlag, 1982), particularly ch. 3 and 4. Less profound but still interesting breaks with the authoritarian tradition in psychology can be found in R. M. LERNER and N. A. BUSCH-ROSSNAGEL, *Individuals as producers of their own development* (London: Academic Press, 1981); by way of contrast see the psychodynamically oriented C. A. COLARUSSO and R. M. NEMIROFF, *Adult development* (New York: Plenum Press, 1981) which, as one might say, buys into all the available reifications of grammar.

Additional works cited in the text are A. BLASI, 'Bridging moral cognition and moral action: a critical review of the literature' (*Psychological Bulletin*, 88, 1980, 1–45); R. BOYD, 'Metaphor and theory change: what is "metaphor" a metaphor for?' (in *Metaphor and thought*, ed. A. Ortony, Cambridge: Cambridge University Press, 1979); G. BREAKWELL, *Threatened identities* (Chichester: John Wiley and Sons, 1983); M. VON CRANACH and R. HARRÉ (eds), *The analysis of action* (Cambridge: Cambridge University Press, 1982); J.-P. DE WAELE and R. HARRÉ, 'Autobiography as a scientific method' (in *Emerging strategies in social scientific research*, ed. G. P. Ginsburg, Chichester: John Wiley and Sons, 1979); S. LUKES, *Individualism* (Oxford: Basil Blackwell, 1973); I. A. RICHARDS, *The philosophy of rhetoric* (New York: Galaxy, 1965); C. R. SNYDER and H. L. FROMKIN, *Uniqueness: the human pursuit of difference* (New York: Plenum Press, 1980).

Index of Subjects

Index of Names